A VOTE FOR WOMEN

CELEBRATING THE WOMEN'S SUFFRAGE MOVEMENT AND THE 19TH AMENDMENT

2020
WOMEN'S VOTE
CENTENNIAL
INITIATIVE™

SJH
St James's House

ISBN: 978-1-906670-88-7

Cover image: Illustrator and portrait painter Neysa McMein carries the American flag during the 1917 woman suffrage parade in New York City.

Sixty-sixth Congress of the United States of America;

At the First Session,

Begun and held at the City of Washington on Monday, the nineteenth day of May, one thousand nine hundred and nineteen.

JOINT RESOLUTION

Proposing an amendment to the Constitution extending the right of suffrage to women.

Resolved by the Senate and House of Representatives of the United States of America in Congress assembled (two-thirds of each House concurring therein), That the following article is proposed as an amendment to the Constitution, which shall be valid to all intents and purposes as part of the Constitution when ratified by the legislatures of three-fourths of the several States.

"ARTICLE ————.

"The right of citizens of the United States to vote shall not be denied or abridged by the United States or by any State on account of sex.

"Congress shall have power to enforce this article by appropriate legislation."

F. H. Gillett

Speaker of the House of Representatives.

Thos. R. Marshall

Vice President of the United States and
President of the Senate.

Above: The Joint Resolution by Congress to send the
19th Amendment to the states to ratify. It became part
of the U.S. Constitution on August 26, 1920.

FOREWORD

The 2020 Women's Vote Centennial Initiative (WVCI) and publisher St James's House are delighted to present *A Vote for Women* to mark the centennial of the ratification of the 19th Amendment to the U.S. Constitution, the amendment that recognized women's right to vote by prohibiting voter discrimination based on gender.

Appropriately, for a book that celebrates the achievements of a movement whose triumphs resulted from the bravery and endeavors of so many women from so many different walks of life, a spirit of collaboration lies at the heart of this publication.

A Vote for Women aims to document and honor the extraordinary accomplishments of women's suffrage; to explore the remarkable stories of individuals and organizations whose drive and perseverance have shaped American society and stand as testament to the nation's democratic ideals.

This book began with the partnership between the WVCI, whose mission is to commemorate the 100th anniversary of the 19th Amendment, educate the public about its impact, and stimulate dialogue around the ongoing fight for equal rights, and publisher St James's House, whose experience of producing titles on women's suffrage, history, and culture made for an ideal match.

The end result, however, represents the combined efforts of a host of contributors. From authors and academics, archives and institutions, to government agencies and departments, sponsors and supporters, all have played their part in chronicling the battle for the ballot, and in reflecting on the equal rights challenges and success stories of the years that followed, up to the present day.

In this book, you'll read profiles of some of the most significant figures in the women's suffrage movement, courtesy of the National Women's History Museum, along with an overview of women's ascent in the world of politics, from the first trailblazers to the current vice-president.

You'll read detailed historical accounts of the suffrage movement's struggles, setbacks and successes across each region of the United States, courtesy of the National Park Service. And, as U.S. government departments and agencies strive to lead the way in equality and diversity, you'll read how the Department of State's Office of Global Women's Issues, for example, is promoting women's political, economic, and social participation in society.

The publishers of this book are grateful to all those who have contributed their time, effort, and visual and editorial resources to make this book possible. A special note of thanks goes to the publication's sponsorship partners and contributors, who can be found listed on page 296, for their support and insights into championing women's rights in a range of sectors, from education to finance, hospitality to corporate management. Without their involvement, this book simply would not have been possible.

The achievements of the generations of women who fought for the right to vote cannot be underestimated. However, milestone as it was, the ratification of the 19th Amendment did not mark the end of the struggle for women. Work remains to be done and hurdles need to be overcome to this day, a fact that makes it all the more important to raise awareness of the suffrage movement's triumphs and of the challenges that still persist.

CONTENTS

"Congratulations"

INTRODUCTION

After winning ratification by one vote in the final state necessary, the 19th Amendment became part of the U.S. Constitution on August 26, 1920, thereby ushering in the largest expansion of the electorate in American history. The amendment officially prohibited voter discrimination by sex, recognizing women's right to vote throughout the country. In 2020 and 2021, the United States has been witnessing a nationwide celebration of the amendment's centennial and the subsequent expansion of women's rights. National events, state exhibits, local programs, statues, films, coins, stamps, books, and more were produced to honor the unsung heroes of the women's suffrage movement. And all this has been accomplished despite the challenges posed by the pandemic.

Anticipating this important year, the 2020 Women's Vote Centennial Initiative (WVCI) was founded in 2015 to prepare for and promote this anniversary of American women winning the constitutional right to vote. The WVCI brings together representatives of national institutions and grassroots groups to recognize the centennial of the 19th Amendment and the complex story behind it. Our mission is to raise the visibility and increase the impact of this historic anniversary by encouraging activities throughout the country, and to highlight the ongoing relevance of the women's suffrage struggle. Under the guidance of a volunteer Steering Committee, the WVCI maintains a robust online presence at www.2020centennial.org and on social media. We offer resources, educational materials, webinars, links, and panels. And we have partnered with St James's House to produce this unique centennial book, *A Vote for Women*.

Organizations in every state are commemorating the centennial by highlighting local suffragists and commemorating the role their state played in the movement. Museums, libraries, historical societies, theaters, galleries, and art facilities of all sorts are also celebrating the long struggle of women to become voters. Throughout the country, local activists began doing new research, profiling forgotten figures, uncovering archives, and creating new curricula. And when the pandemic forced changes, groups and institutions responded immediately with online events, in-depth broadcasts, expanded websites, virtual exhibits, digital publications, panels, conversations, and much more. Like the suffragists being honored, they overcame unexpected obstacles and are continuing their work.

The creative spirit of the centennial is beautifully captured by *A Vote for Women*, which pays tribute to what American women achieved 100 years ago and in the ensuing years. This volume, compiled by our centennial partner St James's House, stands as a welcome and elegant recognition of the breadth and depth of the American women's suffrage movement. Part of that story is the change in terms used to describe it, from "woman suffrage" during that era to the more commonly used "women's suffrage" and "women's rights" today.

The struggle for equal suffrage is woven throughout America's story. It is hard to find a place in the U.S. where women did not actively seek the vote. In these pages, we see suffragists at work in the North, South, East, and West. We learn of fascinating women from a wide range of backgrounds and cultures, rank-and-file as well as leading figures, who dedicated years of their lives to the vision of equality. While women of color are often underrepresented in suffragist history, the evidence shows that there were many who were active during the long struggle for the vote.

Women waged hundreds of separate federal, state, and local electoral campaigns throughout the country to convince male voters and legislators to approve equal suffrage. For decades, suffrage workers faced fierce opposition, outright dismissal, betrayal, corruption, arrest, and worse, all while trying to secure a basic civil right. They endured defeat after defeat before winning stunning victories.

Political opposition came from party bosses and economic opposition emerged from various business interests, particularly those in the brewing industry who feared prohibition. Racial antipathy formed the backbone of opposition in many states. And, not just in Washington D.C. but in states throughout the country, male lawmakers generally derided the very idea of women voting and put off their demand for decades. Some women joined the ranks of the anti-suffragists and worked against passage of the 19th Amendment.

The persistence of the suffragists is a lasting testament to their vision, endurance, and love of democracy. These women, denied a say in their own government, refused to be silent and built a bold, nonviolent movement to enshrine women's right to vote in the Constitution. Nevertheless, some women were still barred from voting because of discriminatory state and federal barriers that took decades to overcome. The majority of Black women, in particular, were prevented from voting until passage of the 1965 Voting Rights Act. Efforts to safeguard the right to vote continue today, efforts as audacious as those prior to 1920.

In the 21st century, female voices are being heard like never before as women acquire greater influence and power. Many look to the suffragists as role models, individuals willing to sacrifice and persevere on behalf of justice, democracy, and equality. These are the values *A Vote for Women* celebrates. We hope you enjoy this enlightening and visually striking volume that honors some of the most inspiring and remarkable Americans.

Nancy E. Tate
Krysta Nicole Jones
Co-chairs
2020 Women's Vote Centennial Initiative

CHAPTER ONE

DEMANDING THE VOTE

WOMEN'S SUFFRAGE BEFORE 1848

In the decades that preceded those of more direct activism, women fought to acquire important skills in the public sphere and to gain knowledge of the rules that guided politics

By Johanna Neuman

Most suffrage histories begin in 1848, the year Elizabeth Cady Stanton convened a women's rights convention in Seneca Falls, New York. There, she unfurled a Declaration of Rights and Sentiments, seeking religious, educational, and property rights for women—and the right to vote. While Seneca Falls remains an important marker in women's suffrage history, in fact women had been agitating for this basic right of citizenship even before the first stirrings of revolutionary fervor in the colonies. Some, like Lydia Chapin Taft, had even voted.

On Josiah Taft's death in 1756 at the age of 47, his wife became a wealthy widow with three minor children still at home—and the largest taxpayer in Uxbridge, Massachusetts. As the town was about to vote for a local militia to fight the French and Indian Wars, civic leaders asked Lydia to cast a vote in her husband's place, as her funds would be critical to the war effort. Her affirmative vote on funding the local militia in 1756 was the first of three she cast as a widow. Two years later, in 1758, she voted on tax issues. In 1765, she again appeared at a town meeting to vote on school districts. Two decades before the colonies declared their independence from Britain, and 30 years before the U.S. Constitution was ratified, she became, according to Uxbridge town records, America's first recorded female voter.

Women who expressed interest in politics were rare, as it was considered unnatural. Exceptions were made, however, for some upper-class women, such as Mercy Otis Warren, who during the war years published anonymously and then used the pseudonym "A Columbian Patriot" in 1788 to oppose ratification of the U.S. Constitution unless it included a Bill of Rights to protect the rights of individuals from a formidable central government. She later penned a lengthy history of the Revolution under her own name. But, once appeals for resistance spread through the colonies, many women asked their husbands or fathers for updates on the war. "Nothing else is talked of," Sarah Franklin wrote her father Benjamin Franklin. "The Dutch talk of the stamp tack, the Negroes of the tamp, in short, everyone has something to say."

As her husband John Adams set off for the Second Continental Congress in Philadelphia in 1776, Abigail Adams wrote him for details of the latest battles. She also urged him, in helping to craft the colonies' Articles of Confederation and Perpetual Union, to "Remember the Ladies," warning that women would foment a rebellion "if attention is not paid" to their interests, that they would "not hold ourselves bound by any laws in which we have no voice or representation." Her husband replied, "To your extraordinary Code of Laws, I cannot but laugh... Depend upon it, we know better than to repeal our Masculine systems."

More than any other founder, John Adams may have foreseen the waves of changes likely in the country's electorate. "There will be no end of it," he wrote to a Massachusetts attorney in 1776. "New claims will arise; women will demand a vote; lads from 12 to 21 will think their rights not enough attended to; and every man who has not a farthing [one-fourth a penny in British coin], will demand an equal voice with any other, in all acts of state."

Before the war, most women were absent from the political scene, constrained by their duties to the home. The work was difficult and included backbreaking duties in the fields, repeated childbirths, taxing meal preparation, and daily efforts to keep dust and dirt from invading primitive homes. Indentured servants, Black and white, suffered from broken bones and pulled muscles from lugging 20-gallon containers of water from well to home,

for bathing and cooking. For enslaved African Americans, one-fifth of the nation, exhausting duties were tinged with the threat of whippings and separation from loved ones on the auction block. But once the war began, women heard the call. All over the colonies, effective boycotts against British products required a buy-in from women. And buy in they did. Women founded anti-tea leagues, meeting to brew concoctions of raspberry, sage, and birch to substitute their herbal mixes for well-regarded English teas. Others shared camaraderie in collective gatherings to weave material from local products. Hundreds of spectators came to

Previous pages: Some women could vote in New Jersey
until 1807. Opposite: Abigail Adams. Above: A satirical
take on the boycotting of English tea, c. 1775.

SARAH MOORE GRIMKÉ

1792–1873

By Kerri Lee Alexander

Even though Sarah Moore Grimké was shy, she often spoke in front of large crowds with her sister Angelina. The two sisters became the first women to speak in front of a state legislature; they did so as representatives of the American Anti-Slavery Society. They also became active writers and speakers for women's rights. Their ideas were so different from most of the ideas in the community that people burned their writings and angry mobs protested their speeches. However, Grimké and her sister would not let that stop them from making a difference for women and African Americans.

Born on November 26, 1792, Sarah Grimké came from a rich family of slaveholders in Charleston, South Carolina. She lived with her mother Mary Smith and her father John Faucheraud Grimké, who was a head judge of the state supreme court. Her parents gave her private tutors and her lessons included painting, sewing, and music. However, she wanted to learn all of the interesting subjects they taught the boys in school. Her older brother Thomas was a student at Yale College (now Yale University) and taught her what he learned in his classes. He taught her many subjects including Latin and Greek, mathematics, and geography. While she spent time reading and learning, the enslaved people on the family plantation were not permitted to learn their letters. She began to teach some of the enslaved people how to read until her father would not allow her to teach them anymore. She began to see how badly people treated African Americans.

In 1819, Sarah visited Philadelphia, Pennsylvania with her father and met many members of the Society of Friends, known as Quakers. The Quakers she met believed that slavery was evil, and that it was their responsibility to help the people that were suffering in society. They also allowed women to become preachers and leaders in the church. Grimké liked their ideas about women and slavery

and decided to move there to become a Quaker in 1821. A few years later, her sister Angelina joined her in Philadelphia. They both became members of anti-slavery groups and began speaking out against the treatment of African Americans. In 1836, Angelina published a booklet called *An Appeal to the Christian Women of the South*, and Sarah published one called *Epistle to the Clergy of the Southern States*. Both booklets argued against slavery. Leaders in the South were so offended by their ideas against slavery that they burned the booklets and warned Sarah and Angelina that they would be arrested if they ever came back to South Carolina. The General Association of Congregational Ministers of Massachusetts objected to their writings and objected to them giving speeches in front of men, and wrote a public statement against the Grimké sisters.

Sarah and Angelina kept writing even though it was dangerous. Their next booklets addressed women's rights and the reasons others should help African American people. Angelina wrote *Appeal to the Women of the Nominally Free States* in 1837, while Sarah wrote *Letters on the Equality of the Sexes and the Condition of Women* in 1838. Now living in New York, Sarah wrote about the poor treatment of women and enslaved people. She continued to speak in front of large crowds with her sister. When her sister Angelina decided to marry an abolitionist named Theodore Dwight Weld, the Quaker Meeting disowned the Grimkés because Weld was not a Quaker. Together, the three of them published *American Slavery As It Is: Testimony of a Thousand Witnesses* in 1839. Shortly after, they moved to New Jersey and began working in education. They started taking in students to live with them in 1848, and by 1851 they were the leaders of a boarding school. They opened a second school in Eagleswood, New Jersey and taught students until 1862. During this time, the American Civil War broke

out over the issue of slavery. Grimké decided to write to support President Abraham Lincoln and the war to end slavery. Shortly after this, the Grimké sisters welcomed their African American nephews Archibald Henry Grimké and Francis James Grimké into their home. The boys were the sons of their brother Henry and a woman he enslaved named Nancy Weston. The Grimké sisters supported the boys as they went on to Harvard Law School (Archibald) and Princeton Theological Seminary (Francis).

Sarah Grimké continued to fight for women's rights and the fair treatment of African Americans for the rest of her life. She was the vice president of the Massachusetts Woman Suffrage Association in 1868. A few years later, she led a group of women in Hyde Park, a neighborhood in Boston, to vote in the local election even though it was against the law. Even at the age of 79, she was known for walking up and down the street, passing out copies of John Stuart Mill's book *The Subjection of Women*. Sarah Grimké died on December 23, 1873.

This article appears courtesy of the National Women's History Museum.

"Two decades before the colonies declared their independence from Britain, and 30 years before the U.S. Constitution was ratified, Lydia Chapin Taft became America's first recorded female voter"

watch. Young women reveled in the task, feeling they were making a contribution to the nation's future. One girl at the spinning parties wrote that she "felt Nationaly," part of "a fighting army of amazons... armed with spinning wheels."

In New Jersey, lawmakers heard the call too, and adopted a state constitution on July 2, 1776 that offered the vote to "all inhabitants of this colony of full age, who are worth £50." The new vote for women applied to only a small proportion of the female population. Coverture laws meant women could not own property unless they were single or widowed, like Lydia Taft. Married women gave up rights to own property, which transferred to their husbands. No one knows how many single or widowed women of 21 years or older in New Jersey had amassed £50 worth in holdings by 1776. Pamphleteer William Griffith, who said he found it "perfectly disgusting" to watch women cast ballots, estimated the number at 10,000 or more.

For more than 30 years, women in New Jersey attended rallies, lobbied for patronage jobs for their male relatives and family friends, raised money for political causes, actively campaigned for candidates, and were invited to public political

events. Politicians sought to endear themselves to these new voters, offering carriages to transport them to the polls.

Despite all these early, significant steps towards women's enfranchisement, the guiding rule of suffrage history is that male politicians never cede power unless it advantages them. John Condict, a Democratic-Republican congressman angered by the votes of 75 Federalist women against him, launched a successful campaign to rescind women's rights in 1807. Legislators did not rewrite the constitution, they merely passed a new election law limiting the vote to white male taxpayers. What historian Rosemary Zagarri dubbed "a revolutionary backlash," when men reclaimed the power of politics, had begun.

If women lost voting rights after the Revolution, one new role was added—what historian Linda Kerber called the Republican Motherhood. Asked to educate the next generation of patriots in the new republic, they pressed this advantage to win new opportunities in education. Advertisements soon appeared for female academies that would, like the one opened by Judith Sargent Murray in Dorchester, Massachusetts, teach "Reading, English, Grammar, Writing, Arithmetic, the French language, Geography, including

the use of Globes, needle work in all its branches, painting and hair work upon ivory." And, once armed with knowledge, women in great numbers entered the political sphere even before they won the vote. In petitions often sent through stealth networks of like-minded women, many women fought against President Andrew Jackson's Indian Removal Policy. They lost, and Native Americans were banished from their homelands to Oklahoma in a naked land grab, which killed many in what historians now call the Long Trail of Tears. In the 1830s, many women demanded an end to slavery and aided the Underground Railroad that helped thousands escape slavery. These nascent acts of politics, cast amid the Second Great Awakening, an evangelical movement that urged Christians to atone for their own sins and that of their nation, set the stage for a wider appeal for the vote in the 1840s.

The first women to make the case for abolition publicly were the Grimké sisters. Born into a slave-owning family in Charleston, South Carolina, Angelina Grimké and her older sister Sarah were eager to give witness to the daily humiliations of slavery. They had fled the South to testify to its cruelties. In a letter to abolitionist William Lloyd Garrison published in his newspaper, *Liberator*, Angelina wrote, "It is my deep, solemn, deliberate conviction that this is a cause worth dying for." In speaking for the slave, the Grimké sisters were regularly assailed for speaking in public at all, as this was a privilege restricted to men. In her *Appeal to the Christian Women of the South* in 1836, Angelina urged women to lobby their legislators on the issue, "as a matter of morals and religion, not of expedience or politics."

Perhaps the greatest spur to female advocacy against slavery and for women's suffrage was Lucy Stone, one of the first female graduates of Oberlin College. In the summer of 1847, Stone began lecturing for the Anti-Slavery Society. The sight of a woman speaking in public provoked much anger by men in the audience, who pelted the stage with prayer books, rotten fruit and—

Above: Charles T. Webber's "The Undergound Railway", 1891, depicts families escaping enslavement arriving at a "station."

ANGELINA GRIMKÉ WELD

1805–79

By Debra Michals

Although raised on a slave-owning plantation in South Carolina, Angelina Grimké Weld grew up to become an ardent abolitionist writer and speaker, as well as a women's rights activist. She and her sister Sarah Moore Grimké were among the first women to speak in public against slavery, defying gender norms and risking violence in doing so. Beyond ending slavery, their mission—highly radical for the times—was to promote racial and gender equality.

Born on February 20, 1805, Angelina was the last of 14 children of prominent jurist John Faucheraud Grimké and Mary Smith. John Grimké owned a home in the city of Charleston, South Carolina, a plantation in the country, and numerous slaves. Believing women should be subordinate to men, John Grimké did not seek to educate his daughters, though his sons shared their lessons with their sisters.

Two facts—a childhood spent witnessing slavery's cruelties and her own experiences with the limitations of gender—would shape Angelina's life and sense of mission. Early on, Angelina and sister Sarah, 13 years her senior, taught some slaves to read and held prayer meetings with others, despite their parents' admonitions against it. Angelina also sought to persuade her family to abandon slavery, to no avail.

Like her elder sister, Angelina converted from her Episcopal religion to the Society of Friends (Quakers), known for its relative egalitarianism and efforts to end slavery. In 1829, she joined Sarah in Philadelphia, where both became members of the Philadelphia Female Anti-Slavery Society. Angelina supported herself as a teacher, and in 1835, wrote a letter to William Lloyd Garrison, an abolitionist publisher who, without her consent, printed it in his newspaper *The Liberator*. The move launched her career as an abolitionist writer and speaker. In 1836, Angelina published her pamphlet *An Appeal to Christian Women of the South*, urging southern women to join the antislavery movement. In South Carolina, leaders threatened Angelina with imprisonment if she returned home.

Though unusual for the times, Garrison welcomed women to his American Anti-Slavery Society (AASS), and in 1837, Angelina and her sister Sarah became its first female agents, touring New York and New Jersey. Their lectures about their first-hand knowledge of slavery's evils—especially to mixed male and female audiences—provoked rebuke from ministers for their "unwomanly behavior." Such reactions drew both women into the women's rights debate, with Weld authoring a series of letters in *The Liberator*. Undeterred, Angelina became the first woman to address the Massachusetts State Legislature in February 1828, bringing a petition signed by 20,000 women seeking to end slavery.

Through the AASS, Angelina met Theodore Weld, a leading agent for Garrison's abolitionist group. The pair married in 1838 and two days later, Angelina spoke at the annual antislavery convention in Philadelphia. Later that night, angry crowds burned the building to the ground.

The Welds retired from speaking but continued to attend antislavery meetings and write abolitionist tracts, including *American Slavery As It Is* (1839). The couple moved with Sarah—who remained with them throughout her life—to New Jersey, where they bought a farm and the sisters made a living as teachers. Angelina had three children: Charles Stuart (1839), Theodore Grimké (1841) and Sarah Grimké Weld (1844). The family moved in 1864 to Boston, Massachusetts, where in 1870, the two sisters attempted to vote in a local election.

This article appears courtesy of the National Women's History Museum.

"Once armed with knowledge, women in great numbers entered the political sphere even before they won the vote"

sometimes on a winter's day—cold water. Once in Cape Cod, an angry crowd stormed the stage. Stone asked one of the attackers to escort her outside. The man not only ushered her to safety, he stood guard as she climbed a tree stump and continued to lecture. In a report, the Anti-Slavery Society said she had been "of very high value," attributing her popularity to the "thoroughness of preparation... and the gentleness of demeanor."

Samuel May, secretary for the society, soon protested her mingling of the two causes. "The people came to hear anti-slavery, and not woman's rights; and it isn't right," he said. To this Stone replied, "I was a woman before I was an abolitionist." They agreed that she would receive a reduced fee—from $6 to $4 a week—for lectures on Saturdays and Sundays to advance the cause of the slave. On weekdays, when fewer came to hear lectures, she would speak about equality for women, and so became the first to make a living as a lecturer for women's rights. Frederick Douglass, the famed abolitionist orator, was also a lifelong suffragist. Late in life he commented on the mingling of the two causes. "When I ran away from slavery, it was for myself; when I advocated emancipation, it was for my people; but when I stood up for the rights of women, self was out of the question, and I found a little nobility in the act."

After the Civil War, the two sides would come to blows over their shared priorities—Douglass, Lucy Stone and other abolitionists supporting the 15th Amendment that granted voting rights to Black adult men, while Elizabeth Cady Stanton and Susan B. Anthony campaigned actively against the measure, arguing that African American men should not win the vote if women couldn't also claim their rights to citizenship. This schism would splinter the women's suffrage cause for several decades. Even today, historians still debate whether this untethering of women's suffrage from abolitionism set back the cause of women's rights or propelled it forward in an autonomous path of its own. But when women first began to speak publicly, they fought to acquire skills of the public sphere, to gain knowledge of the rules that guided politics. As Lucy Stone put it, first they had to learn "to stand and speak." They would showcase that knowledge in the conference in Seneca Falls, where Stanton's declaration that women should be eligible to vote was so controversial that her co-sponsor, Quaker Lucretia Mott, told her, "Why Lizzie, thee will make us ridiculous."

This article was originally published by the United States Women's Suffrage Centennial Commission.

Opposite: Lucy Stone's calm appeals convince members
of an anti-abolitionist mob to hear her speak.

THE FIGHT FOR A RIGHT TO VOTE

The ratification of the 19th Amendment was a landmark moment in the long battle for voting rights for women, but it did not spell an end to the suffrage struggle

By Ann D. Gordon

The year 2020 marks a significant centennial: ratification of a federal constitutional amendment that barred states from excluding women from the electorate solely on the basis of their sex. We pay tribute to the tens of thousands of women who envisaged a government in which men and women had equal voice and who, through agitation and persistent mobilization of citizens, brought about that change. This was a long fight. Historians point to different moments of origin, but their choices fall into the 1830s and 1840s. If dated from the women's rights convention at Seneca Falls, New York, in 1848, 72 years passed before ratification of the federal amendment—and that's the short version.

As we celebrate, it matters that we not overstate the changes wrought by the 19th Amendment. It does not confer voting rights on anyone. This is its pith:

"Section 1. The right of citizens of the United States to vote shall not be denied or abridged by the United States or by any state on account of sex."

Advocates of woman suffrage adopted the model created by Congress to extend voting rights to freedmen after the Civil War in the 15th Amendment of 1870. In that case the section ended "on account of race, color, or previous condition of servitude." The wording was a compromise in both cases: it reinforced the nation's tradition that states set voter qualifications, but it imposed new federal rules about how that would be done. In 1920, states could no longer bar women from voting by writing "male" into a state's qualifications. That change, monumental as it was, left many women with U.S. citizenship still unable to vote and, to this day, vulnerable to state actions that exclude them for reasons other than race, color, or sex.

372

HARPER'S WEEKLY.

[June 11, 1859.

Yᴱ MAY SESSION OF Yᴱ WOMAN'S RIGHTS CONVENTION—Yᴱ ORATOR OF Yᴱ DAY DENOUNCING Yᴱ LORDS OF CREATION.

Previous pages: Suffragist Lucy Branham delivers a speech
wearing prison garb in Washington, D.C., 1919. Above: A satirical
illustration from 1859 of a women's rights convention being heckled
by men in the galleries. Opposite: A popular magazine cover depicts
a young woman adding "and women" to the wording of
the Declaration of Independence, 1915.

"We have declared our right to vote—The question now is how should we get possession of what rightfully belongs to us?"

—Elizabeth Cady Stanton

Early declarations of women's right to vote carried no instructions as to where women might secure it. Writing to a friend a few months after the meeting at Seneca Falls, Elizabeth Cady Stanton wondered: "We have declared our right to vote—The question now is how should we get possession of what rightfully belongs to us?" In the spring of 1850, women in Ohio offered one answer: they called a meeting in anticipation of a state constitutional convention and circulated petitions calling for the enfranchisement of women and Black men. Soon, pioneers in the women's rights movement were presenting their demand to state legislatures and conventions from New England to Kansas.

States controlled access to the ballot box. Their constitutions defined who belonged to the club of voters and, by omission, who was excluded. They were not subtle. Wisconsin's first constitution in 1848 expressed ideas standard to the era:

"Every male person of the age of twenty-one years or upwards, of the following classes, who shall have resided in this State for one year next preceding any election, shall be deemed a qualified elector at such election."

The eligible classes of adult males were "white citizens of the United States," white immigrants who had declared an intention to become citizens, and a small number of Native Americans not deemed to be tribal members. Neither females of those classes nor African Americans of either sex could qualify to vote. Across most of the country at mid-century the electorate was male, white, and over 21.

At the start of the Civil War in 1861, no women had gained voting rights, but this new movement had raised the topic of equal political rights in state and federal legal conversations. At war's end in 1865, that mattered. For women seeking equal rights, the post-war

period of Reconstruction changed the political and legal landscape. The end of slavery required that citizenship be rethought. What is it and whose is it? Prior to ratification of the 14th Amendment in 1868, the United States lacked a definition of who among its residents were citizens. The amendment's opening sentence addressed that gap:

"All persons born or naturalized in the United States, and subject to the jurisdiction thereof, are citizens of the United States and of the State wherein they reside."

Though primarily aimed at recognizing African Americans as citizens, the language also removed any uncertainty about

women's citizenship. Questions remained, however, about what came with citizenship. Are voting rights inherent in citizenship? Is there a federal interest in voting rights? From 1865 to 1870, these questions were major topics of national debate, and for most of that time, suffragists acted within an interracial equal rights movement. In many states of the North and the South, activists pressed to change state laws so that all adult men and women, Black and white, had equal rights to vote.

Of hopes for New York in 1866, Susan B. Anthony told an audience: "now is the hour not only to demand suffrage for the negro, but for every other human being in the Republic." Suffragists petitioned Congress to consider the advantages of universal suffrage tied to citizenship. In December 1868, Congressman George W. Julian of Indiana introduced language for an amendment that would achieve that ideal:

"The right of suffrage in the United States shall be based on citizenship, and shall be regulated by Congress, and all citizens of the United States, whether native or naturalized, shall enjoy this right equally, without any distinction or discrimination whatever founded on race, color, or sex."

Julian envisaged not only a polity of equal rights among adult citizens, but also a federal government with the authority to qualify its voters.

This dream of voting rights for every citizen came to a splintered end. Congress rejected universal suffrage in favor of manhood suffrage, proposing the 15th Amendment as we know it to the states in February 1869, while women in the equal rights alliance were told to stand down. Allies who were willing to campaign for manhood suffrage took that path, African American women made choices between pressing for their individual rights or accepting that votes for freedmen alone was a huge leap forward, and woman suffrage lost its connection to a movement with universal aims. In short order, in March 1869, Congressman Julian introduced a 16th amendment for woman suffrage, repeating his earlier language about suffrage and citizenship and slimming down the prohibitions to "founded on sex." Congress let the matter drop.

Organizations devoted to winning woman suffrage date to this post-war period. Some of them were local groups, like the first one, in St. Louis. Within a few years, dozens of states boasted an

Above, left: National Woman Suffrage Association leaders
Elizabeth Cady Stanton (left) and Susan B. Anthony. Above, right:
American Woman Suffrage Association leader Lucy Stone.

SENECA FALLS WOMAN'S RIGHTS CONVENTION

JULY 19–20, 1848

By Allison Lange

In the 1840s, the women who gained experience in the abolitionist movement became leaders of the emerging women's rights movement. Many of the laws of coverture were still in place: their husbands controlled their finances, children, and property. Women did not have equal access to education. During that era, states were repealing laws that required voters to own land, which increased the number of white male voters. Women, however, were not allowed to cast a ballot. In response, male and female activists began to meet and petition for women's rights, including the right to vote.

In 1848, Lucretia Mott, Elizabeth Cady Stanton, and several other women decided to call a women's rights meeting in Seneca Falls, New York. About 300 people—including the former slave and prominent reformer Frederick Douglass—attended. The Seneca Falls meeting was the first in support of women's rights, though not the first activism for woman suffrage.

The group voted on a set of resolutions—the "Declaration of Sentiments"—written by Stanton. She modeled her declaration after Thomas Jefferson's Declaration of Independence. She asserted: "all men and women are created equal," a provocative statement at that time.

The Declaration of Sentiments called for a long list of women's rights: access to education and job opportunities, more power within the church, and the right to control one's own property and money. Woman suffrage (a woman's right to vote) was the most controversial resolution. The suffrage clause was the only one that attendees did not unanimously adopt. While the vote was not originally the main goal of the reformers, suffrage became central to the women's rights movement in the 1860s.

This article appears courtesy of the National Women's History Museum.

THE FIRST CONVENTION

EVER CALLED TO DISCUSS THE

Civil and Political Rights of Women,

Seneca Falls, N. Y., July 19, 20, 1848.

WOMAN'S RIGHTS CONVENTION.

A Convention to discuss the social, civil, and religious condition and rights of woman will be held in the Wesleyan Chapel, at Seneca Falls, N. Y., on Wednesday and Thursday, the 19th and 20th of July current; commencing at 10 o'clock A. M. During the first day the meeting will be exclusively for women, who are earnestly invited to attend. The public generally are invited to be present on the second day, when Lucretia Mott, of Philadelphia, and other ladies and gentlemen, will address the Convention.*

> * This call was published in the *Seneca County Courier*, July 14, 1848, without any signatures. The movers of this Convention, who drafted the call, the declaration and resolutions were Elizabeth Cady Stanton, Lucretia Mott, Martha C. Wright, Mary Ann McClintock, and Jane C. Hunt.

association, sometimes two, if rivals for leadership could not get along. Two organizations with national ambitions were founded in 1869. One, calling itself the National Woman Suffrage Association, planned to keep pressure on the federal government to enfranchise women. This was the group led by Elizabeth Cady Stanton and Susan B. Anthony, among many others.

The American Woman Suffrage Association, led by Lucy Stone, accepted the decision to leave women's rights to the states and resolved to work in that arena. If a major state campaign was underway, as in Michigan in 1874, both groups stepped up to help with speakers and funds. These two associations survived for 21 years as separate and often arguing entities.

Formal organizations were not the sole drivers of agitation about voting rights. Women took direct action to claim their right to vote in a variety of ways, especially in the hopeful years right after the war. In Vineland, New Jersey, year after year, women installed their own ballot box at the polling place and showed up on election day to vote. In Lewiston, Maine, in fall 1868, a taxpaying widow of

a Union soldier applied to register as a voter, one of many widows whose protests spotlighted their lack of political representation. In Washington, D.C., Frederick Douglass marched with a large group of Black and white women to the registrar of elections.

The idea of a citizen's right to vote did not die with Julian's amendment. Several lawyers argued that women had a right to vote because they were citizens and that activists should challenge their exclusion from the ballot box through test cases in the courts. In the early 1870s, what had been spontaneous actions by women to show up at the polls became more systematic as women planned lawsuits. At least six test cases reached the courts—in California, Connecticut, Illinois, Missouri, Pennsylvania, and the District of Columbia—and, after state courts ruled against women, they appealed two cases to the Supreme Court.

Before the court heard arguments in the case of Virginia Minor of St. Louis, a different sort of case got underway in New York, after 14 women in Rochester successfully registered and voted. The federal government arrested and indicted them and prosecuted them

Opposite: Victoria Woodhull, a controversial free love and
women's rights advocate, addresses congressmen in 1871.
Above: A caricature of Susan B. Anthony, published
prior to her trial in 1873.

ELIZABETH CADY STANTON

1815–1902

Edited by Debra Michals

Author, lecturer, and chief philosopher of the women's rights and suffrage movements, Elizabeth Cady Stanton formulated the agenda for women's rights that guided the struggle well into the 20th century.

Born on November 12, 1815 in Johnstown, New York, Stanton was the daughter of Margaret Livingston and Daniel Cady, Johnstown's most prominent citizens. She received her formal education at the Johnstown Academy and at Emma Willard's Troy Female Seminary in New York. Her father was a noted lawyer and state assemblyman and young Elizabeth gained an informal legal education by talking with him and listening in on his conversations with colleagues and guests.

A well-educated woman, Stanton married abolitionist lecturer Henry Stanton in 1840. She, too, became active in the anti-slavery movement and worked alongside leading abolitionists of the day including Sarah and Angelina Grimke and William Lloyd Garrison, all guests at the Stanton home while they lived in Albany, New York and later Boston.

While on her honeymoon in London to attend the World Anti-Slavery Convention, Stanton met abolitionist Lucretia Mott, who, like her, was also angry about the exclusion of women at the proceedings. Mott and Stanton, now fast friends, vowed to call a women's rights convention when they returned home. Eight years later, in 1848, Stanton and Mott held the first women's rights convention at Seneca Falls, New York. Stanton authored, "The Declaration of Sentiments," which expanded on the Declaration of Independence by adding the word "woman" or "women" throughout. This pivotal document called for social and legal changes to elevate women's place in society and listed 18 grievances, from the inability to control their wages and property or the difficulty in gaining custody in divorce to the lack of the right to vote. That same year, Stanton circulated petitions throughout New York to urge the New York Congress to pass the New York Married Women's Property Act.

Although Stanton remained committed to efforts to gain property rights for married women and ending slavery, the women's suffrage movement increasingly became her top priority. Stanton met Susan B. Anthony in 1851, and the two quickly began collaboration on speeches, articles, and books. Their intellectual and organizational partnership dominated the women's movement for over half a century. When Stanton was unable to travel due to the demands of raising her seven children, she would author speeches for Anthony to deliver.

In 1862, Stanton moved to Brooklyn and later New York City. There she also became involved in Civil War efforts and joined with Anthony to advocate for the 13th Amendment, which ended slavery. An outstanding orator with a sharp mind, Stanton was able to travel more after the Civil War and she became one of the best-known women's rights activists in the country. Her speeches addressed such topics as maternity, child rearing, divorce law, married women's property rights, temperance, abolition, and presidential campaigns.

She and Anthony opposed the 15th Amendment to the U.S. Constitution because it gave voting rights to Black men but did not extend the franchise to women. Their stance led to a rift with other suffragists and prompted Stanton and Anthony to found the National Woman Suffrage Association (NWSA) in 1869. Stanton edited and wrote for NWSA's journal *The Revolution*. As NWSA president, Stanton was an outspoken social and political commentator and debated the major political and legal questions of the day. The two major women's suffrage groups reunited in 1890 as the National American Woman Suffrage Association.

By the 1880s, Stanton was in her sixties and focused more on writing rather than traveling and lecturing. She wrote three volumes of *History of Woman Suffrage* (1881–85) with Anthony and Matilda Joslyn Gage. In this comprehensive work, published several decades before women won the right to vote, the authors documented the individual and local activism that built and sustained a movement for woman suffrage. Along with numerous articles on the subject of women and religion, Stanton published *The Woman's Bible* (1895, 1898), in which she voiced her belief in a secular state and urged women to recognize how religious orthodoxy and masculine theology obstructed their chances to achieve self-sovereignty. She also wrote an autobiography, *Eighty Years and More*, about the great events and work of her life. Stanton died in October 1902 in New York City, 18 years before women gained the right to vote.

This article appears courtesy of the National Women's History Museum.

"Admit this right to deny suffrage to the states, and there is no power to foresee the confusion, discord, and disruption that awaits us"

—Susan B. Anthony

for a criminal violation of federal law—voting without having the right to vote. Because one among them was very well known, the U.S. attorney eventually proceeded only against her, and an associate justice of the Supreme Court presided at her trial.

Associate Justice Ward Hunt's opinion in that trial, United States v. Susan B. Anthony (1873), scoffed at the idea of a citizen's right to vote:

"If the right belongs to any particular person, it is because such person is entitled to it by the laws of the State where he offers to exercise it, and not because of citizenship of the United States."

The states, he went on, could do what they wanted, provided their exclusions did not conflict with the 15th Amendment.

"If the State of New York should provide that no person should vote until he had reached the age of thirty years, ... or that no person having gray hair, ... should be entitled to vote, I do not see how it could be held to be a violation of any right derived or held under the Constitution of the United States."

Susan B. Anthony was convicted of the crime.

Eighteen months later, the Supreme Court heard the case of Virginia Minor. Denied registration as a voter, Minor wanted the court to rule that Missouri's limitation of voting rights to males was unconstitutional. In a unanimous opinion, the justices ruled that women were citizens of the country and thus "entitled to all the privileges and immunities of citizenship." That was a welcome clarification, but it begged the question, what are those privileges and immunities? In the court's view, they did not include voting rights. Writing in 1875, after ratification of the 15th Amendment, the justices could agree: "that the Constitution of the United

States does not confer the right of suffrage upon any one, and that the constitutions and laws of the several States which commit that important trust to men alone are not necessarily void."

The decisions in the cases of Susan B. Anthony and Virginia Minor not only closed a door for women but also opened doors for states. In advance of her trial, Susan B. Anthony had warned about the flawed reasoning:

"It will not always be men combining to disfranchise all women ... Indeed, establish this precedent, admit this right to deny suffrage to the states, and there is no power to foresee the confusion, discord, and disruption that awaits us. There is, and can be, but one safe principle of government—equal rights to all."

Above: Virginia Minor who, denied registration as a voter, took her case to the Supreme Court in 1874.

Once the Supreme Court ruled against Virginia Minor, suffrage activism settled into two streams: federal and state. The National Association returned to advocacy of a federal amendment and used Julian's model with its claim of universal voting rights based on citizenship. However, in 1878, an amendment modeled on the 15th Amendment was introduced in the Senate. Despite the less radical language, opponents blocked its consideration for nine years. On January 25, 1887, a day that coincided with a convention of woman suffragists in the nation's capital, Senator Henry W. Blair of New Hampshire brought the matter to the floor and the Senate finally voted on the issue. Women packed the Senate Gallery to watch senators defeat the resolution. The Senate would not vote again on the amendment until 1914. In the House of Representatives, the amendment did not come up for any vote until 1915.

Meanwhile, the American Association encouraged activists in states to pursue any political rights that fell within a state's power to grant. Suffragists poured enormous resources into state and territorial campaigns, with far more lost than won. But the wins mattered to the women in the West who gained a voice in government through full suffrage.

Woman suffragists did not act in a political vacuum but were influenced and constrained by national politics. In the South, the withdrawal of federal troops as part of the Compromise of 1877 closed Reconstruction and reversed the progress toward political participation made by African Americans in that region. Elections in southern states were occasions of racial violence. Federal enforcement of the 15th Amendment ceased, and white southerners regained power in Congress. States in the former Confederacy set about rewriting their constitutions to put obstacles in the way of African American men registering to vote. Beginning with Mississippi's new constitution of 1890, the states defined an assortment of ways to block or significantly reduce Black enfranchisement.

At about the same time, after the Senate vote on a woman suffrage amendment in 1887, discussion began about merging the two suffrage associations before their leaders died. There were lots

Right: Suffragists put up a poster promoting
a parade in Washington, D.C.

of reasons, but the defeat of the amendment seemed to signal the end of an old divide and a chance for suffragists to unite around state action. Through merger, the National American Woman Suffrage Association came into existence in 1890. Attention to federal protection for a citizen's right to vote or any federal amendment waned.

It happened, then, that in 1890, woman suffragists stopped seeking federal protection for voting rights at the same moment that southern states formalized the exclusion of Black men from the franchise. Their complicity went further. To gain ground in the white South, the National American Woman Suffrage Association affirmed in 1903 its belief in the South's prerogative to legislate white supremacy: the association resolved "to do away with the requirement of a sex qualification for suffrage ... What other qualifications shall be asked for it leaves to each State." The political equality of all citizens was no longer the organized movement's objective.

Woman suffragists turned back to the goal of a constitutional amendment in 1913 and the Senate voted on the measure in 1914—defeating it again. But this time, despite a persistent interest in keeping the focus on state actions and despite a new divide between two suffrage groups, women stayed the course and kept up pressure until both houses of Congress approved the

measure in June 1919. It is this last phase, from 1913 to 1919, that produces the most striking stories and martyrology of woman suffrage history, with jail sentences, hunger strikes, and forced feeding. The images shocked contemporaries and clothed the federal government as oppressor.

Less colorful was the fact that by 1919 women in 15 states had gained full voting rights and were electing senators and members of Congress. The men who were accountable to female constituents voted overwhelmingly in support of the amendment. Like any amendment proposed to the Constitution, this one needed three-quarters of the states (36 at the time) to ratify it. Those many steps took more than a year and came down to one vote in one state—in Tennessee in August 1920. It had taken decades and generations to eliminate the presumption that men had a right to govern for women. Activists had changed both law and political culture because they believed that manhood suffrage—full voting rights for men and only men—made a mockery of self-government.

This huge step toward "a more perfect union" left standing the judicial decisions that a right to vote was not a fundamental right of American citizenship. Although the National Woman's Party had referred to the 19th Amendment as the "Susan B. Anthony Amendment," it did not reflect her convictions about a citizen's

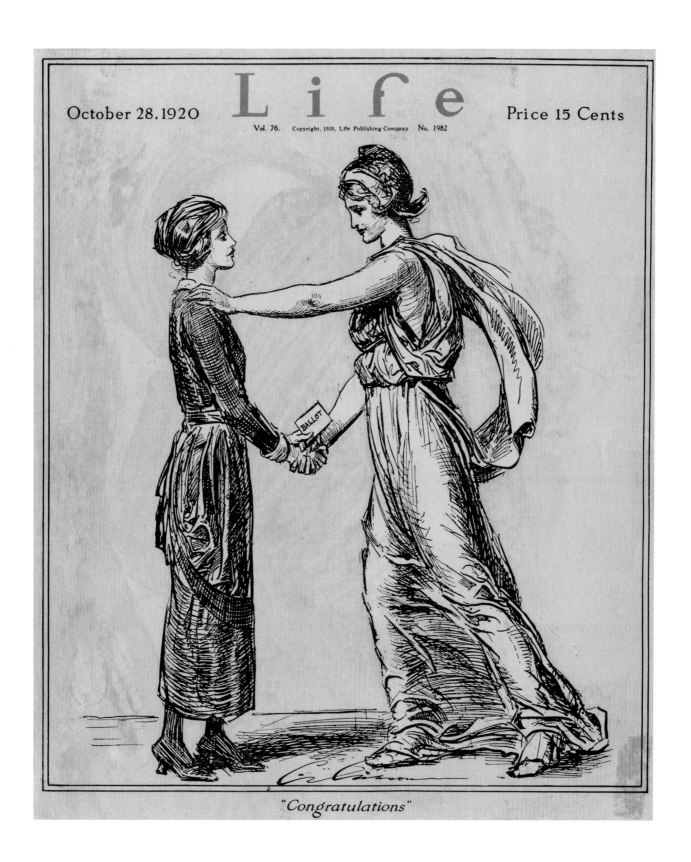

October 28, 1920

Life

Vol. 76. Copyright, 1920, Life Publishing Company No. 1982

Price 15 Cents

BALLOT

"Congratulations"

Opposite: Members of New York's Woman Suffrage Party take part
in the city's 1913 suffrage parade. Above: Columbia, the female
personification of the U.S., offers "Congratulations" to the nation's
women following ratification of the 19th Amendment.

"There is, and can be, but one safe principle of government —equal rights to all"

—Susan B. Anthony

right to vote. The difference was underscored immediately in the fall of 1920 by the federal government's decision that the women of Puerto Rico, despite their U.S. citizenship, were not enfranchised by the amendment because citizenship did not guarantee a right to vote. Their woman suffrage movement lasted until 1935.

The amendment also left in place states' rights to exclude citizens from the rolls of eligible voters provided that the reasons for doing so were not those itemized in the 15th and 19th Amendments. This bow to states' rights was a part of the amendment's political appeal and is a part of its legacy to this day. This amendment simply meant that the state must discriminate equally. As the Equal Suffrage League of Virginia reassured the white public in 1916, speaking of the devices by which African Americans were kept at bay, "as these qualifications restrict the negro man's vote, it stands to reason that they will also restrict the negro woman's vote."

In northern states, African American women embraced their new right to vote and used its power to press for racial justice and equality. The experience of African American women in states of the former Confederacy was not uniform, and it took several years for officials to complete the job of disfranchisement. Some women managed to register and vote in the presidential election in 1920. But across much of the South, equal discrimination subjected African American women to well-practiced tactics designed to discourage and/or disqualify them as voters.

William Pickens, of the National Association for the Advancement of Colored People, reported on voter registration in Columbia, South Carolina, a state where African Americans made up the majority of the population. Registrars were surprised at the high numbers of Black women who lined up to register, he wrote. They relied on a familiar tactic, "white people first," leaving women of color standing for hours. On the second day, these women "were made to read and even to explain long passages from the constitutions and from various civil and criminal codes." White supremacists of South Carolina followed the path etched in Ward Hunt's conviction of Susan B. Anthony, the same one later ratified by the National American Woman Suffrage Association's promise to the South in 1903, that states could invent whatever qualifications for voters they desired, so long as there was no sex qualification. It took 45 years to win the Voting Rights Act of 1965 that protected the rights for people of color, women and men, across the South.

To close the history of woman suffrage at 1920 is to ignore those women left behind in 1920, women who still dreamed of equal political rights. It is also to ignore how precarious the victory, how easily women can lose their ability to vote if the state where they reside exercises its right to exclude people, and to forget that freedom without voting rights is a mockery, whoever you are.

This article was originally commissioned by the National Conference of State Historic Preservation Officers in partnership with the United States National Park Service.

Opposite: Women cast their votes in Pittsburgh, 1950. It would be another 15 years before legislation was signed into law protecting Black voters' rights nationwide.

Elizabeth Cady Stanton and Women's Rights

ELIZABETH CADY STANTON'S SENECA FALLS ADDRESS

In July 1848, Stanton gave this keynote speech
at the first women's rights convention, held
in Seneca Falls, New York

"We have met here today to discuss our rights and wrongs, civil and political, and not, as some have supposed, to go into the detail of social life alone. We do not propose to petition the legislature to make our husbands just, generous, and courteous, to seat every man at the head of a cradle, and to clothe every woman in male attire.

None of these points, however important they may be considered by leading men, will be touched in this convention. As to their costume, the gentlemen need feel no fear of our imitating that, for we think it in violation of every principle of taste, beauty, and dignity; notwithstanding all the contempt cast upon our loose, flowing garments, we still admire the graceful folds, and consider our costume far more artistic than theirs. Many of the nobler sex seem to agree with us in this opinion, for the bishops, priests, judges, barristers, and lord mayors of the first nation on the globe, and the Pope of Rome, with his cardinals, too, all wear the loose flowing robes, thus tacitly acknowledging that the male attire is neither dignified nor imposing.

No, we shall not molest you in your philosophical experiments with stocks, pants, high-heeled boots, and Russian belts. Yours be the glory to discover, by personal experience, how long the kneepan can resist the terrible strapping down which you impose, in how short time the well-developed muscles of the throat can be reduced to mere threads by the constant pressure of the stock, how high the heel of a boot must be to make a short man tall, and how tight the Russian belt may be drawn and yet have wind enough left to sustain life.

But we are assembled to protest against a form of government existing without the consent of the governed—to declare our right to be free as man is free, to be represented in the government which we are taxed to support, to have such disgraceful laws as give man the power to chastise and imprison his wife, to take the wages which she earns, the property which she inherits, and, in case of separation, the children of her love; laws which make her the mere dependent on his bounty. It is to protest against such unjust laws as these that we are assembled today, and to have them, if possible, forever erased from our statute books, deeming them a shame and a disgrace to a Christian republic in the 19th century. We have met to uplift woman's fallen divinity upon an even pedestal with man's. And, strange as it may seem to many, we now demand our right to vote according to the declaration of the government under which we live.

This right no one pretends to deny. We need not prove ourselves equal to Daniel Webster to enjoy this privilege, for the ignorant Irishman in the ditch has all the civil rights he has. We need not prove our muscular power equal to this same Irishman to enjoy this privilege, for the most tiny, weak, ill-shaped stripling of twenty-one has all the civil rights of the Irishman. We have no objection to discuss the question of equality, for we feel that the weight of argument lies wholly with us, but we wish the question of equality kept distinct from the question of rights, for the proof of the one does not determine the truth of the other. All white men in this country have the same rights, however they may differ in mind, body, or estate.

Opposite: Elizabeth Cady Stanton addresses
the audience in the Wesleyan Chapel
in Seneca Falls, New York, 1848.

The right is ours. The question now is: how shall we get possession of what rightfully belongs to us? We should not feel so sorely grieved if no man who had not attained the full stature of a Webster, Clay, Van Buren, or Gerrit Smith could claim the right of the elective franchise. But to have drunkards, idiots, horse-racing, rum-selling rowdies, ignorant foreigners, and silly boys fully recognized, while we ourselves are thrust out from all the rights that belong to citizens, it is too grossly insulting to the dignity of woman to be longer quietly submitted to.

The right is ours. Have it, we must. Use it, we will. The pens, the tongues, the fortunes, the indomitable wills of many women are already pledged to secure this right. The great truth that no just government can be formed without the consent of the governed we shall echo and re-echo in the ears of the unjust judge, until by continual coming we shall weary him.

There seems now to be a kind of moral stagnation in our midst. Philanthropists have done their utmost to rouse the nation to a sense of its sins. War, slavery, drunkenness, licentiousness, gluttony, have been dragged naked before the people, and all their abominations and deformities fully brought to light, yet with idiotic laugh we hug those monsters to our breasts and rush on to destruction. Our churches are multiplying on all sides, our missionary societies, Sunday schools, and prayer meetings and innumerable charitable and reform organizations are all in operation, but still the tide of vice is swelling, and threatens the destruction of everything, and the battlements of righteousness are weak against the raging elements of sin and death.

Verily, the world waits the coming of some new element, some purifying power, some spirit of mercy and love. The voice of woman has been silenced in the state, the church, and the home, but man cannot fulfill his destiny alone, he cannot redeem his race unaided. There are deep and tender chords of sympathy and love in the hearts of the downfallen and oppressed that woman can touch more skillfully than man.

The world has never yet seen a truly great and virtuous nation, because in the degradation of woman the very fountains of life are poisoned at their source. It is vain to look for silver and gold from mines of copper and lead.

It is the wise mother that has the wise son. So long as your women are slaves you may throw your colleges and churches to the winds. You can't have scholars and saints so long as your mothers are ground to powder between the upper and nether millstone of tyranny and lust. How seldom, now, is a father's pride gratified, his fond hopes realized, in the budding genius of his son!

The wife is degraded, made the mere creature of caprice, and the foolish son is heaviness to his heart. Truly are the sins of the fathers visited upon the children to the third and fourth generation. God, in His wisdom, has so linked the whole human family together that any violence done at one end of the chain is felt throughout its length, and here, too, is the law of restoration, as in woman all have fallen, so in her elevation shall the race be recreated.

'Voices' were the visitors and advisers of Joan of Arc. Do not 'voices' come to us daily from the haunts of poverty, sorrow, degradation, and despair, already too long unheeded. Now is the time for the women of this country, if they would save our free institutions, to defend the right, to buckle on the armor that can best resist the keenest weapons of the enemy—contempt and ridicule. The same religious enthusiasm that nerved Joan of Arc to her work nerves us to ours. In every generation God calls some men and women for the utterance of truth, a heroic action, and our work today is the fulfilling of what has long since been foretold by the Prophet—Joel 2:28:

'And it shall come to pass afterward, that I will pour out my spirit upon all flesh; and your sons and your daughters shall prophesy.'

We do not expect our path will be strewn with the flowers of popular applause, but over the thorns of bigotry and prejudice will be our way, and on our banners will beat the dark storm clouds of opposition from those who have entrenched themselves behind the stormy bulwarks of custom and authority, and who have fortified their position by every means, holy and unholy. But we will steadfastly abide the result. Unmoved we will bear it aloft. Undauntedly we will unfurl it to the gale, for we know that the storm cannot rend from it a shred, that the electric flash will but more clearly show to us the glorious words inscribed upon it, 'Equality of Rights.'"

"We are assembled to protest against a form of government existing without the consent of the governed—to declare our right to be free as man is free, to be represented in the government which we are taxed to support"

CHAPTER TWO

ALLIES, STRATEGIES, AND CONFLICTS

WHAT BREAKS UP THE

Unemployment for men.   Bad employment for women and children.

WHAT WILL SAVE TH

The participation of the home-maker in all governmental control of these problems. For

VOTES FOR W

NATIONAL AMERICAN WOMAN SUFFRAGE ASSOCIATION,   505 F

IOME?

NO HANDS
WANTED
TO DAY

"The easiest way."

C HOME?

eason we demand

MEN

H AVENUE, NEW YORK CITY

THE INFLUENCE OF OTHER SOCIAL MOVEMENTS

Women's enfranchisement was closely connected to such causes as the struggle for racial justice, temperance, and the labor movement, all of which were linked at one time or another to the fight for the vote

By Robyn Muncy

American women's struggle for the vote, a profoundly important chapter in the story of American democracy, did not unfold as an independent plot. Instead, the woman suffrage movement emerged from and was continually fed by other social movements and political causes. Between the 1830s and 1920, women's enfranchisement was intimately connected to such crusades as the struggle for racial justice, the women's rights movement, the campaign to regulate alcohol, and the labor movement. For some women, involvement in these social movements created the very desire for the vote; for many, it honed skills necessary to building a political movement. At various points, factions within those social movements became allies of the suffrage campaign, expanding its base of support. Many of these movements circulated ideas about human rights and democracy that prompted increasing numbers of Americans to advocate women's enfranchisement. In all these ways, other reform movements were crucial to the victories of woman suffrage.

The antebellum period (the years before the Civil War), awash in religious fervor, economic upheaval, and debates over the meaning of the American Revolution, generated many potent reform movements. Women's participation in these movements often nudged them beyond the domestic sphere, accepted in the early 19th century as women's natural place, and sometimes eroded their acceptance of social norms that required women's subordination to men. In the 1840s and 1850s, a women's rights movement coalesced from a wide array of antebellum reform drives and eventually produced a sustained struggle for woman suffrage.

The antislavery movement, the most significant antebellum reform effort, proved a powerful generator of women's rights activism. A fundamental institution of American life at the birth of the republic, slavery became ever more central to the U.S. economy during the early 19th century. Organized opposition to slavery emerged first among free Blacks in the North, as well as Quakers, Unitarians, and evangelical Christians, both Black and white. Radical abolitionism publicly debuted in 1829 when African American David Walker published *Walker's Appeal, In Four Articles*, a forceful critique of slavery and racial discrimination. Two years later, white New Englander William Lloyd Garrison began publishing *The Liberator*, and, in 1833, he joined with other opponents of slavery to form the American Anti-Slavery Society (AASS). The AASS demanded the immediate abolition of slavery and full civil rights for African Americans. Its broad commitment to human rights opened the AASS to overtures by women for voice and leadership: over 100 local women's affiliates joined the cause.

The Liberator demonstrated its openness to women in 1831 when it published an essay by Maria Stewart, a free Black woman, who condemned slavery as well as discrimination against free Blacks and women. Stewart urged free Black men, "sue for your rights and privileges," and she asked, "How long shall the fair daughters of Africa be compelled to bury their minds and talents beneath a load of iron pots and kettles?" When a Boston antislavery society invited Stewart to speak in 1832, she became the first American-born woman to address an audience of both women and men.

"The antislavery movement, the most significant antebellum reform effort, proved a powerful generator of women's rights activism"

By doing so, Stewart violated social conventions that forbade women from speaking before what was termed a "promiscuous" audience. Women might speak before a gathering of women in their parlors or churches, but an audience of both women and men outraged propriety. Although Stewart left Boston in 1833, disappointed that the city seemed to reject her leadership, the publication of her works by *The Liberator* assured that her anti-racist, abolitionist feminism reached beyond Boston, and her public addresses set a precedent for other female activists.

Stewart's ideas certainly resonated with those of the interracial Philadelphia Female Anti-Slavery Society founded the very year that Stewart left Boston. Philadelphia was a hotbed of antislavery activism in part because of its vital Quaker community, which was inclined to egalitarian social relations by the belief that God dwelled in every person. Quaker egalitarianism even helped to convert two women born to the southern plantation elite, Angelina and Sarah Grimké, to antislavery activism. In 1836, after living in Philadelphia for several years, the sisters took up the abolitionist cause and soon scandalized many Americans by speaking before gender- and race-integrated audiences, as Maria Stewart had. Their audacity provoked violent opposition.

The belief of many women in the antislavery movement that God called them to the cause weakened their acceptance of cultural prohibitions against women's public activism. Some antislavery activists even began to see the exclusion of women from public life as a violation of women's own human rights. By 1838, Sarah Grimké came to the conclusion that "Men and women were CREATED EQUAL; they are both moral and accountable beings; and whatever is right for man to do, is right for woman." Some of those who could not countenance this perfect equality of women and men nevertheless questioned limitations on women's freedom to work publicly to benefit others. After all, dominant ideals of womanhood assumed women's selflessness and innate moral perspicacity. If God granted women special moral insight, some

Previous pages: A National American Woman Suffrage Association handbill depicting the ills that "Votes for Women" could help overcome. Opposite: An illustration celebrating the emancipation of slaves following the Civil War, and a vision of the life of freedom to come, c. 1865. Above: William Lloyd Garrison.

LUCRETIA MOTT

1793–1880

Edited by Debra Michals

Lucretia Coffin Mott was an early feminist activist and strong advocate for ending slavery. A powerful orator, she dedicated her life to speaking out against racial and gender injustice.

Born on January 3, 1793 on Nantucket Island, Massachusetts, Mott was the second of Thomas Coffin Jr.'s and Anna Folger Mott's five children. Her father's work as a ship's captain kept him away from his family for long stretches and could be hazardous—so much so that he moved his family to Boston and became a merchant when Lucretia was 10 years old.

Mott was raised a Quaker, a religion that stressed equality of all people under God, and attended a Quaker boarding school in upstate New York. In 1809, the family moved to Philadelphia, and two years later, Mott married her father's business partner, James Mott, with whom she would have six children. In 1815, her father died, saddling her mother with a mountain of debt, and Mott, her husband, and her mother joined forces to become solvent again. Mott taught school, her mother went back to running a shop, and her husband operated a textile business.

Mott, along with her supportive husband, argued ardently for the abolitionist cause as members of William Lloyd Garrison's American Anti-Slavery Society in the 1830s. Garrison, who encouraged women's participation as writers and speakers in the anti-slavery movement embraced Mott's commitment. Mott was one of the founders of the Philadelphia Female Anti-Slavery Society in 1833. Not everyone supported women's public speaking. In fact, Mott was constantly criticized for behaving in ways not acceptable for members of her sex, but it did not deter her.

Mott's stymied participation at the World Anti-Slavery Convention in London in 1840 brought her into contact with Elizabeth Cady Stanton with whom she formed a long and prolific collaboration. It also led Mott into the cause of women's rights. As women, the pair were blocked from participating in the proceedings, which not only angered them, but led them to promise to hold a women's rights convention when they returned to the United States. Eight years later, in 1848, they organized the Seneca Falls Convention, attended by hundreds of people including noted abolitionist Frederick Douglass. Stanton presented a "Declaration of Sentiments" at the meeting, which demanded rights for women by inserting the word "woman" into the language of the Declaration of Independence and included a list of 18 woman-specific demands. These included divorce, property and custody rights, as well as the right to vote. The latter fueled the launching of the woman suffrage movement. Mott explained that she grew up "so thoroughly imbued with women's rights that it was the most important question" of her life. Following the convention Mott continued her crusade for women's equality by speaking at ensuing annual women's rights conventions and publishing *Discourse on Women*, a reasoned account of the history of women's repression.

Her devotion to women's rights did not deter her from fighting for an end to slavery. She and her husband protested the passage of the Fugitive Slave Act of 1850 and helped an enslaved person escape bondage a few years later. In 1866, Mott became the first president of the American Equal Rights Association. Mott joined with Stanton and Anthony in decrying the 14th and 15th amendments to the Constitution for granting the vote to Black men but not to women. Mott was also involved with efforts to establish Swarthmore College and was instrumental in ensuring it was coeducational. Dedicated to all forms of human freedom, Mott argued as ardently for women's rights as for Black rights, including suffrage, education, and economic aid. Mott played a major role in the woman suffrage movement through her life.

This article appears courtesy of the National Women's History Museum.

asked, did it make sense to ban women from public life, which so desperately needed moral leadership?

So contentious did women's roles become among abolitionists that they split over the issue in 1840. Those accepting women's rights as a legitimate commitment for their movement remained in the AASS, and those opposed formed the American and Foreign Anti-Slavery Society. From that point on, women such as Lucretia Mott and Lydia Maria Child were elected officers of the AASS, and others, including Susan B. Anthony, were hired as paid organizers. In this way, the antislavery movement became a significant node in the emerging network of activists demanding greater power and scope for American women.

There were many other nodes. One was the labor movement. Textile manufacturing industrialized in the early 19th century and recruited young women from rural families to work in the new cloth-making mills that dotted New England. In the 1830s, those earliest of America's industrial workers staged strikes against deteriorating working conditions, claiming a public voice and presence for working women.

In that same decade, both Black and white women, working and middle class, joined a movement for moral reform. These activists decried social norms that allowed respectable men to frequent brothels while condemning prostitutes as hopeless sinners. Moral reformers wanted men held to the same chaste standard as women and to offer alternative employment opportunities to poor women. This movement critiqued the existing gender system and slid some women reformers into public life.

Like moral reform, the temperance movement urged men to control their desire for pleasure, in this case by abstaining from drunkenness. Some women saw temperance as an issue on which they must take a public stand in order to protect their families from domestic violence and poverty. The antebellum temperance movement became another site for reimagining women's proper place in society and giving some women experience in public speaking and movement organizing.

The antebellum period also witnessed independent campaigns explicitly for women's rights. Frances Wright began lecturing about the equality of women and men soon after her immigration to the

Above: Writer and activist
Lydia Maria Child.

United States from Scotland in the 1820s. Her efforts produced no sustained following, probably because she rejected marriage and supported racial equality. But other, more focused drives won adherents. Calls for equal access to education and employment, for instance, drew broader support. Demands for equal pay resonated powerfully among women teachers.

Agitation for married women's property rights gained momentum when, in 1836, Ernestine Rose, a Jewish immigrant from Poland by way of England, campaigned in New York for a law aimed at securing married women's property rights. The proposal represented change because, when women in the United States married, they generally lost control of their property and even the wages they earned. Husbands controlled all under the legal doctrine of coverture, which said that women had no independent legal identity once married. In the 1840s, emerging feminists Paulina Wright and Elizabeth Cady Stanton joined Rose in lobbying for married women's economic rights in New York, where they achieved partial success in 1848 and a broader triumph in 1860.

At the same time, Stanton, a privileged and brilliant mother deeply dissatisfied with the restrictions on antebellum women's lives, imagined a broader agenda. Strong ties to antislavery Quakers made it possible for Stanton to organize support for her vision of greater equality for women. Her activist friends included Lucretia Mott, whom Stanton had first met in 1840 at the World Anti-Slavery Convention in London, Martha Coffin Wright, Mott's sister, Mary Ann and Elizabeth M'Clintock, and Jane Hunt. Together, these women called the

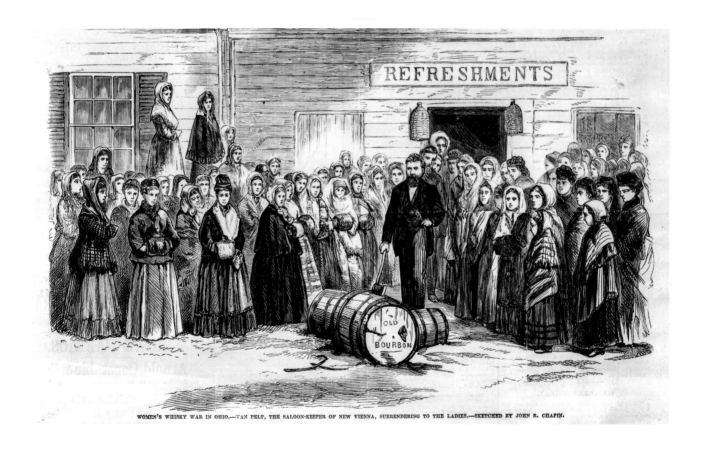

WOMEN'S WHISKY WAR IN OHIO.—VAN PELT, THE SALOON-KEEPER OF NEW VIENNA, SURRENDERING TO THE LADIES.—SKETCHED BY JOHN R. CHAPIN.

Above: Temperance advocates convince an Ohio saloon
keeper to take an axe to his barrels of bourbon. Opposite, left:
Frances Wright. Opposite, right: Paulina Wright.

first women's rights convention in U.S. history. It convened at Seneca Falls, New York, in July 1848. Over 300 participants, men and women, Black and white, attended that historic two-day meeting. They debated the Declaration of Sentiments, a sweeping list of demands for women's advancement, which ranged from equal access to education and professions to married women's property rights and access to divorce—as well as the vote. All the demands passed unanimously except the call for suffrage. Only passionate advocacy by Stanton and antislavery activist Frederick Douglass saved that item from the scrap heap. Clearly, suffrage was not, in the 1840s, a central issue even for many women's rights advocates. Nevertheless, the vote commonly appeared on the agendas of national women's rights conventions that began in 1850.

Suffrage became a central concern of the women's rights movement because of the allied movement for racial justice. The U.S. Civil War interrupted the campaign for women's rights between 1861 and 1865, but once slavery was legally abolished and the U.S. Congress began to debate the civil and political rights of freed people, women's rights agitation reemerged. During a congressional push for the protection of Black men's voting rights, some advocates of African American and women's rights formed the American Equal Rights Association to press for the simultaneous enfranchisement of Black men and all women. (By that point, the states had generally enfranchised all white men.)

When it became clear, however, that Congress would, through the 15th Amendment, protect the voting rights of Black men but not those of women, some women's rights activists, including Elizabeth Cady Stanton and Susan B. Anthony, refused to support it and formed the National Woman Suffrage Association to push for a 16th Amendment enfranchising women. Activists committed to maintaining the alliance between the movements for racial justice and women's rights, especially Lucy Stone and Julia Ward Howe, formed the American Woman Suffrage Association, which supported the 15th Amendment and mounted state-level battles for women's enfranchisement. Not until 1890 would the two groups reunite in the National American Woman Suffrage Association, which became the principal woman suffrage organization in the decades leading to ratification of 19th Amendment. By that time, the alliance between the movements for racial justice and women's rights was severely attenuated.

As women's rights advocates split over their relationship to racial justice, the woman suffrage effort received a boost from another social movement, the temperance crusade. Founded in the 1870s, the Woman's Christian Temperance Union (WCTU) became the largest women's organization in the late 19th century. Especially strong in the Midwest and South, the WCTU focused on closing saloons through nonviolent direct action and laws limiting the sale of alcohol. In 1876, one of the WCTU's leaders, Frances Willard, concluded that women would have greater power to win temperance legislation if they had the vote. She did not claim the franchise as a right, however, but as a necessity for fulfilling women's domestic duties. While in prayer, Willard wrote in her autobiography, she received the revelation that she should "speak for the woman's ballot as a weapon of protection to her home." With that framing, in 1881 Willard convinced the WCTU to endorse woman suffrage. As a result, many socially conservative women began to support their own voting rights, expanding the movement's base. Indeed, because so many women backed temperance, the Prohibition Party endorsed woman suffrage in 1872 and remained a staunch supporter of the movement for decades.

The Populist Party was another third-party advocate of votes for women. A coalition of farmers, workers, and small business owners opposed to the control of the U.S. economy by an eastern corporate elite, the Populist Party in 1892 proposed a set of policies intended to broaden American democracy and democratize the U.S. economy. The enfranchisement of women was on that agenda. The victory of woman suffrage in Colorado in 1893 can be directly credited to the Populists, and several men in Colorado, including juvenile court judge Benjamin Lindsey, became national spokesmen for women's enfranchisement.

Although the Populist Party disappeared into the Democratic Party in 1896, many of its commitments were absorbed by the Progressive movement that emerged in the 1890s and dominated

Above: Members of the Woman's Christian
Temperance Union, New Hampshire.

SUSAN B. ANTHONY

1820–1906

Edited by Nancy Hayward

Champion of temperance, abolition, the rights of labor, and equal pay for equal work, Susan Brownell Anthony became one of the most visible leaders of the women's suffrage movement. Along with Elizabeth Cady Stanton, she traveled around the country delivering speeches in favor of women's suffrage.

Susan B. Anthony was born on February 15, 1820 in Adams, Massachusetts. Her father, Daniel, was a farmer and later a cotton mill owner and manager, and was raised as a Quaker. Her mother, Lucy, came from a family that fought in the American Revolution and served in the Massachusetts state government. From an early age, Anthony was inspired by the Quaker belief that everyone was equal under God. That idea guided her throughout her life. She had seven brothers and sisters, many of whom became activists for justice and the emancipation of slaves.

After many years of teaching, Anthony returned to her family who had moved to New York State. There she met leading abolitionists William Lloyd Garrison and Frederick Douglass, who were friends of her father. Listening to them moved Anthony to want to do more to help end slavery. She became an abolition activist, even though most people thought it was improper for women to give speeches in public, and made many passionate speeches against slavery.

In 1848, a group of women held a convention at Seneca Falls, New York. It was the first women's rights convention in the United States and is recognized widely as the beginning of the suffrage movement. Her mother and sister attended the convention but Anthony did not. In 1851, Anthony met Elizabeth Cady Stanton. The two women became good friends and worked together for over 50 years fighting for women's rights. They traveled the country and Anthony gave speeches demanding that women be given the right to vote. At times, she risked being arrested for sharing her ideas in public.

Anthony was good at strategy. Her discipline, energy, and ability to organize made her a strong and successful leader. Anthony and Stanton co-founded the American Equal Rights Association. In 1868, they became editors of the Association's newspaper, *The Revolution*, which helped to spread the ideas of equality and rights for women. Anthony began to lecture to raise money to publish the newspaper and to support the suffrage movement. She became famous throughout the county—many admired her, yet others hated her ideas.

When Congress passed the 15th Amendment, which gave voting rights to African American men, Anthony and Stanton believed the legislation should have included the right to vote for women. Suffragists divided over support for the 15th Amendment. Anthony, Stanton and others went on to form the National Woman Suffrage Association to push for a constitutional amendment giving women the right to vote.

In 1872, Anthony was arrested for voting. She was tried and fined $100 for her crime—a judgment that angered many people and

brought national attention to the suffrage movement. In 1876, she led a protest at the Centennial Celebration of our nation's independence. She took to the stage and gave a speech—"Declaration of Rights of the Women of the United States"—written by Stanton and another suffragist, Matilda Joslyn Gage.

Anthony spent her life working for women's rights. In 1890, she helped to merge the two largest suffrage associations into one: the National American Woman Suffrage Association. She led the group until 1900. She traveled around the country giving speeches, gathering thousands of signatures on petitions, and lobbying Congress every year for women. Anthony died in 1906, 14 years before the passage of the 19th Amendment in 1920 included women's right to vote in the U.S. Constitution.

This article appears courtesy of the National Women's History Museum.

Above: Social reformer and activist Jane Addams.
Opposite: Typographical Union members take
part in a Labor Day parade, New York, 1909.

American politics in the early 20th century. The Progressive movement began in diffuse local initiatives aimed to diminish the egregious inequalities of wealth and power created by new national corporations. By the 1890s, these economic behemoths controlled entire sectors of the U.S. economy and wielded substantial political power. Women were prominent among local reformers who tried to rein in corporate power through state laws to limit working hours, regulate child labor, and institute factory safety measures. Those same reformers also expanded public education, built public playgrounds, and created a juvenile justice system. They eventually created a federal income tax and public programs to reduce maternal and infant mortality. By the 1910s, many women in the Progressive movement were national political leaders, including Mary Church Terrell, first president of the National Association of Colored Women; Jane Addams, champion of working-class families; Florence Kelley, head of the National Consumers League; and Ida B. Wells-Barnett, anti-lynching crusader and cofounder of the National Association for the Advancement of Colored People (NAACP).

As millions of American women worked passionately in the Progressive movement, many came to believe, as had so many female abolitionists and temperance advocates, that they needed the vote in order to succeed in their other reform efforts. Some also believed that women deserved the vote as a matter of right. Either way, these reformers swelled the ranks of the woman suffrage movement. Their visibility and effectiveness as reformers also meant that Progressive men increasingly supported votes for women. In fact, the Progressive Party of 1912, an enormously important third-party effort, endorsed woman suffrage, and its presidential nominee, former president Theodore Roosevelt, proclaimed that women would participate in the Progressive Party on a basis of "absolute equality" with men.

Although African American suffragists worked vigorously for the cause in the early 20th century, the deterioration of

U.S. race relations after 1890—embodied in brutal measures to segregate the races and disenfranchise African American men in the South—meant that suffragists worked mostly in racially segregated organizations between 1890 and 1920. While white suffragists, including some who expressly opposed the enfranchisement of Black women, increased the membership of NAWSA to two million, many Black women worked for the vote through multifocus organizations such as the National Association of Colored Women or the Women's Convention of the Black Baptist Church. Ida B. Wells-Barnett founded the Alpha Suffrage Club in Chicago, which contributed mightily to the victory of woman suffrage in Illinois (1913). The NAACP, organized in 1909–10, became an important forum for suffrage activism that included both woman suffrage and the reenfranchisement of Black men in the South.

Women in the labor movement and Socialist Party also expanded support for woman suffrage in the early 20th century.

Immigrant women in New York's garment industry, including Clara Lemlich, Rose Schneiderman, and Pauline Newman, agitated for the vote. Although many male labor leaders and socialists supported woman suffrage in principle, they did not make it a priority. Indeed, many belittled woman suffrage as a middle-class issue. But leaders among the dramatically increasing group of working women argued that wage-earning women needed the vote. Only with suffrage, they insisted, could working women hope for equal pay, safe work places, and humane hours.

In 1909, working-class suffragists generated a major debate about their cause within New York's labor community, and in 1911 they formed the Wage Earners' Suffrage League. One of the league's flyers asked, "Why are you paid less than a man? Why do you work in a fire trap? Why are your hours so long?" The answer: "Because you are a woman and have no vote. Votes make the law. The law controls conditions. Women who want better conditions must vote." Woman suffrage

Above: Young women picket in New York City
during the 1909 garment workers strike.

IDA B. WELLS-BARNETT

1862–1931

By Arlisha R. Norwood

Ida B. Wells-Barnett was a prominent journalist, activist, and researcher in the late 19th and early 20th centuries. In her lifetime, she battled sexism, racism, and violence. As a skilled writer, Wells-Barnett also used her skills as a journalist to shed light on the conditions of African Americans throughout the South.

Ida Bell Wells was born in Holly Springs, Mississippi on July 16th, 1862. She was born into slavery during the Civil War. Once the war ended Wells-Barnett's parents became politically active in Reconstruction Era politics. Her parents instilled into her the importance of education. Wells-Barnett enrolled at Rust College but was expelled when she started a dispute with the university president. In 1878, Wells-Barnett went to visit her grandmother. While she was there Wells-Barnett was informed that a yellow fever epidemic had hit her hometown. The disease took both of Wells-Barnett's parents and her infant brother. Left to raise her brothers and sister, she took a job as a teacher so that she could keep the family together. Eventually, Wells-Barnett moved her siblings to Memphis, Tennessee. There she continued to work as an educator.

In 1884, Wells-Barnett filed a lawsuit against a train car company in Memphis for unfair treatment. She had been thrown off a first-class train, despite having a ticket. Although she won the case on the local level, the ruling was eventually overturned in federal court. After the lynching of one of her friends, Wells-Barnett turned her attention to white mob violence. She became skeptical about the reasons Black men were lynched and set out to investigate several cases. She published her findings in a pamphlet

and wrote several columns in local newspapers. Her expose about an 1892 lynching enraged locals, who burned her press and drove her from Memphis. After a few months, the threats became so bad she was forced to move to Chicago, Illinois.

In 1893, Wells-Barnett joined other African American leaders in calling for the boycott of the World's Columbian Exposition. The boycotters accused the exposition committee of locking out African Americans and negatively portraying the Black community. In 1895, Wells-Barnett married famed African American lawyer Ferdinand Barnett. Together, the couple had four children. Throughout her career Wells-Barnett, balanced motherhood with her activism.

Wells-Barnett traveled internationally, shedding light on lynching to foreign audiences. Abroad, she openly confronted white women in the suffrage movement who ignored lynching. Because of her stance, she was often ostracized by women's suffrage organizations in the United States. Nevertheless, Wells-Barnett remained active in the women's rights movement. She was a founder of the National Association of Colored Women's Clubs, which was created to address issues dealing with civil rights and women's suffrage. Although she was in Niagara Falls for the founding of the National Association for the Advancement of Colored People (NAACP), her name is not mentioned as an official founder. Late in her career Wells-Barnett focused on urban reform in the growing city of Chicago. She died on March 25, 1931.
This article appears courtesy of the National Women's History Museum.

"Why are you paid less than a man? Why do you work in a fire trap? Why are your hours so long? Because you are a woman and have no vote"

—Wage Earners' Suffrage League

triumphed in New York in 1917 partly because so many working-class men voted yes.

Similar agitation occurred elsewhere to such an extent that throughout the 1910s, working-class men petitioned Congress to pass a woman suffrage amendment to the Constitution. Likewise in the territories, where Puerto Rican labor activist Luisa Capetillo argued so effectively for woman suffrage that by 1908 the island's Free Federation of Workers endorsed women's enfranchisement, and wage-earning women and the Socialist Party were among the most ardent suffrage activists.

Relationships between the woman suffrage movement and other social movements were sometimes wrenching: witness the conflict over the 15th Amendment and the racial and class segregation of most suffrage organizations in the early 20th century. Even so, the suffrage movement owed its existence and much of its gradually increasing strength to other reform movements. A host of antebellum reform efforts drew female adherents out of the domestic sphere, challenging prevailing gender conventions and motivating many to ask questions about all the restrictions on their lives.

The accumulation of those questions—and experience with writing, speaking, and organizing—produced a women's movement that eventually put suffrage front and center. Moreover, the fervent desire to change American life—whether by increasing women's wages or decreasing alcohol consumption—encouraged many women between the 1830s and 1920 to desire the vote as an important tool in their quest to perfect the union. Male colleagues in those reform movements increasingly perceived the value to their own political causes of enfranchising the women who worked alongside them. In sum, other reform movements were crucial to the victory of votes for women.

This article was originally commissioned by the National Conference of State Historic Preservation Officers in partnership with the United States National Park Service.

Opposite, top: Trade Union leader Rose Schneiderman.
Opposite, bottom: Members of the National Women's
Trade Union League attend a convention
in Chicago, 1909.

FLEXING FEMININE MUSCLES

The suffrage movement represents an extraordinary effort on the part of women to change not only their role in political life, but also the perception of women as civic-minded citizens

By Susan Goodier

Winning women's right to vote took the energies of three generations of women, the support of a few men, and nearly a century to accomplish. The process necessitated that suffragists ally with groups holding other priorities—abolitionists, temperance and maternalist reformers, and eventually political and third-party reformers—in their effort to broaden support.

When they began in the early 19th century, suffragists argued from a natural rights perspective; after the Civil War, during Reconstruction, suffragists cited the importance of women's unique characteristics as justification for the vote while also demanding the vote for themselves as citizens. Then, as suffragists observed the success of women's enfranchisement in the West, they increasingly focused on justice and equality arguments. Meanwhile, southerners' tightening of Jim Crow legal restrictions, which constrained African American voting and other rights, led some suffragists to develop arguments that played upon racial fears.

Over the course of the movement, suffragists continually modified their strategies, relying on state and national conventions, parlor meetings, petitions, promotional stunts, and print culture. Conflict, inherent to all social justice movements, stimulated ever greater creativity and influenced the strategies women drew upon. By the first two decades of the 20th century, suffragists had become experts at marketing their movement, overcoming most conflicts with careful strategizing.

A century earlier, during an era of "parlor politics," women sought to influence powerful men in private settings. A few daring women, such as Fanny Wright, spoke on lecture circuits and published their ideas. In these early years of the movement, suffragists looked back to the American Revolution to ground

their idea that women were citizens and had the same natural rights as men. Because the government derived from the "consent of the governed," as stated in the Declaration of Independence, women must be included in the electorate. The cry "no taxation without representation" applied to women as well as men.

Democratic ideals of equality between races, as well as the growing abolition movement, also influenced ideas related to gender equality. Wright, a freethinker, demanded that women be given an education equal to that of men; African American abolitionist Maria W. Stewart argued for the need to educate young women of color; abolitionists and women's rights activists Sarah and Angelina Grimké, who spoke to mixed audiences, and Margaret Fuller, author of *Woman in the Nineteenth Century* (1845), called for equality between women and men.

By 1846, six property-owning women submitted a petition to the New York State Constitutional Convention demanding it confer upon women the same "equal, and civil and political rights" white men enjoyed. Two years later, in July 1848, five women, including Quakers Lucretia Mott, her sister Martha Coffin Wright, Jane Hunt, and Mary M'Clintock, along with Elizabeth Cady Stanton, organized a women's rights convention in Seneca Falls, New York. Three hundred women and men responded to the call and traveled from across the state to discuss the "social, civil and religious condition and rights of woman."

The organizers drafted a Declaration of Sentiments—based on the wording of the Declaration of Independence—and called for greater civic and political rights for women.

During two days of debate, attendees supported most of the declaration's resolutions. Mott had forewarned Stanton that a demand for women's enfranchisement would likely put other goals of the convention at risk. As predicted, activists argued strenuously over inclusion of a demand for woman suffrage. Frederick Douglass and a few others finally convinced those in attendance to support the resolution—although they expected "misconception, misrepresentation, and ridicule." They determined to circulate tracts, petition legislators, curry the support of religious leaders and the press, and travel the speaking circuits. Immediately planning for additional conventions, activists eventually expected to hold them nationwide. For a dozen years, women's rights conventions drew the curious and the interested.

Efforts to gain women's rights, however, stalled during the Civil War. Rather than continue to petition and hold conventions for woman suffrage, many women chose to prove they were essential to the war effort, and by extension, to the political process. Stanton and Susan B. Anthony founded the Women's Loyal National League in 1863 to support the war and the end of slavery. Women served as nurses in field hospitals, while others ran farms or businesses left behind when men enlisted or were drafted. Energetic women organized fairs under the auspices of the United States Sanitary

Previous pages: Suffragists prepare to hike from New York to Washington, D.C. on a 295-mile Votes for Women Pilgrimage, 1913. Opposite: Two activists make themselves seen and heard. Above: Elizabeth Cady Stanton (left) and Susan B. Anthony.

Commission to raise money to support the Union. Although they wholeheartedly supported the Union cause, women's rights activists expected to be rewarded for their efforts with full citizenship rights, which they believed should include the right to vote.

At war's end, the link between women's rights and rights for freed people remained, shaping postwar strategies and conflicts. At the 1866 national women's rights convention, the first since before the war, white and Black reformers founded the American Equal Rights Association (AERA) to secure suffrage "irrespective of race, color, or sex." Lucretia Mott, known for her commitment to equal rights and her ability to mediate between opposing factions, served as president. Association members traveled the lecture circuit, even influencing some southern states to consider equal rights.

However, when, with the 14th Amendment, legislators tied representation in Congress to the number of male voters, suffragists divided over their loyalties. By the 1869 AERA convention, during congressional debates on the 15th Amendment to enfranchise Black men, Douglass, Stanton, Anthony, and Massachusetts suffrage leaders Lucy Stone and Henry Blackwell argued vehemently. Stone reasoned that enfranchisement for Black men signified progress, while Stanton and Anthony

contended that woman suffrage was equally important and should not be sacrificed. The AERA underwent a painful split.

Two new organizations resulted that grew in strength and political expertise as their leadership developed increasingly effective ways to promote woman suffrage. Anthony and Stanton immediately established the National Woman Suffrage Association (NWSA) with an all-female membership, demanding a 16th amendment enfranchising citizens without regard to sex. Their weekly newspaper, *The Revolution*, publicized their views on woman suffrage, politics, labor, and other subjects. By September, rivals Stone and Blackwell founded the less militant American Woman Suffrage Association (AWSA). Its members, which included women and men, focused on state campaigns to demand or expand woman suffrage, staying away from other issues. Stone also began the *Woman's Journal* in 1870, which became the most successful and longest lasting suffrage newspaper. Whether states or the federal government should dictate who had the right to vote remained a contentious issue throughout the movement.

Black women activists divided their allegiance between the AWSA and the NWSA. Sojourner Truth and Harriet Tubman attended NWSA conventions, while Charlotte Forten Grimké and

---

Above, left: Harriet Tubman.
Above, right: Charlotte Forten Grimké.

CARRIE CHAPMAN CATT

1859–1947

By Debra Michals

A skilled political strategist, Carrie Clinton Lane Chapman Catt was a suffragist and peace activist who helped secure for American women the right to vote. She directed the National American Woman Suffrage Association (NAWSA) and founded the League of Women Voters (1920) to bring women into the political mainstream.

Born January 9, 1859 in Ripon, Wisconsin, Catt was the second of three children of Maria Clinton and Lucius Lane, farmers in Potsdam, New York. When she was seven, her family relocated to Iowa, where she later became the only woman in her graduating class at Iowa State Agricultural College (now Iowa State University). She advanced from teacher to superintendent of schools, working in Mason City, Iowa. In 1885, she married newspaper editor Leo Chapman who died a year later of typhoid fever. In 1890, she married successful engineer George Catt.

Catt became involved with the suffrage movement in the late 1880s joining the Iowa Woman Suffrage Association, though her interest dated back to her teen years when she realized her mother lacked the same voting rights her father had. She also became involved with the National American Woman Suffrage Association (NAWSA), and, an outstanding speaker, she was soon tapped to give speeches nationwide and help organize local suffrage chapters. In 1900, she was elected NAWSA president, filling the seat vacated by the aging Susan B. Anthony.

Recognizing the international dimensions of the suffrage issue, in 1902, Catt founded the International Woman Suffrage Alliance to spread democracy around the globe. In 1904, she retired briefly to care for her dying husband, who passed away a year later making Catt a wealthy widow. But that loss, combined with those of her brother, mother, and activist Susan B. Anthony, left her emotionally drained. To heal, she spent several years traveling abroad and serving as president of the International Woman Suffrage Alliance. She also helped found the Woman's Peace Party in 1915.

Catt resumed the NAWSA presidency from 1915 to 1920, during which time the suffrage amendment (the 19th) became part of the U.S. Constitution. She devised the "Winning Plan," which carefully coordinated state suffrage campaigns with the drive for a constitutional amendment—the plan which helped ensure final victory. Meanwhile, however, Catt faced strategic challenges from younger recruits such as Alice Paul and Lucy Burns, who favored militant tactics and focused exclusively on a U.S. constitutional amendment. Catt also differed with Paul and Burns over picketing the White House during the First World War; Catt threw her support toward Wilson's war effort and continued her state-by-state suffrage campaigns. She consolidated New York City suffrage groups into the Woman Suffrage Party, greatly contributing to the New York state suffrage victory in 1917 after previous failed attempts.

With the vote won, Catt founded the League of Women Voters to educate women on political issues and served as the organization's honorary president until her death in 1947. She published a history of suffrage in 1923, *Woman Suffrage and Politics: The Inner Story of the Suffrage Movement.* She also gave her attention to other issues such as child labor and world peace. After the horrors of the First World War, she organized the Committee on the Cause and Cure of War (1925). Concerned about Hitler's growing power, she worked on behalf of German Jewish refugees and was awarded the American Hebrew Medal (1933).

This article appears courtesy of the National Women's History Museum.

Frances Ellen Watkins Harper supported the AWSA. Although most Black women's benevolent and literary clubs supported suffrage for women, Sarah Garnett founded the first known organization of Black women devoted specifically to suffrage, the Brooklyn Colored Woman's Equal Suffrage League, in the late 1880s. African American suffragists operated in dynamic networks of support in Black communities in cities throughout the nation but tended to work outside the mainstream movement, in part because white women, particularly in the South, rarely welcomed their Black sisters.

Suffragists employed ever more complex strategies to promote women's enfranchisement. Suffrage leaders formulated a legal strategy they called the "new departure," which argued that voting was one of the "privileges or immunities" of citizenship protected by the 14th Amendment. From 1868 to 1872, hundreds of Black and white women suffragists registered and voted, hoping to bring the issue before the courts. Officials arrested many of these women, who then filed suit—or were charged with a crime. Sojourner Truth, Sarah Grimké, her niece Angelina Grimké Weld, Matilda Joslyn Gage, and many other less well-known women engaged in this strategy.

The most famous of these was Susan B. Anthony, who, along with 14 other women, voted in an 1872 election in Rochester, New York. Her trial resulted in a guilty verdict and a fine she refused to pay. Virginia Minor of Missouri further tested the understanding of citizenship as plaintiff in Minor v. Happersett, decided by the United States Supreme Court in 1874. Justices unanimously determined that the 14th Amendment did not intend that woman suffrage be guaranteed. The case marked a serious setback not just for the woman suffrage movement, but for civil rights of all citizens, and refocused attention on a federal amendment.

After years of hard work, in 1887 members of the NWSA and legislative supporters finally brought a proposal for a federal amendment to a vote in Congress. It failed, prompting suffragists to revise their strategies yet again, beginning with uniting disparate suffrage factions. Lucy Stone and her daughter, Alice Stone Blackwell, began negotiations with Susan B. Anthony to merge the AWSA and the NWSA. The process took more than two years, and many leaders, such as Matilda Joslyn Gage of New York and Olympia Brown of Wisconsin, who feared the loss of attention to a federal amendment, opposed the merger. Nevertheless, the two groups became the National American Woman Suffrage Association (NAWSA) in February 1890. Many state and local political equality and suffrage clubs, once

"Though observers increasingly realized the illogic of the dire predictions of social disruption once expected of woman suffrage, some women actively resisted enfranchisement"

affiliated with one or the other of the former associations, formalized their affiliation with the new association.

NAWSA had a total of four presidents: Elizabeth Cady Stanton, Susan B. Anthony, Carrie Chapman Catt in two separate terms, and Anna Howard Shaw, each with her own strategy. Stanton, chosen primarily to honor her, spent most of her term in England with her daughter. Anthony, who had already taken on presidential duties, hoped the organization would prioritize a federal amendment, although state and local suffrage activity often siphoned energy and attention from a national focus. She also had the support of Frances Willard's Woman's Christian Temperance Union. The largest women's organization in the world, the union endorsed woman suffrage on the premise that having the vote would help protect women and children from problems related to alcohol.

Catt, who served from 1900 until 1904, then again beginning in 1908, focused on attracting elite women's money and support, as well as educating confident suffrage speakers and organizers tasked with establishing suffrage clubs. Shaw, who spoke before an estimated million people during her tenure, challenged the "Southern strategy" of the 1890s, which explicitly connected woman suffrage to white supremacy to court southern support. Shaw understood the hypocrisy of a strategy that would exclude any race or class from the right to vote.

In the late 19th century, as the country industrialized and urbanized, and as immigration brought increasing diversity, class and ethnic divisions undermined an assumed male equality. White supremacist rule returned to the southern states, increasing racially based violence. Simultaneously, suffragists argued that the nation would benefit from women's selflessness, devotion to family, and

social benevolence. Some women, especially those who also supported temperance, claimed they needed the ballot for self-protection or to meet social reform goals. Many elite, white suffragists advocated for restricted suffrage, promoting the idea of enfranchising educated white women but not the "undesirable" classes (immigrants and Blacks) as a solution. So, while many women had come to support suffrage, they sometimes did so from dramatically different perspectives.

As the United States expanded westward, new territories and states entered the union, often with women entitled to the vote. Strategies women in the West utilized mirrored those used in the East, including lobbying, participating in parades and meetings, supporting the party that endorsed woman suffrage, forming coalitions, and increasing the respectability of women's voting. Campaigns in the West also benefited from eastern women who traveled west to organize suffrage support. Organizations sent observers to the West to

Opposite: Suffragists rally support in Chicago, 1880.
Above: NAWSA president Anna Howard Shaw (right).

determine the success or failure of women's enfranchisement, putting to rest some of the arguments that claimed disaster if women regularly went to the polls. Although the population of the western states was small, they represented a steadily growing number of women voters. With women holding increasing political power, state and federal legislatures paid more attention to women's demands.

As more women attended college, they increasingly sought professions in the public sphere. Oberlin College in Ohio had opened its doors to Black men in 1835 and women in 1837, but for a long time it remained rare for either group to complete college degrees. New colleges, such as Vassar (1861), Wellesley (1870), and Bryn Mawr (1885) opened as women's institutions. Even as critics of woman suffrage advocated for "true womanhood," the ideology based on women's role in the domestic sphere, people supported higher education for women. But when the 1900 federal census showed that the birth rate had dropped while immigrant women continued to have large families, some, including Theodore Roosevelt, argued that educated women who shirked their "duty" to procreate engaged in "race suicide." Nevertheless, the ultimate success of suffrage would depend on the involvement and support of women (and men) of all of races, ethnicities, and classes.

Though observers increasingly realized the illogic of the dire predictions of social disruption once expected of woman suffrage, some women actively resisted enfranchisement. Women opposed to woman suffrage published articles in lady's magazines; others frustrated suffragists by their indifference. However, as more prominent people announced their support for suffrage, it prompted those who opposed it to acknowledge the need to organize. In 1890, a Massachusetts anti-suffrage organization began the journal *Remonstrance* to publicize the dangers of women in politics. The anti-suffrage *Woman's Protest*, which eventually became the *Woman Patriot*, began in 1912 and continued until 1932.

Ever ready to meet new challenges head on, suffrage leaders paid attention to anti-suffrage views and continued to revise their strategies to reach more people, including across class lines. They published articles and books to express their arguments, disseminating them broadly. They held conventions and meetings regularly, seeking to educate women on their civic rights, political participation, and on how to speak before the public. Suffragists also took to the road, traveling year-round to reach women and men in rural and urban areas. Activists toured the country in horse-drawn vehicles, then in automobiles, and they rode trolleys and trains as they spoke before large audiences. Local suffragists assisted with renting halls and lodging guest speakers. Many communities founded local clubs in response to these visits.

Suffragists established ever more sophisticated patterns of organization to reach voters, especially in advance of a referendum, a question posed by legislators to the voters to decide if women could vote. Suffragists had success with referenda in Colorado (1893) and Idaho (1896). They also used telephones and telegraphs, marched in parades wearing clothing that evoked ideas of women as feminine and pure, and appropriated modern

---

Opposite, top: New Yorkers read notices displayed in the window of an anti-suffrage organization. Opposite, bottom: Activists Nell Richardson (left) and Alice Burke pictured during a cross-country tour for the suffrage amendment, 1916.

Above and opposite: Suffragists employed a variety
of promotional materials, including postcards (above),
playing cards (opposite, top), and calendars (opposite,
bottom), to advance their cause.

marketing techniques. Influenced by consumer capitalism, suffragists designed and distributed buttons, pennants, ribbons, calendars, sheet music, fans, playing cards, toys, dolls, china dishes, and other souvenirs. They mailed thousands of postcards, and they used yellow, a common suffrage color, for letters and promotional literature. Suffragists spoke on street corners, organized motorcades and hikes, and held beautiful baby contests. They showed the electorate that women could be beautiful and domestic as they carried out their political duties. Suffragists staged mock daring feats, such as rescuing an anti-suffragist who fell into the sea, or piloted planes while they scattered suffrage literature. When the *Titanic* sank in 1912, suffragists, referring to rumors of men who wore women's coats to slip onto lifeboats, declared that women could not depend on men to protect them. Anything that happened became fodder for suffrage publicity.

Having learned from the Civil War experience, suffragists knew better than to set aside their reform vision when the nation entered the First World War. They used their political expertise to promote war preparedness and patriotism, sell Liberty Bonds, offer Red Cross service, and gather information for the government. Others, however, refused to do war work, since their government denied them political equality; peace activists

ALICE PAUL

1885–1977

Edited by Debra Michals

A vocal leader of the 20th century women's suffrage movement, Alice Paul advocated for and helped secure passage of the 19th Amendment to the U.S. Constitution, granting women the right to vote. Paul next authored the Equal Rights Amendment in 1923, which has yet to be adopted.

Born on January 11, 1885 in Mount Laurel, New Jersey, Paul was the oldest of four children of Tacie Parry and William Paul, a wealthy Quaker businessman. Paul's parents embraced education for women. Paul's mother, a suffragist, brought her daughter with her to women's suffrage meetings.

Paul attended Swarthmore College, a Quaker school cofounded by her grandfather, graduating with a biology degree in 1905. She attended the New York School of Philanthropy (now Columbia University) and received a Master of Arts degree in sociology in 1907. She then went to England to study social work, and after returning, earned a PhD from the University of Pennsylvania in 1910.

While in England, Paul met American Lucy Burns, and joining the women's suffrage efforts there, they learned militant protest tactics, including picketing and hunger strikes. Back in the United States, in 1912, Paul and Burns joined the National American Woman Suffrage Association (NAWSA); Paul was appointed to lead NAWSA's Congressional Committee in Washington, D.C. NAWSA primarily focused on state-by-state campaigns; Paul preferred to lobby Congress for a constitutional amendment. Such differences led Paul and others to split with NAWSA and form the National Woman's Party.

Borrowing from her British counterparts, Paul organized parades and pickets in support of suffrage. Her first—and the largest—was in Washington, D.C., on March 3, 1913, the day before President-elect Woodrow Wilson's inauguration.

Approximately 8,000 women marched with banners and floats down Pennsylvania Avenue from the Capitol to the White House, while a half million spectators watched, supported and harassed the marchers. On March 17, Paul and other suffragists met with Wilson, who said it was not yet time for an amendment to the Constitution. On April 7, Paul organized a demonstration and founded the Congressional Union for Woman Suffrage to focus specifically on lobbying Congress.

In January 1917, Paul and over 1,000 "Silent Sentinels" began 18 months of picketing the White House, standing at the gates with such signs as, "Mr. President, how long must women wait for liberty?" They endured verbal and physical attacks from spectators, which increased after the U.S. entered the First World War on April 6, 1917. Instead of protecting the women's right to free speech and peaceful assembly, the police arrested them on the flimsy charge of obstructing traffic. Paul was sentenced to jail for seven months, where she organized a hunger strike in protest. Doctors threatened to send Paul to an insane asylum and force-fed her, while newspaper accounts of her treatment garnered public sympathy and support for suffrage. By 1918, Wilson announced his support for suffrage. It took two more years for the Senate, House, and the required 36 states to approve the amendment.

Afterward, Paul and the National Woman's Party focused on the Equal Rights Amendment (ERA) to guarantee women constitutional protection from discrimination. Paul spent her life advocating for this and other women's issues. The ERA was ratified by 35 states in the 1970s, but by the 1982 deadline was three states short of 38 needed to become a constitutional amendment. *This article appears courtesy of the National Women's History Museum.*

opposed war entirely. Members of NAWSA, like Progressives and socialists, saw opportunities to demonstrate women's importance to the state in war work. Anti-suffragists, on the other hand, almost to a woman, devoted themselves to patriotic service and asked suffragists to put the campaign on hold. Both suffragists and anti-suffragists portrayed themselves as ideal citizens, since citizenship required service to the state.

By the end of 1912, suffrage strategies changed again, influenced by Alice Paul and Lucy Burns's involvement in NAWSA. Paul, inspired by her work with the radical branch of the British movement, became frustrated with what she saw as the stagnation of the U.S. movement. Deeming the strategy of state-by-state campaigns ineffective, she and Lucy Burns took over NAWSA's Congressional Committee and focused on obtaining a federal amendment.

As its first major event, the Congressional Committee held an enormous pageant and march on the day before Woodrow Wilson's inauguration. Fifty African American women marched in the parade despite NAWSA leadership's attempt to marginalize them. The pageant drew national attention and, because many of the marchers suffered taunts and physical abuse from parade watchers, public sympathy. However, Catt accused Paul and Burns of defying the national leadership in their organizing and fundraising efforts, especially after they formed a concurrent affiliate group called the Congressional Union (CU). Paul and Burns soon left NAWSA and the Congressional Committee and ran the CU independently. The union, headquartered in Washington, D.C., held daily meetings, established branches in different states, and published *The Suffragist* newspaper, featuring articles by prominent authors. In 1916, the Congressional Union established the National Woman's Party.

Holding the political party in power responsible for women's disenfranchisement, as well as highlighting the hypocrisy of "fighting for democracy abroad," a phrase Wilson often repeated, members of the National Woman's Party picketed the White House from 1917 to early 1919. Critics resented the

Above: Lucy Burns street
speaking in New York.

"Once passed, the amendment required ratification by at least 36 states, and suffragists and anti-suffragists campaigned vigorously"

women picketing a wartime president; authorities arrested some 500 women, and as many as 170 suffered imprisonment and forced feeding. Yet, women from all over the United States traveled to Washington to take their places on the picket lines. Because both groups vied for membership and media attention as they worked for the same goal, their competing strategies won greater overall support for woman suffrage.

During these same years, NAWSA president Carrie Chapman Catt implemented her "winning plan," advocating for state enfranchisement as well as a federal amendment. By 1917, women had won the vote in 11 western states. After New York voters approved a woman suffrage referendum, suffragists shifted their focus to Congress and a federal constitutional amendment. Persuaded by suffrage arguments, some congressmen claimed that enfranchising women should be a war measure, and Wilson, surely moved by the determination of the militant suffragists, increased suffrage agitation, and widening support from politicians, finally declared he would back a federal amendment. It still took several votes, however, before both the House of Representatives and the Senate passed the measure.

Once passed, the amendment required ratification by at least 36 states, and suffragists and anti-suffragists campaigned vigorously. They gathered wherever a state legislature convened to debate the amendment, speaking directly with legislators. They sent a flurry of telegrams to press their views, and each side kept a tally of states as legislatures voted on the amendment. Tennessee ("Armageddon," to suffragists) became the last state to ratify the amendment and did so by a single vote. Secretary of State Bainbridge Colby signed the certificate of ratification for the 19th Amendment to the Constitution on August 26, 1920, with no suffragists present.

The suffrage movement represents an extraordinary effort on the part of women to change not only their role in the polity, but also the perception of women as engaged civic-minded citizens. Never again would women, as a class of citizens, be content with lives defined by domesticity. Although the process had been long and complicated, and the movement steeped in conflict and controversy, suffragists used ever more effective strategies that ultimately won them the right to full political participation.

This article was originally commissioned by the National Conference of State Historic Preservation Officers in partnership with the United States National Park Service.

Opposite: The *Washington Evening Star* announces Secretary of State Bainbridge Colby's signing of the certificate of ratification for the 19th Amendment, August 26, 1920. Above: Marchers herald the president's newly asserted support for woman suffrage.

CHAPTER THREE

THE STORY LESS TOLD

Above: A group of Haudenosaunee
in upstate New York, c. 1914.

THE INFLUENCE OF THE HAUDENOSAUNEE

The rights and sovereignty of the indigenous women of the Native Nations informed the suffragist movement, and sustains to this day

By Dr. Sally Roesch Wagner

"Will your husband like to have you give the horse away?" Alice Fletcher asked. This early anthropologist was recounting an experience she'd had with a Native American woman of the Omaha Nation. The woman had just given away a "fine quality horse" and, hearing Fletcher's question, she broke "into a peal of laughter, and she hastened to tell the story to the others gathered in her tent, and I became the target of many merry eyes," Fletcher continued. "Laughter and contempt met my explanation of the white man's hold upon his wife's property."

Fletcher is telling this story to a women's rights audience from around the Western world at the 1888 International Council of Women. Married women, they knew, had no legal right to their own possessions or property in most states and countries, but that was just the tip of the iceberg. Married women had no legal identity. A wife ceased to exist in the eyes of the law once she promised to obey and uttered the words "I do." The two became one and the one was the man.

A wife lost control of her body. She had the legal obligation to submit to her husband's sexual demands; rape laws defined "an act of unlawful sexual intercourse with someone other than the wife of the perpetrator." Husbands had the legal right to beat disobedient wives, provided they didn't inflict permanent damage. Children belonged to their father, who dying could even will away his unborn child to someone other than the mother to raise. With most jobs closed to women and the few available paying half (or less) of men's wages, marriage was the only option open to women who wouldn't inherit. The founding document

"Haudenosaunee women 'were the great power among the clan, as everywhere else,' Stanton told the National Council of Women in 1891"

of America's women's movement, the 1848 "Declaration of Sentiments," summed it up well: "He has made her, if married, in the eye of the law, civilly dead."

Elizabeth Cady Stanton and Matilda Joslyn Gage were the primary writers of the early women's rights movement and, along with Susan B. Anthony, formed the leadership triumvirate of the National Woman Suffrage Association. Stanton and Gage lived on the homelands of the six nations of the Haudenosaunee (Iroquois) confederacy and knew their native neighbors. Both wrote extensively about the social, religious, economic, and political position of indigenous women as far superior to their own. "Never was justice more perfect; never was civilization higher," Gage wrote. Violence against women and children was rare and dealt with harshly.

Women had the absolute right to their bodies and their children; they had the final say in matters of war and peace and land. Women raised the food for their communities and controlled the collective economy; everyone had their own private property as well. While no Christian denomination allowed women to preach, Indigenous women had the responsibility for planning the spiritual ceremonies.

Propertied women had voted in the colonies, but after the revolution state laws declared it illegal for women to vote. Susan B. Anthony and others were arrested for attempting to exercise their right of citizenship, while Haudenosaunee women "were the great power among the clan, as everywhere else," Stanton told the National Council of Women in 1891. "The original nomination of the chiefs also always rested with the women," she told the audience. "They did not hesitate, when occasion required, 'to knock off the horns,' as it was technically called, from the head of a chief and send him back to the ranks of the warriors."

Clan mothers and male chiefs (sachem) shared political responsibility, with each clan mother having the responsibility for nominating and holding in office her chief; these appointed men carried out the business of government. A man who had stolen, was a warrior or had abused a woman could not become a chief. The clan mother had the responsibility of removing a chief who did not listen to the people and make decisions considering seven generations in the future.

"Division of power between the sexes in this Indian republic was nearly equal," Gage told *The New York Evening Post* readers in 1875. Clan mothers in the six Haudenosaunee nations continue to have the political voice they have exercised since the founding of the Iroquois Confederacy in 909, long before Columbus or the Pilgrims.

While women in the United States are celebrating 100 years of constitutionally-guaranteed voting, Native Nation women have had political voice on this land for over 1,000 years.

Indigenous women of numerous Native Nations had more rights, sovereignty and integrity long before Europeans arrived on these shores than we in the United States have today. As we non-native feminists listen to them, we can follow their leadership and learn from their centuries of experience just as our suffrage foremothers did.

Dr. Sally Roesch Wagner is the author of several books including Sisters in Spirit, *and editor of* The Women's Suffrage Movement *from which this article is adapted. This article appears courtesy of the author and the National Women's History Alliance.*

Above: More members of the group of
Haudenosaunee pictured previously.

AFRICAN AMERICAN WOMEN AND THE 19TH AMENDMENT

Black women were active in the fight for suffrage from the very start but faced prejudice and discrimination from many within the movement as well as from those opposed to it

By Sharon Harley

African American women, though often overlooked in the history of woman suffrage, engaged in significant reform efforts and political activism leading to and following the ratification in 1920 of the 19th Amendment, which barred states from denying American women the right to vote on the basis of their sex. They had as much—or more—at stake in the struggle as white women. From the earliest years of the suffrage movement, Black women worked side by side with white suffragists. By the late 19th century, however, as the suffrage movement splintered over the issue of race in the years after the Civil War, Black women formed their own organizations to continue their efforts to secure and protect the rights of all women, and men.

The U.S. women's rights movement was closely allied with the antislavery movement and, before the Civil War, Black and white abolitionists and suffragists joined together in common cause. During the antebellum period, a small cohort of formerly enslaved and free Black women, including Sojourner Truth, Harriet Tubman, Maria W. Stewart, Henrietta Purvis, Harriet Forten Purvis, Sarah Parker Remond, and Mary Ann Shadd Cary, were active in women's rights circles. They were joined in their advocacy of women's rights and suffrage by prominent Black men, including Frederick Douglass, Charles Lenox Remond, and Robert Purvis, and worked in collaboration with white abolitionists and women's rights activists, including William Lloyd Garrison, Elizabeth Cady Stanton, and Susan B. Anthony.

Following the 1848 women's rights convention in Seneca Falls, New York, prominent free Black women abolitionists and suffragists attended, spoke, and assumed leadership positions at multiple women's rights gatherings throughout the 1850s and 1860s. In 1851, former slave Sojourner Truth delivered her famous "Ain't I A Woman" speech at the national women's rights convention in Akron, Ohio. Sarah Parker Remond and her brother Charles won wide acclaim for their pro-woman suffrage speeches at the 1858 National Woman's Rights Convention in New York City.

With the end of the Civil War, arguments for woman suffrage became entwined with debates over the rights of former slaves and the meaning of citizenship. Sisters Margaretta Forten and Harriet Forten Purvis, who helped to establish the interracial Philadelphia Suffrage Association in 1866, and other Black women were active in the new American Equal Rights Association (AERA), an organization formed by former abolitionists and women's rights advocates that endorsed both women's and Black men's right to vote. Purvis served on the AERA executive committee. Abolitionist Frances Ellen Watkins Harper spoke on behalf of woman suffrage at the founding meeting of the AERA, and Sojourner Truth gave a major address at its first anniversary meeting.

But with the proposal of the 15th Amendment, which would enfranchise Black men but not women, interracial and mixed-gender coalitions began to deteriorate. Suffragists had to choose between insisting on universal rights or accepting the priority of

Opposite: Women's rights advocates pose for
a portrait in Newport, Rhode Island, c. 1899.

SOJOURNER TRUTH

1797–1883

Edited by Debra Michals

A former slave, Sojourner Truth became an outspoken advocate for abolition, temperance, and civil and women's rights in the 19th century. Her Civil War work earned her an invitation to meet President Abraham Lincoln in 1864.

Truth was born Isabella Bomfree, a slave in Dutch-speaking Ulster County, New York in 1797. She was bought and sold four times, and subjected to harsh physical labor and violent punishments. In her teens she married another slave with whom she had five children, beginning in 1815. In 1827—a year before New York's law freeing slaves was to take effect—Truth ran away with her infant Sophia to a nearby abolitionist family, the Van Wageners. The family bought her freedom for 20 dollars and helped Truth successfully sue for the return of her five-year-old son Peter, who was illegally sold into slavery in Alabama.

Truth moved to New York City in 1828, where she worked for a local minister. By the early 1830s, she participated in the religious revivals that were sweeping the state and became a charismatic speaker. In 1843, she declared that the Spirit called on her to preach the truth, renaming herself Sojourner Truth.

As an itinerant preacher, Truth met abolitionists William Lloyd Garrison and Frederick Douglass. Garrison's anti-slavery organization encouraged Truth to give speeches about the evils of slavery. She never learned to read or write. In 1850, she dictated what would become her autobiography—*The Narrative of Sojourner Truth*—to Olive Gilbert, who assisted in its publication. Truth survived on sales of the book, which also brought her national recognition.

She met women's rights activists, including Elizabeth Cady Stanton and Susan B. Anthony, as well as temperance advocates—both causes she quickly championed.

In 1851, Truth began a lecture tour that included a women's rights conference in Akron, Ohio, where she delivered her famous "Ain't I A Woman?" speech. In it, she challenged prevailing notions of racial and gender inferiority and inequality by reminding listeners of her combined strength (Truth was nearly six feet tall) and female status. Truth ultimately split with Douglass, who believed suffrage for formerly enslaved men should come before women's suffrage; she thought both should occur simultaneously.

During the 1850s, Truth settled in Battle Creek, Michigan, where three of her daughters lived. She continued speaking nationally and helped slaves escape to freedom. When the Civil War started, Truth urged young men to join the Union cause and organized supplies for Black troops. After the war, she was honored with an invitation to the White House and became involved with the Freedmen's Bureau, helping freed slaves find jobs and build new lives. While in Washington, D.C., she lobbied against segregation, and in the mid 1860s, when a streetcar conductor tried to violently block her from riding, she ensured his arrest and won her subsequent case. In the late 1860s she collected thousands of signatures on a petition to provide former slaves with land, though Congress never took action. Nearly blind and deaf towards the end of her life, Truth spent her final years in Michigan.

This article appears courtesy of the National Women's History Museum.

Black male suffrage. The split in the suffrage movement over the 15th Amendment prompted Elizabeth Cady Stanton and Susan B. Anthony to sever ties with the AERA and form the National Woman Suffrage Association (NWSA), which promoted universal suffrage, insisting that Black men should not receive the vote before white women. Stanton and Anthony's racist remarks about Black men evoked intense anger on the part of Black suffragists, including long-time allies Frederick Douglass and Frances Ellen Watkins Harper. As a result, Harper supported the 15th Amendment—this from a fiercely independent woman who believed women were equal, indeed, superior to men in their level of productivity; men were talkers, while women were doers. Harper joined the new American Woman Suffrage Association (AWSA), which supported both Black suffrage and woman suffrage and took a state-by-state approach to securing women's right to vote. As Harper proclaimed in her closing remarks at the 1873 AWSA convention, "much as white women need the ballot, colored women need it more." As many whites, including some white female suffragists, publicly denounced Black male suffrage, Black women incorporated Black male suffrage as an important component of their suffrage goals.

Black women, however, did become members of both woman suffrage groups—the Stanton and Anthony-led NWSA and the Lucy Stone and Julia Ward Howe-led AWSA. Hattie Purvis was a delegate to the NWSA (as well as a member of the executive committee of the Pennsylvania State Suffrage Association). Among the prominent African American reformers and suffragists who joined the AWSA were Charlotte Forten and Josephine St. Pierre Ruffin, a member of the Massachusetts Woman Suffrage Association.

Black women attended and spoke out at political and religious meetings and public rallies. Their enthusiasm and political engagement within and outside suffrage campaigns was particularly concerning to whites in the post-emancipation South. The suffrage work of Charlotte ("Lottie") Rollin shows the long history of African American women's political activism outside the Northeast and beyond women's rights conferences and organizations. In 1866, a year before chairing the inaugural meeting of the South Carolina Woman's Rights Association, Rollin courageously proclaimed her support for universal suffrage at a meeting of the South Carolina House of Representatives. In 1870, she was the elected secretary of the South Carolina Woman's Rights Association, an affiliate of the

Above, left: Harriet Tubman.
Above, right: Frederick Douglass.

"We ask justice, we ask equality, we ask that all the civil and political rights that belong to citizens of the United States be guaranteed to us and our daughters forever"

—Mary Ann Shadd Cary

AWSA. Rollin, along with her sisters Frances and Louisa and other local women, figured prominently in Reconstruction politics and woman suffrage campaigns at the local and national levels in the early 1870s. South Carolina's African American woman suffrage advocates were encouraged by African American men. In certain 1870 South Carolina district elections, Black election officials encouraged Black women to vote—an action the Rollin sisters and some other African American women were already assuming (or attempting) on their own.

In 1871, pioneer suffragist, newspaper editor, and first female law school student at Howard University Mary Ann Shadd Cary, with several other women, attempted, unsuccessfully, to register to vote in Washington, D.C. This failure notwithstanding, they insisted upon and secured an official signed affidavit recognizing that they had attempted to vote.

Like white suffragists, African American women linked suffrage to a multitude of political and economic issues in order to further their cause, and they engaged in multiple strategies to secure women's political and voting rights within and outside the organized suffrage movement. At the same time, they combated anti-Black discrimination in the southern United States and within the predominantly white national woman suffrage organizations.

Over time, tensions between Stanton, Anthony, and Douglass subsided. The discrimination against Black women in the woman suffrage movement continued as certain white woman suffragist leaders sought southern white male and female support. The anti-Black rhetoric and actions of NWSA leaders Susan B. Anthony and Elizabeth Cady Stanton persisted but so did African American women's courageous battles for both gender and racial equality. In 1876, Mary Ann Shadd Cary wrote to leaders of the National

Woman Suffrage Association urging them to place the names of 94 Washington, D.C. Black woman suffragists on their Declaration of the Rights of the Women of the United States issued on the 100th anniversary of American independence. The declaration concluded, "we ask justice, we ask equality, we ask that all the civil and political rights that belong to citizens of the United States be guaranteed to us and our daughters forever." While unsuccessful in having their names added, Cary remained a committed suffrage activist, speaking at the 1878 NWSA meeting. Two years later, she formed the Colored Woman's Franchise Association in Washington, D.C., which linked suffrage not just to political rights but to education and labor issues.

Late 19th-century Black women believed there was an inextricable link between effective reform work and women's right to vote. Many Black suffragists were active in the temperance movement, including Hattie Purvis, Frances Ellen Watkins Harper, and Gertrude Bustill Mossell. Purvis and Harper served as Superintendent of Work among Colored People in the Woman's Christian Temperance Union. Purvis also served, from 1883 to 1900, as a delegate to the National Woman Suffrage Association. Mossell wrote pro-suffrage articles for the Black press. In her 1881 article, "Woman's Suffrage," reprinted in an 1885 issue of *New York Freeman*, Mossell urged readers to become more knowledgeable about suffrage history and women's rights. Purvis, Harper, Mossell, and other Black woman suffragists and reformers argued that intemperance was a major obstacle to racial advancement and that the passage of federal woman suffrage would significantly reduce this and other social ills.

Despite all this important work by Black suffragists, the mainstream suffrage movement continued its racially

Above: Members of the Phyllis Wheatley Club
of Buffalo, NY, an affiliate of the National
Association of Colored Women's Clubs.

FRANCES E. W. HARPER

1825–1911

By Kerri Lee Alexander

As a poet, author, and lecturer, Frances Ellen Watkins Harper was a household name in the 19th century. Not only was she the first African American woman to publish a short story, but she was also an influential abolitionist, suffragist, and reformer who co-founded the National Association of Colored Women's Clubs.

Frances Ellen Watkins Harper was born on September 24, 1825 in Baltimore, Maryland. An only child, Harper was born to free African American parents. Unfortunately, by the time she was three years old, both of her parents died and she became an orphan. Harper's aunt and uncle, Henrietta and William Watkins, raised her after her parent's death. Her uncle was an outspoken abolitionist, practiced self-taught medicine, organized a black literary society and established his own school in 1820 called the Watkins Academy for Negro Youth. Frances Harper learned from her uncle's activism and she attended the Watkins Academy until she was 13 years old. At that age, children were typically expected to join the workforce. Harper took a job as a nursemaid and seamstress for a white family that owned a bookshop. Her love for books blossomed as she spent any free time she had in the shop. By age 21, Harper wrote her first small volume of poetry called *Forest Leaves*.

When she was 26 years old, Harper left Maryland and became the first woman instructor at Union Seminary, a school for free African Americans in Wilberforce, Ohio. She taught domestic science for a year and then moved to a school in York, Pennsylvania. Shortly after she began working as a teacher, her home state of Maryland passed a law stating that free African Americans living in the North were no longer allowed to enter the state of Maryland. If found, they would be imprisoned and sold into slavery. Harper was now unable to return to her own home. She decided to devote all of her efforts to the antislavery cause. Harper moved in with William and Letitia George Still who were abolitionists and friends of her uncle. William Still became known as the father of the Underground Railroad while he served as chairman of the Vigilance Committee of the Pennsylvania Anti-Slavery Society. Supported by the Stills, Harper began writing poetry for antislavery newspapers. Her poem "Eliza Harris," was published in *The Liberator*, and in *Frederick Douglass' Paper*. By the time Harper left Philadelphia in 1854, she had compiled her second small volume of poetry called *Poems on Miscellaneous Subjects* with an introduction by abolitionist William Lloyd Garrison.

For the next eight years, Harper traveled across the United States and Canada as a lecturer. After her first speech entitled, "The Elevation and Education of our People," she was hired as a traveling lecturer for various organizations including the Maine Anti-Slavery Society and the Pennsylvania Anti-Slavery Society. In addition to her antislavery lectures, Harper was committed to the struggle for women's rights and the temperance movement. She included her observations from her travels in her writings and began to publish novels, short stories, and poetry focused on issues of racism, feminism and classism. In 1859, Harper published a short story in the *Anglo-African Magazine* called "The Two Offers." This short story about women's education was the first short story published by an African American woman.

On November 22, 1860, Frances married Fenton Harper and the couple had a daughter named Mary. Unfortunately, Fenton Harper died four years later. After her husband's death, Frances Harper began touring again and formed alliances with prominent women's rights activists. In 1866, Harper spoke at the National Woman's Rights Convention in New York. Her famous speech entitled "We Are All Bound Up Together" urged her fellow attendees to include African American women in their fight for suffrage. She emphasized that Black women were facing the double burden of racism and sexism at the same time, therefore the fight for women's suffrage must include suffrage for African Americans. The next day, the Convention held a meeting to organize the American Equal Rights Association to work for suffrage for both African Americans and women. However, the organization soon split over the decision to support the 15th Amendment, granting African American men the right to vote. Harper, along with Frederick Douglass and many others supported the amendment and helped to form the American Woman Suffrage Association.

Harper spent the rest of her career working for the pursuit of equal rights, job opportunities, and education for African American women. She was a co-founder and vice president of the National Association of Colored Women's Clubs, and the director of the American Association of Colored Youth. She was also the superintendent of the Colored Sections of the Philadelphia and Pennsylvania Women's Christian Temperance Unions. Frances Ellen Watkins Harper died on February 22, 1911 in Philadelphia, Pennsylvania. *This article appears courtesy of the National Women's History Museum.*

discriminatory practices and even condoned white supremacist ideologies in order to garner southern support for white women's voting rights. Consequently, African American women and men became increasingly marginalized and discriminated against at woman suffrage meetings, campaigns, and marches. Even after the NWSA and the AWSA reconciled to form the National American Woman Suffrage Association (NAWSA) in 1890, Anthony and other white suffragists in the South and the North continued to choose expediency over loyalty and justice when it came to Black suffragists. In 1895, Anthony asked her "friend" and veteran woman suffrage supporter Frederick Douglass not to attend the upcoming NAWSA convention in Atlanta. As she later explained to Ida B. Wells-Barnett, Douglass's presence on the stage with the honored guests would have offended the southern hosts. Wells-Barnett and other suffragists reprimanded Anthony and other white women activists for giving in to racial prejudice. During the 1903 NAWSA meeting in New Orleans, the *Times Democrat* denounced the organization's anti-Black states' rights strategy for its negative impact on Black women's quest for suffrage.

There were exceptions to the discriminatory traditions among suffragists. In New England, Josephine St. Pierre Ruffin claimed she had been warmly welcomed by Lucy Stone, Julia Ward Howe, and others. Some African American women, such as internationally prominent women's rights activist and speaker Mary Church Terrell, belonged to and participated in NAWSA meetings and activities, even as the new organization discriminated against them to woo southern and white male support for woman suffrage.

In the closing decades of the 19th century more Black women formed their own local and regional woman suffrage clubs and, in 1896, the National Association of Colored Women (NACW). The NACW, which elected Terrell as its first national president, provided Black women a national platform to advocate for woman suffrage and women's rights causes. From the organization's inception and throughout the 20th century, Terrell, Ruffin, Barrier Williams, Wells-Barnett, and numerous NACW members and leaders fought for woman suffrage, sharing their pro-suffrage sentiments and activities at regional and national NACW conventions and in the white and Black press.

Above: Civil rights and suffrage
activist Mary Church Terrell.

"White woman suffrage organizations claimed racial inclusivity, but the actions and policy statements of their leaders reflected a very different racial reality"

Despite the discrimination Black women experienced, including the rejection of Josephine St. Pierre Ruffin's effort to represent the NACW in the General Federation of Women's Clubs, Black women cautiously joined interracial efforts to secure the ballot for women and to expand women's engagement in electoral politics as canvassers, organizers, and voters. Prominent anti-lynching activist, NACW member, and suffragist Ida B. Wells-Barnett organized, in 1913, the first Black woman suffrage club in Illinois, the Chicago-based Alpha Suffrage Club. She and other midwestern women participated in nonpartisan NACW, NAWSA, and Alpha Club campaigns and political rallies; most Black women, however, also supported Republican Party platforms and candidates.

As the suffrage movement moved into its final phase in the early decades of the 20th century, local and national white woman suffrage organizations claimed racial inclusivity and did have African American women as active members, but the actions and policy statements of their leaders reflected a very different racial reality—one that worsened over time. When NAWSA organized a woman suffrage parade in 1913, scheduled a day before the inauguration of Woodrow Wilson, the first U.S. president from the South since the Civil War, its accommodating acquiescence to white racism typified the worsening racial climate within the suffrage movement. Prior to the parade, Wells-Barnett, representing the Alpha Suffrage Club, was asked to march with other Black women rather than with the white Chicago delegation. In keeping with her resistant and radical personality, Wells-Barnett refused. Instead, as the all-white Chicago delegation passed, Wells-Barnett

emerged from the crowd and entered the line between two white Chicago women and marched with them.

NACW founder Mary Church Terrell later told Walter White, of the National Association for the Advancement of Colored People (NAACP), in denouncing the anti-Black stance of some white woman suffrage leaders, that she believed if white suffrage leaders could pass the amendment without giving Black women the vote, they would—a claim white suffragists denied while persisting in

Opposite: Frances "Fannie" Barrier Williams, who helped found
the National Association of Colored Women. Above: Prominent
anti-lynching activist and suffragist Ida B. Wells-Barnett.

organizing white women exclusively in various southern states. The opposition African American women faced was the subject of NACW and NAACP leader Mary B. Talbert's 1915 *Crisis* article, "Women and Colored Women." As Talbert pointed out, "with us as colored women, this struggle becomes two-fold, first, because we are women and second, because we are colored women."

Talbert's essay was one of several by a small cadre of Black female and male intellectuals and public figures who had participated in a symposium on "Votes for Women" and whose remarks appeared in the August 1915 issue of the *Crisis*, the national organ of the NAACP. In her essay, Black feminist leader and educator Nannie Helen Burroughs offered a cryptic but profound response to a white woman's query about what Black women would do with the ballot, retorting, "What can she do without it?" Expressing a common line of thinking, Burroughs and other Black women political activists proclaimed that the Black woman "needs the ballot, to reckon with men who place no value upon her virtue, and to mould [sic] healthy sentiment in favor of her own protection." Burroughs echoed an idea previously expressed by Adella Hunt Logan, a life member of the National American Woman Suffrage Association and active member of the Tuskegee Woman's Club, in an earlier monthly Black publication, *Colored American Magazine*:

"If white American women, with all their natural and acquired advantages, need the ballot, that right protective of all other rights; if Anglo Saxons have been helped by it... how much more do black Americans, male and female need the strong defense of a vote to help secure them their right to life, liberty and the pursuit of happiness?"

These arguments notwithstanding, on the eve of ratification of the 19th Amendment, white suffragists, fearing offending white southerners, continued their racially discriminatory practices toward Black suffragists. In 1919, NAWSA president Carrie Chapman Catt opposed admitting the Northeastern Federation of Women's Clubs, a regional body of Black clubwomen, as a member of the national suffrage organization out of fear of offending white voters. When at last the 19th Amendment was ratified, African American women voters in the Jim Crow South encountered the very same disenfranchisement strategies and anti-Black violence that led to the disfranchisement of Black men, so that Black women had to continue their fight to secure voting privileges, for both men and women.

Racism and discrimination within and outside organized woman suffrage campaigns and anti-Black racial violence forced Black women early on to link their right to vote to the restoration

Above: National Association of Colored Women leader Mary B. Talbert. Opposite: Black feminist leader and educator Nannie Helen Burroughs (left) pictured with Woman's National Baptist Convention attendees.

of Black male suffrage and civil rights activism. African American suffragist and radical activist Angelina Weld Grimké, named for her great aunt, suffragist Angelina Grimké Weld, boldly and optimistically asserted, "injustices will end" between the sexes when woman "gains the ballot." But instead, the struggle continued.

Black women's political engagement from the antebellum period to the opening decades of the 20th century helped to define their post-1920 political activism. Following ratification of the 19th Amendment, the battle for the vote ended for white women. For African American women the outcome was less clear. Hoping to combat post-First World War anti-Black racial violence and the disenfranchisement of Black men, particularly in the South, Black women's engagement in electoral politics and radical activism continued, indeed, expanded, after ratification.

An examination of Black women's post-1920 political life reveals that rather than ending, the 19th Amendment was a starting point for African American women's involvement in electoral politics in the years to come. Oscar De Priest credited Black women with being the deciding factor in his election, in 1928, as the first African American elected to the United States House of Representatives since Reconstruction. Woman suffrage struggles in the United States were one part of a long and impressive history of African American women's political engagement to promote women's rights and to share equally in the advancement of the race.

This article was originally commissioned by the National Conference of State Historic Preservation Officers in partnership with the United States National Park Service.

FRANCES E. W. HARPER'S "WE ARE ALL BOUND UP TOGETHER" SPEECH

The poet and civil rights activist Frances Ellen Watkins Harper delivered this address to the 11th National Woman's Rights Convention in New York In May 1866

"I feel I am something of a novice upon this platform. Born of a race whose inheritance has been outrage and wrong, most of my life had been spent in battling against those wrongs. But I did not feel as keenly as others, that I had these rights, in common with other women, which are now demanded. About two years ago, I stood within the shadows of my home. A great sorrow had fallen upon my life. My husband had died suddenly, leaving me a widow, with four children, one my own, and the others stepchildren. I tried to keep my children together. But my husband died in debt, and before he had been in his grave three months, the administrator had swept the very milk crocks and wash tubs from my hands. I was a farmer's wife and made butter for the Columbus market; but what could I do, when they had swept all away? They left me one thing and that was a looking glass! Had I died instead of my husband, how different would have been the result! By this time he would have had another wife, it is likely; and no administrator would have gone into his house, broken up his home, and sold his bed, and taken away his means of support.

I took my children in my arms, and went out to seek my living. While I was gone, a neighbor to whom I had once lent five dollars, went before a magistrate and swore that he believed I was a non-resident, and laid an attachment on my very bed. And I went back to Ohio with my orphan children in my arms, without a single feather bed in this wide world, that was not in the custody of the law. I say, then, that justice is not fulfilled so long as woman is unequal before the law.

We are all bound up together in one great bundle of humanity, and society cannot trample on the weakest and feeblest of its members without receiving the curse in its own soul. You tried that in the case of the negro. You pressed him down for two centuries; and in so doing you crippled the moral strength and paralyzed the spiritual energies of the white men of the country. When the hands of the black were fettered, white men were deprived of the liberty of speech and the freedom of the press. Society cannot afford to neglect the enlightenment of any class of its members. At the South, the legislation of the country was in behalf of the rich slaveholders, while the poor white man was neglected. What is the consequence today? From that very class of neglected poor white men, comes the man who stands today, with his hand upon the helm of the nation. He fails to catch the watchword of the hour, and throws himself, the incarnation of meanness, across the pathway of the nation. My objection to Andrew Johnson is not that he has been a poor white man; my objection is that he keeps 'poor whits' all the way through. That is the trouble with him.

This grand and glorious revolution which has commenced, will fail to reach its climax of success, until throughout the length and breadth of the American Republic, the nation shall be so color-blind, as to know no man by the color of his skin or the curl of his hair. It will then have no privileged class, trampling upon and outraging the unprivileged classes, but will be then one great privileged nation, whose privilege will be to produce the loftiest manhood and womanhood that humanity can attain.

Above: Frances Ellen Watkins Harper shared the platform
with Elizabeth Cady Stanton and Susan B. Anthony at
the 1866 Woman's Rights Convention in New York.

"I do not believe that giving the woman the ballot is immediately going to cure all the ills of life. I do not believe that white women are dew-drops just exhaled from the skies. I think that, like men, they may be divided into three classes: the good, the bad, and the indifferent"

I do not believe that giving the woman the ballot is immediately going to cure all the ills of life. I do not believe that white women are dew-drops just exhaled from the skies. I think that, like men, they may be divided into three classes: the good, the bad, and the indifferent. The good would vote according to their convictions and principles; the bad, as dictated by prejudice or malice; and the indifferent will vote on the strongest side of the question, with the winning party.

You white women speak here of rights. I speak of wrongs. I, as a colored woman, have had in this country an education which has made me feel as if I were in the situation of Ishmael, my hand against every man, and every man's hand against me. Let me go tomorrow morning and take my seat in one of your street cars—I do not know that they will do it in New York, but they will in Philadelphia—and the conductor will put up his hand and stop the car rather than let me ride.

Going from Washington to Baltimore this Spring, they put me in the smoking car. Aye, in the capital of the nation, where the black man consecrated himself to the nation's defence, faithful when the white man was faithless, they put me in the smoking car! They did it once; but the next time they tried it, they failed; for I would not go in. I felt the fight in me; but I don't want to have to fight all the time.

Today I am puzzled where to make my home. I would like to make it in Philadelphia, near my own friends and relations. But if I want to ride in the streets of Philadelphia, they send me to ride on the platform with the driver. Have women nothing to do with this? Not long since, a colored woman took her seat in an Eleventh Street car in Philadelphia, and the conductor stopped the car and told the rest of the passengers to get out, and left the car with her in it alone, when they took it back to the station. One day I took my seat in a car, and the conductor came to me and told me to take another seat. I just screamed 'murder.' The man said if I was black I ought to behave myself. I knew that if he was white he was not behaving himself. Are there no wrongs to be righted?

In advocating the cause of the colored man, since the Dred Scott decision, I have sometimes said I thought the nation had touched bottom. But let me tell you there is a depth of infamy lower than that. It is when the nation, standing upon the threshold of a great peril, reached out its hands to a feebler race, and asked that race to help it, and when the peril was over, said, 'You are good enough for soldiers, but not good enough for citizens.' When Judge Taney said that the men of my race had no rights which the white man was bound to respect, he had not seen the bones of the black man bleaching outside of Richmond. He had not seen the thinned ranks and the thickened graves of the Louisiana Second, a regiment which went into battle nine hundred strong, and came out with three hundred. He had not stood at Olustee and seen defeat and disaster crushing down the pride of our banner, until words was brought to Colonel Hallowell, 'The day is lost; go in and save it,' and black men stood in the gap, beat back the enemy, and saved your army.

We have a woman in our country who has received the name of 'Moses,' not by lying about it, but by acting out—a woman who has gone down into the Egypt of slavery and brought out hundreds of our people into liberty. The last time I saw that woman, her hands were swollen. That woman who had led one of Montgomery's most successful expeditions, who was brave enough and secretive enough to act as a scout for the American army, had her hands all swollen from a conflict with a brutal conductor, who undertook to eject her from her place. That woman, whose courage and bravery won a recognition from our army and from every black man in the land, is excluded from every thoroughfare of travel. Talk of giving women the ballot box? Go on. It is a normal school, and the white women of this country need it. While there exists this brutal element in society which tramples upon the feeble and treads down the weak, I tell you that if there is any class of people who need to be lifted out of their airy nothings and selfishness, it is the white women of America."

Above: Mabel Ping-Hua Lee who, at the age of 16, rode in
the honor guard of the 1912 New York suffrage parade.

HOW CHINESE AMERICAN WOMEN HELPED SHAPE THE SUFFRAGE MOVEMENT

Anti-Chinese immigration policies meant that the numbers of Chinese American suffragists were small, but they played an important role in the suffrage struggle, advocating for equality of sex and race and teaching white suffrage leaders about the global scope of the fight for women's rights

By Cathleen D. Cahill

Mabel Ping-Hua Lee was a feminist pioneer. She was the first Chinese woman in the United States to earn her doctorate and an advocate for the rights of women and the Chinese community in America. However, due to discriminatory immigration laws, she was unable to become a citizen of the United States. Despite this injustice, she played an important part in the fight for voting rights both in the United States and in China.

In 1912, suffrage leaders in New York invited 16-year-old Mabel to ride in the honor guard that would lead their massive suffrage parade up Fifth Avenue. In order to understand why they asked and why Mabel agreed, we have to enlarge the scope of our vision and realize that conversations about women's rights and suffrage were happening all over the world. Suffragists in the United States were part of these transnational discussions.

Mabel Lee was one of the very few Chinese women who lived in the United States in the early 20th century. Records show that, of the 89,837 Chinese migrants who lived in the U.S. in 1900, only 4,522 were women. This was because Congress had passed harsh laws aimed at keeping Chinese immigrants out of the United States. In the mid-19th century, men from China came to work in the mines and to build the railroads. White Americans held many negative stereotypes about the "Oriental" Chinese, fueled by the prevalent bias of the period, assuming the Chinese had inherently "passive" or "servile" natures that made them unable to participate in democratic governments. Immigration laws codified these racist ideas about who could be an American citizen. Specifically, Congress passed two laws to exclude Chinese people from entering the United States.

The first law, the Page Act of 1875, was aimed at Chinese women, though it used the language of excluding prostitutes (many

Americans believed any Chinese woman who was immigrating was coming to the United States for the purpose of serving as a prostitute). The second law, the 1882 Exclusion Act, dramatically shrunk the number of Chinese immigrants (men and women) admitted into the United States and denied them from becoming naturalized citizens. This made the Chinese the only people in the world who were ineligible to become U.S. citizens. This law was renewed every ten years and extended to other Asian countries in 1924. As a result, most of the Chinese people in the United States at the beginning of the 20th century were men, and the vast majority lived on the West Coast or in Hawaii Territory.

Mabel Lee immigrated to the United States from Canton (now Guangzhou), China, around 1900 when she was roughly five years old. Her family lived in New York City, where her father served as the Baptist minister of the Morningside Mission in Chinatown. Her parents, Lee Towe and Lee Lai Beck (their names were spelled the Chinese way with surnames first) were able to immigrate under one of the very few exceptions to the Exclusion Act, because they were teachers working for the Baptist Church. As a teacher in China, Mabel's mother was aware of the conversations that feminists in that country were having about women's rights. Both she and Mabel's father raised their only child as a modern woman. For example, they chose not to bind Mabel's feet (though Lai Beck's mother had bound hers) and encouraged her education. Her father taught her Chinese classics, but they also sent her to public school in New York. She was the only Chinese student in her graduating class.

Under the terms of the Exclusion Act, the Lee family and the few other Chinese people who immigrated to the United States in this period could not become citizens. As a result, they paid close attention to events back home in China and maintained a vibrant dialogue between the two countries. Many of the Chinese in the U.S. were supporters of the republican revolutionary, Dr. Sun Yat-sen, and shared his goal of modernizing China. His vision included women's rights, such as equal education and political participation, and in the United States some Chinese women actively supported him by giving speeches at his fundraisers. Chinese women in the United States were also active in their local communities in a variety of ways. For example, along with their work at the Morningside Mission, Mabel Lee and her mother raised money for Chinese famine victims, worked with the YWCA (the Young Women's Christian Association), and participated in Chinatown parades. They closely followed the events in China, especially in 1911 when the Chinese Revolution overthrew Chinese imperial rule, eventually leading to the establishment of the Republic of China (1912–49).

White suffrage leaders were also interested in the Chinese Revolution. News spread that the Chinese government had enfranchised women (it was actually more complicated; each province was initially free to determine their own rules on the issue). White suffragists were "glad, but irritated, too," according to an article in the *New York Daily Tribune*, dated March 23, 1912, that women in China had won the vote before them. They also wanted to hear more. They turned to local Chinese communities to find out more. Leading Chinese women from cities like Portland, Oregon, Cincinnati, Ohio, Boston, Massachusetts, and New York City were invited to speak at white suffrage meetings in the spring of 1912. Eager for an audience, Chinese women seized the opportunity to share the news of women's contributions to the founding of their new nation. They told of the women's brigade that fought side-by-side with men in the revolution and celebrated the enfranchisement of Chinese women. At the same

time, they appealed to the white women in the audience to help address the needs of Chinese communities in the United States, especially the demeaning immigration laws that they faced.

In New York City in 1912, not too long before the parade, Mabel Lee and several other members of the Chinatown community joined national and state suffrage leaders for a meeting at the Peking Restaurant at the corner of 7th Avenue and 47th Street. The white suffragists were well-known and included Harriet Laidlaw, chairman of the Manhattan branch of the Women's Suffrage Party, Anna Howard Shaw, president of the National American Woman Suffrage Association (NAWSA), and wealthy patron of the cause, Alva Belmont. The representatives of the Chinese community were Mabel Lee and her parents; Grace Yip Typond, wife of a powerful merchant, Yip Typond; and Pearl Mark Loo (Mai Zhouyi), a teacher and missionary. It is worth noting that the latter all were immigrants to the U.S. from China, and therefore none were eligible to become U.S. citizens. Nonetheless, they cared about women's rights. They also hoped that by working with white suffragists, they could convince white Americans that their biased stereotypes about China and Chinese people were wrong and they should all work together to change the situation of Chinese people in the United States.

When she spoke to these famous suffrage leaders, Mabel Lee was only 16 years old and still a high school student, but she had recently been accepted to Barnard College. She reminded her audience that Chinese women in the United States suffered under the burden of not only sexism, but also racial prejudice. She especially urged more equitable educational opportunities for Chinese girls and boys in New York City, as did Grace Typond. Their colleague from Chinatown, Pearl Mark Loo (Mai Zhouyi), called for U.S. citizenship for Chinese women, likely regaling the audience with her own harrowing tale. Before coming to the

Opposite: Women and the Chinese community are left
"Out in the cold" in this 1884 magazine cover.

"Leading Chinese women from cities like Portland, Oregon, Cincinnati, Ohio, Boston, Massachusetts, and New York City were invited to speak at white suffrage meetings in the spring of 1912"

United States, she had lived in Canton and worked as a teacher. She had been involved in the woman's movement there and had edited the *Lingnan Women's Journal*. Despite her advanced education, she had been detained by the Immigration and Naturalization Service in San Francisco for months. She, too, believed education was the key to both women's rights and the strength of a nation, be it China or the United States.

Mabel Lee impressed suffrage leaders so much that they asked her to help lead the parade they were planning later that spring. She agreed. Newspapers across the nation reported on her participation and printed her picture, suggesting great interest from the American audience. Nor was she the only Chinese suffragist in the parade. Her mother and the other women from Chinatown also participated in another section. They proudly carried the striped flag of their new nation as well as a sign stating "Light from China." Though Americans widely believed that their cultural values were superior and needed to be shared with China, this slogan reversed that idea. Chinese suffragists hoped their participation would refute racist stereotypes and help change U.S. policies towards Chinese immigrants.

White suffragists also emphasized the reversal of roles. Anna Howard Shaw, the president of NAWSA, marched directly in front of the Chinatown contingent. She carried a banner that read: "NAWSA Catching Up with China." This slogan was directed primarily at shaming American men into supporting women's suffrage. Although Americans considered themselves modern and China backwards, the enfranchisement of Chinese women

suggested otherwise. Shaw's banner suggested that the U.S. was behind China in this arena. This idea remained one that white suffragists periodically invoked over the next few years.

That fall, Mabel Lee matriculated to Barnard College in New York City; she also remained in the midst of conversations about women's rights in both countries. While she was often asked to talk to white suffrage audiences and give them updates on women's rights in China—which she happily did—she also exerted a great deal of energy advocating for those rights among Chinese students studying in America. For example, in 1915, Mabel Lee herself was invited by the Women's Political Union to give a speech at one of their Suffrage Shops. Her speech "The Submerged Half," covered by *The New York Time*s, urged the Chinese community to promote girls' education and women's civic participation. The U.S. had created a college scholarship program, the Boxer Indemnity Program, to train future Chinese political and business leaders in U.S. institutions. Mabel Lee became heavily involved in the Chinese Students' Alliance, a national organization for those students that published a journal for its members. She urged the future leaders of China to incorporate women's rights into their new republic, writing articles for *The Chinese Students' Monthly*.

In one such article, titled "The Meaning of Woman Suffrage," she focused on the importance of women's rights to the new nation. "Are we going to build a solid structure" by including women's rights from the beginning, she asked readers. Not doing so would "leave every other beam loose for later readjustment," as she had learned from her experiences in the American suffrage

movement. After all, she concluded, "the feministic movement" was not advocating for "privileges to women," instead it was "the requirement of women to be worthy citizens and contribute their share to the steady progress of our country."

When New York state enfranchised women in 1917, Mabel Lee, still not a U.S. citizen, was unable to vote. However, she vowed to become a feminist "pioneer" by entering a Ph.D. program in Columbia University's Department of Political Science, Science, and Philosophy. She earned her doctoral degree in economics from Columbia in 1921, the first Chinese woman in the United States to do so. Although Chinese suffragists hoped that their actions would help to change U.S. immigration policy, they were disappointed. In fact, in 1924 Congress passed the Johnson-Reed Immigration Act that further restricted Chinese immigration and expanded those restrictions to all the countries of Asia. Some American-born Chinese women were able to exercise the right to vote (especially in California), but their numbers were small and remained so until immigration policy changes after the Second World War, when China fought as an ally alongside the United States.

After earning her degree, Mabel Lee found that there were few opportunities for highly educated Chinese women in the United States. Many of her peers—both U.S. and Chinese-born—moved back to China, where they had more options in the new republic. Indeed, she was offered a teaching position at a Chinese university, but ultimately chose to remain in the United States. When her father died, she took over the administration of his mission, which later became the First Chinese Baptist Church in New York. Mabel Lee continued to work with the Chinatown community in that position until her own death in 1965. Members of her church and community fondly remember her and recently dedicated the local post office to her. But, for the most part, the role of Chinese suffragists in the United States was overlooked for the majority of the past century. Centennial celebrations are bringing more and more stories like Mabel Lee's to light. To be sure, the numbers of Chinese and Chinese American suffragists in the United States were small, but they played a visible and important role in the suffrage struggle. They advocated for a movement that fought for equality of sex and race; they taught white suffrage leaders about the global scope of the fight for women's rights; and they advocated for women's rights in the new Chinese Republic.

This article was originally published by the United States Women's Suffrage Centennial Commission.

Above: Leading advocate for the rights of women and the Chinese in the U.S., Mabel Ping-Hua Lee, c. 1937.

CHAPTER FOUR

SUFFRAGE BY REGION

WOMAN SUFFRAGE IN THE WEST

The West led the way for the enfranchisement of women in the United States, with the establishing of partnerships and coalitions proving crucial to the success of western suffragists' campaigning efforts

By Jennifer Helton

Women of the West were the first in the United States to enjoy full voting rights. As new territories and states organized, many considered, and most granted, women the right to vote. Decades before passage of the 19th Amendment, western women voted and served in public office. In the diverse West, woman suffragists campaigned across mountains, plains, and deserts, finding common cause with a variety of communities and other political movements. Though they experienced setbacks along with their early victories, their successes were crucial to the eventual passage of a federal suffrage amendment.

The first attempt to secure woman suffrage in the West took place in 1854, when the territorial legislature of Washington considered a suffrage measure, only to defeat it by a single vote. However, it wasn't until the Reconstruction era, after the end of the Civil War, that the suffrage movement in the West truly began. The abolition of slavery in 1865 prompted a national deliberation about citizenship and voting rights. During the debates on the 14th and 15th Amendments, women's rights advocates lobbied—unsuccessfully—to enshrine woman suffrage in the Constitution. As attention then turned to the states, many supporters saw the West, with its young governments, as fertile territory for experiments with political reforms.

In February 1868, suffragist Laura De Force Gordon created a sensation by lecturing about woman suffrage in San Francisco. Gordon followed up by giving several suffrage talks in Nevada before returning to California to organize suffrage societies. Perhaps inspired by Gordon, the 1869 Nevada legislature passed an amendment to eliminate the words "male" and "white" from the voting requirements in the state constitution. Nevada law required that constitutional changes be passed in two sessions of the legislature; suffrage advocates would have to wait until 1871 to see if the amendment would be confirmed.

So, it was the women of Wyoming Territory, on December 10, 1869, who were the first to gain the vote. Several suffragist women in the territory, including Esther Morris and Amalia Post, likely lobbied behind the scenes for the law. But Reconstruction politics also played a role. Though Governor John Allen Campbell, Territorial Secretary Edward Lee, and other federally appointed Republican officials supported universal equal rights, it was Democrat William Bright who introduced the voting rights bill in the legislature. A southerner, Bright—whose wife, Julia, supported woman suffrage—opposed voting rights for African Americans and had vehemently spoken out against the 14th Amendment, fearing it would enfranchise Black men. If Black men were to be given the vote, Bright believed, women—and particularly white women—should be as well. Once enfranchised, Wyoming women enthusiastically exercised their new rights. They voted, ran for office, and eventually served in elected positions. Esther Morris became the first woman in the United States to serve as a judge, and Amalia Post was one of the first to serve on a jury.

Utah's predominantly Mormon territorial legislature enfranchised its women soon after, on February 12, 1870. Though Mormon women generally did not espouse radical views about female equality, they had long held the right to vote within church assemblies. In late 1869, Congress attempted to eliminate polygamy in Utah Territory by proposing the Collum Act, which proposed to deny suffrage to men who supported plural marriage. On January 13, 1870,

three thousand Utah women gathered in the Salt Lake Tabernacle at a "Great Indignation Meeting" to protest the law. Fourteen women rose to speak in defense of polygamy and women's rights, including several who called for the right to vote. After the legislature passed the woman suffrage bill, Utah women immediately began to exercise their rights— they voted in a Salt Lake City municipal election only two days after the bill passed. Eliza Snow, who had been the wife of both Joseph Smith and Brigham Young, deemed it "as necessary to vote as to pray."

These early successes can be attributed partly to lack of organized opposition. In Wyoming, woman suffrage was supported by politicians from both parties, though for different reasons. In Utah, suffragists were supported by the Mormon Church. After these victories, many hoped that the 1871 Nevada legislature would reaffirm the suffrage act it had passed in 1869. But despite lobbying efforts by Laura De Force Gordon and Emily Pitts Stevens, also of California, the measure failed. Nevada's women would wait until 1914 to vote. In the other states and territories of the West, too, suffragists would encounter active resistance.

By 1870, women who hoped to spread suffrage through the West began to organize. In some areas, suffragists formed chapters of the national suffrage organizations. In others, they worked through women's clubs. Black clubwomen were particularly committed to the cause, organizing suffrage societies in Idaho, Montana, North Dakota, Nevada, Arizona, Oklahoma, and New Mexico. The Woman's Christian Temperance Union (WCTU), which had chapters across the West, also supported suffrage. The temperance movement inspired many women to agitate for the vote, but it also motivated well-funded opponents, in particular, the "liquor interests."

In the 1870s and 1880s, women's organizations fought many campaigns, but they had limited success. In 1870, the governor of Colorado Territory, Edward McCook, announced his support for woman suffrage, but after heated debate, the legislature rejected a suffrage measure. When Colorado became a state in 1876, activists' efforts to include suffrage in the state constitution failed, as did a subsequent 1877 referendum. Two more unsuccessful legislative attempts followed in 1881 and 1891. Opposition of the liquor interests contributed to these defeats. Anti-Chinese racism was also a factor. One anti-suffrage argument warned: "the poor, degraded Chinese women who might reach our shores, would also be admitted to the voting list, and what then would become of our proud, Caucasian civilization?" Better not to enfranchise any women at all.

In California, too, suffragists regularly lobbied the legislature to approve women's voting rights, but it steadfastly refused. As in Colorado, anti-Chinese racism was strong, even among suffragists.

Previous pages: Women representing California, Wyoming,
and Montana parade up Fifth Avenue in New York, 1915.
Opposite: California-based lawyer, newspaper publisher, and
suffragist Laura De Force Gordon. Above: Esther Morris—
the country's first woman justice of the peace.

FRANK LESLIE'S ILLUSTRATED NEWSPAPER

Entered according to Act of Congress, in the year 1888, by MRS. FRANK LESLIE, in the Office of the Librarian of Congress at Washington.—Entered at the Post Office, New York, N. Y., as Second-class Matter.

No. 1,732.—VOL. LXVII.]   NEW YORK—FOR THE WEEK ENDING NOVEMBER 24, 1888.   [PRICE, 10 CENTS.

WOMAN SUFFRAGE IN WYOMING TERRITORY.—SCENE AT THE POLLS IN CHEYENNE.
FROM A PHOTO, BY KIRKLAND.—SEE PAGE 233.

Above: An illustrated newspaper cover depicts women voting in
Wyoming—the first territory or state in which women won the
vote in 1869; Opposite, left: Oregon activist Abigail Scott Duniway;
Opposite, right: Leading Utah suffragist Emmeline Wells.

At the 1879 California constitutional convention, suffrage leaders embraced the anti-Chinese rhetoric of the Workingmen's Party, hoping to gain its support. In the end, woman suffrage was not included in the new constitution, though anti-Chinese provisions were.

Further north, in the Pacific Northwest, Oregon activist Abigail Scott Duniway and national suffrage leader Susan B. Anthony embarked upon a two thousand–mile journey across Oregon and Washington in 1871, delivering lectures and organizing suffrage clubs as they went. Duniway and other suffragists succeeded in getting bills introduced in the Oregon legislature in 1871, 1873, 1875, and 1884, but the only success for Oregon women in this era was passage in 1877 of a school suffrage law.

For a time, the situation in Washington Territory looked brighter. Activist Mary Olney Brown attempted to vote in 1869, and in 1870 a few women successfully voted, arguing that as citizens it was their right under the 14th Amendment. This prompted the legislature to pass a bill forbidding voting for women. Attempts to pass suffrage bills in 1878 and 1881 failed.

Nonetheless, suffragists pressed on, and in 1883 the Washington territorial legislature passed woman suffrage. For four years, women voted. Then, in 1887, Washington's Supreme Court invalidated the suffrage law on a technicality. When the legislature responded by passing a new suffrage law, opponents, supported by the anti-temperance machine, fired back with a lawsuit. The Supreme Court again declared woman suffrage invalid, on the shakiest of grounds. In 1890, like Oregon women, Washington women were granted school suffrage in place of full voting rights.

Washington women were not alone in losing voting rights. Congress deprived Utah women of the right to vote with the Edmunds-Tucker Act of 1887. This law disenfranchised all Utah women, as well as men who practiced polygamy. Utah suffragist Charlotte Godbe and Belva Lockwood, one of the first female lawyers in the United States, tried unsuccessfully to lobby against this bill. When it passed, in the words of Utah suffragist Emmeline Wells, it "wrested from all the women, Gentile and Mormon alike, the suffrage which they had exercised for 17 years." In response, women founded the Woman Suffrage Association of Utah.

Despite these frustrations and defeats, in the 1870s and 1880s, western activists laid the groundwork for later successes. An important step was their establishment of regional suffrage newspapers. Woman suffrage papers laid out the arguments for suffrage and helped to create a community of activists. They connected western women to the suffrage work that was happening around the world. Western women also wrote for national papers, keeping the women back East informed about progress in the West. In Colorado, for example, Elizabeth Ensley was a correspondent for the *Woman's Era*, a nationwide African American women's paper. Though the achievements of the 1870s and 1880s were limited, the struggles of this period gave activists the experience, networks, and knowledge they would need for later efforts.

By the 1890s, these factors, combined with new political alliances, contributed to new gains. Wyoming entered the Union as a state in 1890 with woman suffrage intact. It was the first state, as it had been the first territory, to guarantee its women the right to vote. The federal government became receptive to Utah's application for

"Woman suffrage papers laid out the arguments for suffrage and helped to create a community of activists. They connected western women to the suffrage work that was happening around the world"

statehood once the Mormon Church outlawed polygamy in 1890. At the Utah constitutional convention in 1895, Utah's suffragists lobbied to ensure that women were included. When Utah became a state in 1896, Utah women regained the right to vote.

It was not until 1893, however, that the West saw its first successful statewide referendum campaign, in Colorado. There, local and national suffrage societies partnered with new labor and political organizations to win support. In the early 1890s, six Denver women, including African American activist Elizabeth P. Ensley, founded the Colorado Equal Suffrage Association (later known as the Non-Partisan Equal Suffrage Association). Ensley, who served as treasurer of the association during the 1893 campaign, ensured that African American activists were connected to the movement. Suffragists also made common cause with the Knights of Labor and the Populist Party. These organizations had women leaders and members and were influential in farming and mining communities.

The support of national suffrage leaders also contributed to the Colorado victory. Carrie Chapman Catt, who arrived in Colorado to organize on behalf of the National American Woman Suffrage Association (NAWSA), traveled over one thousand miles across the state, lecturing and founding suffrage clubs. Coalition politics proved successful; woman suffrage passed in Colorado with 55 percent of the vote. In Idaho, too, woman suffrage passed by referendum and depended on broad support. All three major parties in Idaho—Populists, Republicans, and Democrats—endorsed suffrage, and on election day in November 1896, support from Populists, the labor movement, and Mormons helped the referendum win by a two-to-one margin.

These successes, however, took place against a background of continued setbacks elsewhere. In 1896, a hard-fought referendum campaign in California failed, despite the organizing efforts of Anthony, Catt, and African American suffragist Naomi Anderson. Attempts to re-enfranchise Washington's women were unsuccessful in 1889 and 1898. In Oregon, suffrage was on the ballot in 1900, 1904, 1906, 1908, and 1910 and lost each time. In other states, women continued to organize. The Montana Woman Suffrage Association, established in the 1890s, grew rapidly under the leadership of Populist Ella Knowles, Montana's assistant attorney general. Arizona women founded the Arizona Woman's Equal Rights Association in 1887. In Nevada, educator Eliza Clapp and others formed the Nevada Equal Suffrage Association (NESA) in 1895. In all these states, suffrage organizations lobbied their legislatures nearly every session, with few results.

Finally, after a 14-year gap, a wave of enfranchisements took place the 1910s. The western suffrage campaigns of this era often rejected the involvement of NAWSA, whose methods had

Above, top: Women register to vote, San Francisco, 1911.
Above, bottom: May Arkwright Hutton, the first vice
president of the Washington Equal Suffrage Association.

been unsuccessful in the 1890s and early 1900s. Instead, the new generation formed partnerships with the Progressive and socialist movements, and having learned the hard lessons of earlier failures, disassociated themselves from temperance.

The breakthrough came in 1910, when Washington became the fifth state to grant full suffrage. Led by Emma Smith DeVoe and May Arkwright Hutton, a new generation of suffragists took up the fight. Dr. Cora Smith Eaton led a group of suffragists up Mount Rainier, where they staked a green pennant proclaiming "VOTES FOR WOMEN" at the peak. Campaigners rented billboards, participated in parades, and even sponsored a whistle-stop train tour. Strong links with the labor movement, which was fighting for an eight-hour-day bill for women, were also critical. The campaigners were quick to connect woman suffrage to popular Progressive causes and steered clear of temperance. Finally, 56 years after the first attempt to enfranchise Washington women, the measure passed with nearly 64 percent of the vote.

In California, Progressive legislators placed a woman suffrage measure on the 1911 ballot. The massive campaign that followed favored bold approaches: building suffrage parade floats, presenting stereopticon shows to amazed audiences, and plastering suffrage posters on every available surface. Clubwomen, Progressives, and Socialists all worked for the cause, and the College Equal Suffrage League and the Wage Earners Suffrage League played important roles. California's diverse communities provided essential support. Suffrage articles appeared in Spanish, Chinese, German, Portuguese, and Italian. Maria de Lopez, a Los Angeles clubwoman, campaigned and translated at rallies in Southern California, where suffragists distributed tens of thousands of pamphlets in Spanish. In Oakland, members of the Colored Women's Suffrage League monitored polling stations to prevent fraud. And though hostility to Chinese Americans lingered among some white activists, others courted their support. A majority of Chinese voters supported suffrage on election day. Woman suffrage passed with a mere 50.7 percent of the vote. Once again, coalitions had worked.

Opposite: A personification of justice adorns a sheet music cover, presenting the seals of the four western states that had equal suffrage by the date of publication in 1908. Above: Members of the Women's Union Label League in San Diego on a Labor Day float, 1910.

Oregon finally enfranchised its women via referendum in 1912, after campaigners embraced parades, publicity, and coalitions. At least 23 suffrage clubs existed in Portland alone. Jewish women held key leadership roles on the Portland Central Campaign Committee. The Colored Women's Equal Suffrage Association organized Black churchwomen. The Chinese American Suffrage Club mobilized Portland's Chinese neighborhoods. Politicians and labor leaders dominated the Men's Equal Suffrage Club. Portland suffragists also had a boys' club, a Quaker club, and a stenographers' club. Unions, farmers, Socialists, and the WCTU all endorsed voting rights for women. In the end, the measure squeaked through with 52 percent of the vote. As in California, diverse coalitions were essential to overcome the opposition of liquor interests and old-guard machine politics.

Women in Arizona and the new territory of Alaska also won the right to vote in 1912. When Arizona became a state in 1912, its constitution did not guarantee woman suffrage. After an attempt to secure a referendum failed, the Arizona Equal Suffrage Association (AESA) gathered enough signatures on petitions to place an initiative on the ballot. The AESA secured the support of both the Republican and Democratic Parties and reached out to Progressives, socialists, and the labor movement. Some suffragists also used racist and nativist arguments, claiming that native-born American white women deserved the right to vote more than foreign-born immigrant men. At the same time, however, the AESA worked with Mexican American organizations, Spanish newspapers, and immigrant miners. The measure passed by a two-to-one margin. Support from Mormons and Progressives was key to its success. In Alaska, things were a bit easier. NAWSA sent literature to legislators of the new territory, who quickly proposed a bill. Woman suffrage was the first law signed by the governor.

Two years later, Montana granted women the vote. Jeannette Rankin, a Montanan and NAWSA organizer who had worked on suffrage efforts across the country, led the campaign, sending speakers into nearly every mining community in the state. One of her organizers, Maggie Smith Hardaway, delivered 55 talks and traveled 2,375 miles over seven weeks. At the state fair in September, the Montana State Men's League for Woman Suffrage marched in

Miss Caly Fornia one lovely day
And Mr. Mass A. Chusetts met on the highway
"Where are you going to my pretty maid?"
"Going a-voting Sir" she said
"May I go with you?" "Yes if you will
Give the vote to my sisters on Beacon Hill."

Opposite: Suffragists gather to support the drive for equal
suffrage in California in 1911. Above: A pro-suffrage
postcard depicting a "Miss Caly Fornia" encouraging
a "Mr. Mass A. Chusetts" to pass women's rights.

"Not all western women received the vote with ratification of the 19th Amendment. Many Native American women were not considered U.S. citizens and thus were not able to vote"

a suffrage parade; the WCTU was not allowed to make an appearance for fear of rousing the saloon lobby. The referendum squeaked by, with 52.2 percent of voters approving it.

The Nevada legislature finally passed successive woman suffrage referenda in 1911 and 1913, sending the measure to the voters for a final decision. Anne Martin of the Nevada Equal Suffrage Association (NESA) led the Nevada campaign. Martin, who had been involved with the radical suffrage movement in Britain, led the NESA in establishing new clubs, publicizing the cause in the press, and distributing suffrage literature across the state. Margaret Foley, a labor organizer from Boston, "talked in the depths of eight mines, attended fifty dances, made one thousand speeches, and [wore] out three pairs of shoes." The Socialist, Democratic, and Progressive Parties endorsed woman suffrage at their conventions. These efforts paid off; the referendum passed by a wide margin, finally ending the struggle that had begun in 1869.

With Nevada's vote, only New Mexico, of the continental western states, did not grant women full voting rights before the 19th Amendment. Attempts to gain woman suffrage failed in 1871 and 1891, and the state constitution of 1910 granted only school suffrage. Hispano delegates to the 1910 constitutional convention secured stringent protections for Spanish American (male) voting rights. To protect themselves against any future attempts at Jim Crow-style disenfranchisement, Hispano delegates demanded measures that made voting provisions practically unamendable. These measures also made it impossible to enfranchise New Mexico's women by referendum. A different strategy was needed.

The Congressional Union (CU), founded by radical suffragist Alice Paul, began organizing in New Mexico in the early 1910s. In 1917, the CU, by then renamed the National Woman's Party (NWP), recruited Adelina Otero-Warren, a member of a prominent Republican Hispano family, to oversee its work in New Mexico. Otero-Warren led the NWP's New Mexico campaign for ratification of the 19th Amendment. Suffrage pamphlets were printed in Spanish, and Otero-Warren, along with Aurora Lucero and other local suffragists, promoted the cause. New Mexico ratified the 19th Amendment in February 1920.

Opposite, top: A National Woman's Party poster calls for women of Colorado to support national suffrage at the ballot box, 1916.
Nevada's Governor, Emmet D. Boyle, signs the resolution for ratification of the 19th Amendment, February 7, 1920.

Not all western women, however, received the vote with ratification of the 19th Amendment. Many Native American women were not considered U.S. citizens and thus were not able to vote. Nor did state suffrage laws enfranchise indigenous women, unless they had renounced their connection to their tribe. Suffragists only infrequently reached out to native communities; however, some indigenous leaders believed that voting rights could be a powerful tool for protecting native rights. In 1924, Zitkala-Sa, a Lakota writer and activist, lobbied Congress to secure suffrage for indigenous Americans. Partly as a result of her efforts, Congress passed the Indian Citizenship Act, which defined Native Americans as U.S. citizens. Even after passage of this law, however, many western states continued to disenfranchise indigenous people. Zitkala-Sa went on to cofound the National Council of American Indians, which focused on civil rights for native peoples.

The Territory of Hawai'i also exemplified the challenges faced by indigenous women. After the last indigenous ruler of Hawai'i, Queen Lili'uokalani, was deposed by the United States in 1893, local WCTU activists lobbied for the inclusion of women in the territorial government. When the Territory of Hawai'i was created in 1898, however, woman suffrage was specifically excluded, partly because indigenous women significantly outnumbered white women in the territory.

For women who were able to vote, enfranchisement paved the way for their entry into politics. Across the West, women won election to office, most often for school boards or as county superintendent of schools. In the 1890s, Colorado, Idaho, and Utah all elected women to their state legislatures. The West produced the first woman governor, Nellie Tayloe Ross of Wyoming, who later served as director of the U.S. Mint. It also sent the first woman to Congress, Jeannette Rankin of Montana.

The enfranchisement of women in the United States began in the West. Early successes there were connected to the complex politics of Reconstruction and polygamy. Later victories stemmed from suffragists' ability to build partnerships with other movements that shared their desire for reform and increased democratization of politics. Over time, suffragists discovered that campaigns were most likely to succeed when they had the support of broad coalitions and diverse groups of voters. Through decades of campaigning, debating, and lobbying, western women won the right to vote, and they used their experience and knowledge to support the expansion of women's rights across the country.

This article was originally commissioned by the National Conference of State Historic Preservation Officers in partnership with the United States National Park Service.

Opposite: The nation's first woman governor, Nellie Tayloe Ross,
pictured in her subsequent role as director of the U.S. Mint. Above:
Montana suffragist Jeannette Rankin, the first woman in Congress.

WOMAN SUFFRAGE IN THE MIDWEST

Despite facing organized, well-funded opposition, suffragists in the Midwest galvanized support through various local and national alliances to great effect

By Elyssa Ford

Unlike other regions of the country where it is possible to see clear patterns in the woman suffrage story, such as the West with its early successes or the South where racism impeded the expansion of voting rights, the Midwest has no single dominant narrative of the woman suffrage campaign. Though by the passage of the 19th Amendment in 1920 all midwestern states had extended some form of suffrage to women, only a few granted women full voting rights. Several others offered women presidential and municipal suffrage, others allowed presidential suffrage alone. While two states had approved woman suffrage measures in the early 1910s, most of these states acted only shortly before the federal amendment passed.

Despite such variation, there were several common threads in the midwestern fight for woman suffrage. The values of piety, morality, and domesticity led to strong and complicated ties to other social movements. Issues of race, ethnicity, and class, as well as the rural–urban divide, created internal divisions and provided opportunities for expanded support. At times, midwestern suffragists found themselves at odds with the national leadership, even as they sometimes depended on them for guidance and financial support. These threads demonstrate why suffrage success was difficult, though not impossible, to achieve in these states.

Discussion of woman suffrage first began in the Midwest's eastern states as suffragists from the East toured the region. In 1845 and 1846, Ernestine Rose of New York campaigned for social reform and women's rights, even speaking in the hall of the Michigan House of Representatives on these controversial issues. In 1853, Lucy Stone, an organizer from Massachusetts, began a speaking tour of what she called "the West"—Ohio, Kentucky, Indiana, Missouri, Illinois, and Wisconsin. Even in her radical bloomer outfit, she received a warm welcome in these midwestern states. In St. Louis, the newspaper reported that her talk drew the largest crowd ever assembled for

a speaker. A medical college suspended classes so faculty and students could attend, and a local minister even cancelled the Christmas Eve service so that the congregation could hear Stone's lecture instead.

Midwestern women began to organize local suffrage societies and campaigns in the 1860s and 1870s, after the disruption of the Civil War. One of the first was the Missouri Suffrage Association, founded in 1867. In that same year, supporters of both Black and woman suffrage organized the Impartial Suffrage Association in Kansas to fight for two proposed amendments to the state constitution, one to strike "white" and another to strike "male" from the state's voting requirements. After a brutal campaign that ended up pitting supporters of African American and woman suffrage against one another, the electorate defeated both amendments. Soon, other state legislatures and constitutional conventions across the Midwest also considered the question of woman suffrage. At times, success was achingly close, but all failed. In 1870, Michigan legislators approved woman suffrage, only for the measure to be vetoed by the governor, and in 1872 woman suffrage lost by a single vote in the Dakota Territory. By that time, women in most midwestern states had created their own statewide societies to support these suffrage efforts.

Like other regions of the country, the Midwest faced the challenge of trying to coordinate the various suffrage groups. In many states, local and state organizing preceded national campaigns. While national groups saw themselves as directing the suffrage movement from above, in many ways national organizing was a response to pre-existing grassroots efforts, and the national organizations at times struggled to influence state campaigns as state and local organizations tried to remain independent. For instance, when divisions led to the separate formation of the American Woman

Suffrage Association (AWSA) from the National Woman Suffrage Association (NWSA) in 1869, the Missouri Suffrage Association refused to join either group, though later the Missouri organization became badly divided by affiliations with both AWSA and NWSA. Iowa formed its first state-level organization in 1870 and, despite the presence of national representatives from both groups, decided to remain independent. Just a year later, the Indiana Woman Suffrage Association chose to withdraw from AWSA and become independent.

Tensions between national, state, and local suffragists came to the fore in Michigan in 1874 when the question of woman suffrage was sent to male voters. Susan B. Anthony increasingly believed that state strategies like this hurt the national effort but still decided to go to Michigan. To her surprise, she received an unenthusiastic welcome. Local suffrage workers were concerned that Anthony's ties to the controversial "free love" advocate Victoria Woodhull would provide fodder for anti-suffragists. Even newspapers traditionally in support of woman suffrage wrote attack articles about Anthony and Woodhull and condemned the outside, eastern presence and their immoral values. In the end, suffrage lost by a vote of 135,000 to 40,000. Local organizers blamed Anthony and other national leaders for tainting the campaign, while national groups blamed local suffragists for being poorly organized.

Despite these tensions, many midwestern suffragists were leaders in the national movement. Unsuccessful in securing the vote through state legislatures and constitutional conventions, midwestern suffragists pioneered a strategy that became known as the New Departure. In 1869 at a national suffrage convention in St. Louis, Virginia Minor and her husband, Francis, pointed to the 14th Amendment to argue that women, as citizens, already had the

Previous pages: Members of the Equal Suffrage Club,
University of Minnesota, 1913. Opposite: Suffragists
pictured in Chicago, c. 1910. Above: Temperance
advocates pray in front of an Ohio saloon, 1874.

Above: Suffragists in Kansas solicit
votes at the polls, April 1887.

"In some areas it was the passage of state prohibition laws that finally allowed woman suffrage to gain traction"

right to vote. In answer to the Minors' call for women to simply use this right, hundreds of women across the country went to the polls. Most were denied and some, including Susan B. Anthony, were arrested. In 1872, Virginia Minor sued after she was refused voter registration in Missouri. Minor v. Happersett advanced to the U.S. Supreme Court, which ruled unanimously that voting was not a right of citizenship. This seminal case ended the New Departure and forced suffragists to redouble their efforts on state legislatures and a national amendment.

Throughout their fight for the vote, one constant remained. Midwestern suffrage groups, much like those in the East, focused on morality, piety, and domesticity—the values women promised to bring to the political arena. As one male Iowa state senator said in support of woman suffrage in 1865, "Do you want all grogshops, gambling houses, and corrupt houses of ill-fame banished from the State? If so, let women vote. They will elect men who will execute the laws, and legislators who will enact laws." Yet this emphasis on morality proved to be problematic. The Woman's Christian Temperance Union (WCTU) was founded in 1874 in Cleveland, Ohio, a city known as "the Mecca of the Crusade" against alcohol. Under president Frances Willard's "Do Everything" campaign, unveiled in 1882, the WCTU encouraged members to support woman suffrage, making the WCTU an important ally of the suffrage movement. However, suffragists' alignment with the WCTU also created powerful enemies.

The liquor industry actively opposed the temperance movement and, through extension, voting rights for women. Wisconsin brewers provided the nation's best-funded opposition to woman suffrage.

The German-American Alliance also was hostile to woman suffrage because of its connection to the brewing industry. By 1914, the alliance had a membership in the millions and a powerful lobby in Washington. Germans provided significant opposition to suffrage throughout the Midwest, and they were not the only ethnic group to align with liquor interests. At the 1880 Democratic convention in South Dakota, a large delegation of Russian immigrants wore liquor-industry badges that proclaimed "Against Woman Suffrage and Susan B. Anthony."

A particularly crushing defeat at the hands of the liquor industry came in Michigan in 1912. After decades of organizing, the governor called for a vote, and the measure had strong support from various interests, including farmers. Victory seemed assured until alcohol lobbyists pressed for a recount. There was a strong suspicion of ballot tampering during that process, and suffrage lost by seven hundred votes. Women in Michigan had to wait until 1917 for presidential suffrage and 1918 for full suffrage.

As suffragists realized the problems that came with their relationship with prohibitionists, they moved away from working closely with the temperance movement. In South Dakota, suffrage proponents ended their alliance with temperance advocates in the mid-1910s and began sending the German community copies of their suffrage paper. Still, the association between temperance and woman suffrage lingered. In some areas it was the passage of state prohibition laws that finally allowed woman suffrage to gain traction because only then did the opposition from the liquor industry cease. Following a divisive and ultimately unsuccessful battle for suffrage in Kansas in 1867, proponents were hopeful following the passage of state prohibition in 1879. With that success, the WCTU held significant influence in the state, and their ties to the Kansas Equal Suffrage Association helped lead to passage of the country's first state-level municipal woman suffrage law in 1887.

Something similar happened in South Dakota. In 1916, men in the state voted on both prohibition and woman suffrage. Prohibition won while woman suffrage garnered 48 percent of the vote, an unprecedented high. Suffrage supporters believed their success was now assured because the liquor vote had been silenced. They were right; at their next attempt, in 1918, South Dakota women finally achieved full suffrage.

Midwestern suffragists adopted arguments of female morality, piety, and domesticity as justifications for the vote beyond their connection with temperance. Jane Addams promoted a variation of this argument with her call for municipal housekeeping (also called civic or public housekeeping). Drawing upon her experience with settlement houses in Chicago, Addams argued not that women were different from men and, thus, could purify politics, but that women's household tasks actually made them uniquely qualified to be city leaders and to clean up the problems caused by industrialization. "The ballot," she said, "would afford the best possible protection to working women and expedite that protective legislation which they so sadly need and in which America is so deficient."

Addams's argument resonated best in the region's cities, such as Chicago, Omaha, Minneapolis, and St. Louis, where most suffrage activities were centered. But midwestern states also had significant rural populations with somewhat different concerns. Organizations like the Grange, Farmers' Alliance, and Populist Party routinely endorsed woman suffrage in the Midwest, and by the 1890s, suffrage groups became more adept at leveraging that support. This was especially true in Kansas where these rural associations all promoted the role of women within their organizations and supported a more democratic and egalitarian society. In 1892, shortly after the founding of the Populist Party in Kansas, rural publications targeted women as farmers and as political actors. Its paper the *Farmer's Wife* declared a "Women's War" and vowed to fight any suffrage opponents until the vote was won.

Leaders in other states also targeted farm women with their publications and grassroots campaigns. Following decades of defeat in Nebraska, urban-based suffrage organizations changed their approach in 1914 and included rural women in their push.

Opposite, left: Susan Fitzgerald and Louise Hall glue up suffrage
posters at Main and Canal Street in Cincinnati, Ohio, on May 17,
1912, as part of the statewide suffrage campaign. Opposite, right:
Social worker and suffragist Jane Addams, c. 1910, who went on
to win the Nobel Peace Prize in 1931. Above: A 1912 magazine
pictures a Chicago suffrage rally on its cover.

WHEN WOMEN VOTE -IN- MISSOURI

Men will have a **LIVING WAGE**; Our babies will have **PURE MILK**; Our Social Centers will keep our Young People in the Rural District **ON THE FARM** and Missouri will give **EVERY CHILD** An equal opportunity to become a **GOOD CITIZEN.**

They wrote articles that targeted farm wives and specifically asked their opinions. They even expanded their donation policy to accept crops and farm animals to encourage rural involvement. The message was received positively. As one rural woman wrote to a suffrage paper, "The woman farm owner is considered a citizen only when the taxes fall due, but on election day she may not say how those taxes are spent." Despite their differences, rural and urban Nebraska women were able to see that they both were without an important voice—the vote. Nebraska suffragists' ability to broaden their message to include rural areas helped them win partial suffrage in 1918.

Something similar happened in Iowa. In the late 19th century, urban suffrage leaders preferred to work within their own social circles. When their efforts garnered few results, they looked to new ways to attract rural support, including an automobile tour of small communities and speakers on the Chautauqua circuit. In 1916, with this dual rural–urban approach, suffragists undertook one of the largest grassroots campaigns in Iowa's history. The vote for the suffrage referendum failed in the end, but the change in tactic contributed to a closer vote than previous ones in 1872 and 1909.

The organizing and mobilizing by the region's African American women also contributed to suffrage successes. At times, Black women were supported by white suffrage leaders. For instance, when Lucy Stone learned that Black women had been denied entrance to her talk in Indiana while on her 1853 tour of the Midwest, she demanded that African Americans be permitted to attend the following night and was steadfast in her decision even when told this would mean some of the local white population would refuse to attend. More frequently, it was Black women who had to demand that white suffragists include their voices and perspectives.

Josephine St. Pierre did this at the 1900 meeting of the General Federation of Women's Clubs in Wisconsin when she pushed for Black and white women to unify. Instead, she was taunted, and other leading Black women, such as Mary Church Terrell from the National Association of Colored Women, were not even allowed to speak. Often excluded from white women's suffrage meetings, Black women organized among themselves to advance suffrage rights for all African Americans. Even though Black women in the Midwest did not face the same hostility as those in the South, they still endured discrimination within the suffrage movement.

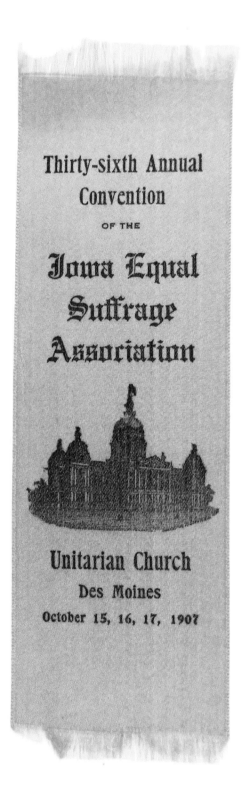

Opposite: A pro-suffrage card rallies support in rural
Missouri. Above, left to right: Yellow suffrage ribbons
produced by the *Farmer's Wife* newspaper and the Iowa
Equal Suffrage Association, respectively.

Above: Prominent activist Grace Wilbur Trout marching in
Chicago on Suffrage Day, May 2, 1914. Opposite: A ballot box
used in the 1912 primary referendum in Cook County, Illinois
about "extending suffrage to women." The referendum was not
passed but the following year women voters won the right
to presidential suffrage throughout the state.

Once they gained suffrage, Black women proved to be an influential voting bloc. Illinois women gained local suffrage in 1914, and Black leaders such as Ida B. Wells-Barnett immediately began to mobilize Black women as voters, partly because they feared that the state planned to offer broader suffrage but only to white women. Wells wanted to ensure that Black women were aware of their rights. They had largely been left out of the Illinois Woman Suffrage Association, but due to Wells's work and the potential threat to their voting rights, Black women created the Alpha Suffrage Club. They gained the support of Black men by arguing that they wanted the vote to help elect Black men into office. Through their efforts to register men and women, Chicago's predominately Black Second Ward soon was sixth out of the city's 35 wards for voter registration. The Alpha Suffrage Club then put those voters to work. The group helped elect the city's first Black alderman and defeat a candidate supported by white suffragists.

Black women also demonstrated the power of their collective action in Ohio. In 1919, the Colored Women's Republican Club changed its name to the Colored Women's Independent Political League as a public repudiation of that party when the Republican-dominated Ohio legislature defeated an equal rights bill. This successful work by Black women made other groups take notice. Anti-suffragists in the South used the Illinois example to demonstrate the danger of extending the vote and, thereby, expanding Black voting potential.

By the start of the 20th century, the national woman suffrage movement had come together with the creation of the National American Woman Suffrage Association (NAWSA) in 1890, which united NWSA and AWSA. Yet new divisions appeared with the formation of the more radical Congressional Union in 1913. Its leader Alice Paul quickly began to make movements into the Midwest, where she was met with varied responses. The Ohio Woman Suffrage Association invited both NAWSA and the Congressional Union to set up offices in the state in 1915. Carrie Chapman Catt of Iowa, president of NAWSA, said that the Ohio group had "lost its senses" and urged the state to oppose the Congressional Union. Leaders in Wisconsin and Minnesota also called for an end to the divisions and tried to work with both national groups. Despite the national divisions, groups in the Midwest—just as they had earlier with AWSA and NWSA—often wanted to see less fighting and more collaboration.

By 1915, ten western states and Kansas—the first in the Midwest—had adopted full woman suffrage. Successful on their third attempt in 1912, Kansas suffragists adopted a wide range of tactics. They held bazaars and teas to raise money, worked with local communities to stage the play *How the Vote Was Won*, and held essay contests in public schools, where children competed for prizes but the real purpose was to convert their parents to the suffrage cause. With a margin of almost 20,000 votes, Kansas became "the seventh star" of woman suffrage in the country and the first in the Midwest.

"Despite the national divisions, groups in the Midwest—just as they had done with AWSA and NWSA—often wanted to see less fighting and more collaboration"

Throughout this period, national speakers continued to travel the Midwest. In 1914, Alice Paul sent Congressional Union organizers to the states with full suffrage. In this campaign, Paul's goal was to organize women and men to support a federal suffrage amendment and to vote against Democratic candidates as a means of opposing the party's anti-suffrage tendencies. One organizer reported from Kansas that she was well-received in the state and shared accounts that, upon hearing her message, people were planning to change their life-long affiliation with the Democratic Party. Despite this push, Democratic presidential candidate Woodrow Wilson won re-election in 1916 in almost all of the suffrage states, including Kansas.

The Congressional Union—by 1917 known as the National Woman's Party (NWP)—was disappointed with its two-year effort. By 1918, the NWP was doing limited on-the-ground work in the Midwest, other than a few scattered speaking tours that, according to the speakers, had little impact in a region that seemed to be without hope. That year, Alice Henkle, an NWP representative, wrote home to the organization's headquarters, "I hope this is my last week here. Kansas City [Missouri] is the limit, but I hope I am bringing something out of the chaos I found here. At least we have a lot of activity and that has stirred up the women to really take an interest."

The reality of the suffrage push in Missouri—like in much of the Midwest—was stronger and more active than Alice Henkle understood. After early initial success in the West, suffragists won no new states between 1896 and 1910. Then, in the short time from 1910 to 1916, they achieved victories across the West and in Kansas. They organized intensely throughout the region in that period, with referenda in Ohio, Wisconsin, Michigan, South and North Dakota, Missouri, and Nebraska. These votes failed, but suffragists in Michigan and South Dakota soon achieved their goal with the passage of full suffrage in 1918, and by 1919 all other midwestern states had extended partial suffrage to women.

Though not as successful as their sisters in the West, suffragists in the Midwest achieved extraordinary victories despite organized and powerful opposition. They led almost constant suffrage campaigns and adeptly changed their tactics as circumstances dictated. Through signature gathering, parades, automobile tours, theatric tableaus, speeches, tabling at county fairs, and publications, suffragists in the Midwest worked within their local communities, struggled to bridge the rural–urban divide, allied with friendly political parties and organizations, devised strategies to counter their well-funded opposition, and drew guidance and inspiration from national organizations. These diverse approaches made the Midwest one of the most varied and successful regions in the country in the campaign for woman suffrage.

This article was originally commissioned by the National Conference of State Historic Preservation Officers in partnership with the United States National Park Service.

Above: Members of the Woman's Party picket
the president in Chicago, October 19, 1916.

WOMAN SUFFRAGE IN NEW ENGLAND

While New England suffragists struggled to gain votes for women in their respective states, they provided vital political skills in the push for a federal amendment

By Heather Munro Prescott

Although many histories of woman suffrage use the 1848 convention in Seneca Falls, New York as a starting point for the movement, New York State was not the only place women fought for the right to vote during the mid-19th century. Women and men from the New England states of Maine, Vermont, New Hampshire, Massachusetts, Connecticut, and Rhode Island also mobilized for women's rights in the 1840s. Because Susan B. Anthony and Elizabeth Cady Stanton's history of the suffrage movement emphasized Seneca Falls and downplayed or even left out suffragists from other parts of the country, the significance of the New England region in the national suffrage campaign has been neglected. An examination of the history of woman suffrage in New England not only uncovers examples of critical suffrage activism on the state and local level, it demonstrates how suffragists from the region helped build the suffrage cause into a national movement.

As in other parts of the country, the women's rights movement in New England grew out of efforts to abolish slavery. In 1837, noted female abolitionists Angelina and Sarah Grimké toured New England and staunchly defended a woman's right to speak out against slavery in public. The Grimké sisters persuaded women and men from the region to join the fight against slavery and inspired a small number of New England women to use the abolitionist cause as a platform for advancing the rights of women.

New England's most notable early suffragist was Lucy Stone of Massachusetts. Ten years after the Grimkés toured the region, Stone delivered her first lecture on behalf of women's rights at her brother's church in Gardner, Massachusetts. Soon after, she moved to Boston to begin a position as a paid lecturer for the Massachusetts Anti-Slavery Society. Stone enraged some audiences by daring to criticize women's lack of rights

"The NEWSA soon became embroiled in the national debate over the 15th Amendment to the U.S. Constitution, which would prohibit denying the franchise based on 'race, color, or previous condition of servitude'"

alongside her condemnation of slavery. Declaring, "I was a woman before I was an abolitionist," Stone defended her actions. Stone's renown as a speaker soon extended beyond New England. Following the 1848 women's rights convention in Seneca Falls, Elizabeth Cady Stanton suggested that convention organizers enlist Stone as a national lecturer on women's rights. Although no one took up this proposition, Stone, along with Stanton and Susan B. Anthony, soon became among the most prominent suffrage leaders in the country.

In 1850, Stone and several other New England women, including Abby Kelley Foster of Massachusetts and Paulina Wright Davis of Rhode Island, organized the first national women's rights convention in Worcester, Massachusetts, to see if they could generate support for suffrage around the country. Nearly one thousand men and women from 11 states attended. All but two of the attendees were native-born, white Protestants. The exceptions were Sojourner Truth, a former slave and prominent abolitionist, and Ernestine Rose, a Jewish immigrant from Poland. In an impassioned speech, Foster declared women had the same duty to rise up against tyranny as their ancestors had against King George III. In 1851, another national convention held in Worcester drew an even larger audience. These meetings, along with lectures by Stone and other suffrage leaders, inspired women throughout the nation to organize their own local efforts on behalf of women's rights.

Like their counterparts elsewhere, women's rights activists in New England put their cause on hold during the Civil War. After the war, they resumed their activism and began planning the formation of a regional suffrage organization. In 1868, they founded the New England Woman Suffrage Association (NEWSA), naming noted poet and author Julia Ward Howe, best known for writing "Battle Hymn of the Republic," president, and Lucy Stone a member of the executive committee. Other founding members included Paulina Wright Davis of Rhode Island and Isabelle Beecher Hooker of Connecticut.

The NEWSA soon became embroiled in the national debate over the 15th Amendment to the U.S. Constitution, which would prohibit denying the franchise based on "race, color, or previous condition of servitude." One of the founders of the NEWSA, Olympia Brown, favored Anthony and Stanton's insistence that woman suffrage be pursued alongside the enfranchisement of African American men. But Howe declared she would not demand the vote for herself until the freedman first obtained that right. Stone, while disagreeing with Frederick Douglass's claim that "the cause of the negro was more pressing than that of woman's," nevertheless agreed that Black male suffrage should come first.

Previous pages: Activists selling the weekly newspaper *The
Suffragist* in Boston, 1919. Above: Suffrage campaigner Lucy
Stone, c. 1860. Overleaf: Prior to the 19th Amendment, women in
certain states held the right to vote in some municipal elections.

The NEWSA formed the basis of the American Woman Suffrage Association (AWSA), founded in 1869 as an alternative to the National Woman Suffrage Association (NWSA) led by Stanton and Anthony. Unlike the NWSA, the AWSA protested both gender-based and race-based discrimination and prioritized the struggle for Black male suffrage. In order to avoid putting the fight for woman suffrage in direct conflict with Black suffrage, the AWSA abandoned efforts to include woman suffrage in the same constitutional amendment as Black suffrage. Instead, it focused its efforts on changing state laws that prohibited women from voting. Only when Black men had the right to vote would the AWSA seek a separate constitutional amendment for woman suffrage.

This schism between the AWSA and the NWSA continued even after passage of the 15th Amendment in 1870. The two organizations disagreed primarily over political strategies. The NWSA insisted that an amendment to the U.S. Constitution was the best way to achieve woman suffrage. The AWSA, on the other hand, argued that Congress would not support woman suffrage until a critical number of states had granted women the right to vote. The AWSA encouraged the growth of state organizations that would campaign for woman suffrage on a state-by-state basis. Stone and her husband, Henry Blackwell, also created the weekly newspaper the *Woman's Journal*, which served as the AWSA's principal means of communicating with affiliated state organizations.

Stanton and Anthony considered the state-based tactic foolhardy: leaving woman suffrage to the states, Stanton argued, would "defer indefinitely its settlement." Nevertheless, most women from New England agreed with the AWSA strategy and formed their own state organizations to pressure their respective legislatures to extend the vote to women. Since most New

LUCY STONE

1818–93

Edited by Debra Michals

A leading suffragist and abolitionist, Lucy Stone dedicated her life to battling inequality on all fronts. She was the first Massachusetts woman to earn a college degree and she defied gender norms when she famously wrote marriage vows to reflect her egalitarian beliefs and refused to take her husband's last name.

Born on August 13, 1818 in rural Massachusetts, Stone was one of Francis and Hannah Matthews Stone's nine children. Her parents were farmers with deep roots in New England. The first Stones arrived in 1635 pursuing religious freedom and her grandfather was a Patriot captain in the American Revolution. She was raised in the Congregational Church and embraced her father's anti-slavery zeal.

Much brighter than her brothers, Stone was frustrated by the inequality that encouraged them to attend college while discouraging women from becoming educated. At age 16, she worked as a teacher, saving her money so she could attend college. In 1839, she spent a semester at Mount Holyoke, but was forced to return home due to a sister's illness. Then, in 1843, she attended Oberlin College in Ohio. Even progressive Oberlin, however, did not permit Stone to explore her interest in public speaking. When she graduated in 1847, she declined the "honor" of writing a commencement speech that would be read by a man.

Almost 30 when she completed her education, Stone's career prospects seemed dim since few professions were open to women. Renowned abolitionist William Lloyd Garrison, however, hired her for his American Anti-Slavery Society. She wrote and delivered abolitionist speeches, while also becoming active in women's rights. Like other female abolitionists, Stone was often heckled and at least once was physically attacked by a mob. Nevertheless,

she proved so popular that soon she was out-earning many male lecturers.

In 1850, two years after the Seneca Falls women's rights convention, Stone organized the first national Woman's Rights Convention in Worcester, Massachusetts. Her speech there was reprinted in the international press. For five years, Stone traveled throughout the U.S. and Canada on the lecture circuit. She continued to attend annual women's rights conventions and presided over the seventh one. She met Henry Blackwell, the brother of physicians Elizabeth and Emily Blackwell, who convinced her to marry him by promising they could create an egalitarian marriage. Intended for publication, their 1855 vows omitted the then-common reference to wifely obedience and included a protest against marital law. She also set a new standard by retaining her maiden name. While living in New Jersey, Stone gave birth to two children, though the second one did not survive. Daughter Alice Stone Blackwell became a feminist and abolitionist, working alongside her parents.

Stone set another precedent in 1858 when she reminded Americans of the "no taxation without representation" principle. Her refusal to pay property taxes was punished by the impoundment and sale of the Stones' household goods. At the end of the Civil War, Stone went to Kansas to work on the referendum for suffrage there. She also served as president of the New Jersey Woman Suffrage Association and helped organize the New England association, in which she would be active after the family moved to Boston in 1869. At the same time, Stone served on the executive committee of the American Equal Rights Association.

In 1869, Stone broke with suffragists Elizabeth Cady Stanton, Susan B. Anthony, and others over passage of the 14th and 15th

Amendments to the Constitution, which granted voting rights to Black men but not to women. Stone was willing to accept this measure for her abolitionist goals while continuing to work for women's suffrage. Anthony and Stanton formed the National Woman Suffrage Association (NWSA). Stone, Julia Ward Howe, and others formed the American Woman Suffrage Association (AWSA). Stone edited the AWSA publication, the *Woman's Journal*. In 1879, Stone registered to vote in Massachusetts, since the state allowed women's suffrage in some local elections, but she was removed from the rolls because she did not use her husband's surname.

Stone lived to see the reunification of the two suffrage associations in 1890; both her daughter and Stanton's daughter, Harriot Stanton Blatch, played important roles in healing their mothers' wounds. Stone gave her last speech in 1893 at the World's Columbian Exposition, and died later that year at age 75.

This article appears courtesy of the National Women's History Museum.

Above: Boston women line up to vote in a school board
election, 1888. Opposite: Alice Stone Blackwell holds a copy
of the newspaper that she edited, dated May 4, 1912.

Englanders considered the education of children and youth to be within women's proper sphere, New England suffrage activists were most successful in campaigns for school suffrage and for the right of women to sit on school boards and to elect its members. New Hampshire was the first to approve school suffrage for women, in 1878, followed by the other New England states in the next few years.

New England suffragists used the argument of "social housekeeping"—that women would clean up urban politics and social ills—to make a case for allowing women to vote in municipal elections. Frequently these campaigns for municipal suffrage drew on anti-immigrant and anti-Catholic bigotry. In Massachusetts, for example, anti-immigrant Republican men believed that native-born Protestant women would be more likely to vote than Catholic women, who would be discouraged from voting by their husbands. Thus, woman suffrage would save the state from "rum and Romanism" by diluting the Catholic vote and promoting the cause of temperance. Despite these appeals, the Republican Party as a whole did not support municipal suffrage for women. The Democratic Party, especially its Irish Catholic wing, which linked woman suffrage to nativism, temperance, and anti-family radicalism, also opposed enfranchising women.

Vermont was the only New England state to grant women the right to vote in municipal elections. The municipal suffrage campaign in the Green Mountain State was successful largely because, as a rural state, Vermont lacked a sizable urban immigrant population to mount an anti-suffrage attack. On the other hand, the temperance movement, considered an appropriate political cause for women to embrace, was extremely popular in the state. Vermont suffragists convinced state legislators that female voters would help make the state dry. In 1917, the Vermont state legislature approved granting women the right to vote in municipal elections.

The work of New England suffragists eventually contributed to a rapprochement between the AWSA and the NWSA. Lucy Stone's daughter, Alice Stone Blackwell, was instrumental in unifying the competing national suffrage organizations. Negotiations between Blackwell, representing the AWSA, and Rachel Foster, of the NWSA, led to the formation of the National American Woman Suffrage Association (NAWSA) in 1890. The new organization elected Stanton president, Anthony vice president, Stone chair of executive committee, and Blackwell corresponding secretary. The *Woman's Journal* became NAWSA's official publication and remained based in Boston. NAWSA retained the AWSA strategy of campaigning for woman suffrage on a state-by-state basis. Although this tactic had limited success in New England, it led to a number of suffrage victories in the far and middle West. This strategy also reinvigorated state and regional suffrage organizations in New England and other areas of the country.

Julia Ward Howe expressed concern that the merger would lead to the abandonment of the AWSA's commitment to racial equality. Howe's fears proved correct: NAWSA dedicated itself solely to woman suffrage. It also adopted a racist and nativist strategy of "educated suffrage," which argued that educated, usually white and native-born women were more deserving of the vote than "ignorant" Black and immigrant men. Although educated suffrage could, theoretically, include the small number of educated Black women in the country, white suffrage organizations excluded or marginalized Black women.

During the 1890s, middle-class Black women founded their own organizations dedicated to fighting both gender and race discrimination. Among the leaders in this endeavor was Josephine Ruffin of Boston, founder of the city's Woman's Era Club and the monthly newsletter *The Woman's Era*, dedicated to providing a venue for "intercourse and sympathy" for women of all races but especially "the educated and refined, among the colored women." The pages of *The Woman's Era* expressed strong support for Ida B. Wells's campaign against lynching and chastised NAWSA for its tacit support of white supremacy. In 1895, the Woman's Era Club organized a convention in Boston for representatives from Black women's clubs around the nation. Attendees created the National Federation of Afro-American Women, forerunner of the National Association of Colored Women (NACW). The NACW established a woman suffrage department to educate members about the suffrage cause, but it received no support from NAWSA, which continued its policy of ignoring and refusing aid to Black suffragists.

NAWSA and its regional affiliates did reach out to white working-class women in an effort to expand its membership and win the support of white working-class male voters. This cross-class alliance was epitomized by the creation of the Women's Trade Union League (WTUL) at the American Federation of Labor's national convention in Boston in 1903. The WTUL elected Mary Morton Kimbell Kehew, a wealthy woman from Boston and descendant of a former Massachusetts governor, president and Mary Kenney O'Sullivan, an Irish Catholic labor organizer and resident of Denison Settlement house in Boston, secretary and first vice president. O'Sullivan's leadership was instrumental in persuading working-class men to support the suffrage cause. The WTUL, dedicated to improving pay and working conditions for women workers, served as an umbrella organization for other women's trade unions. Its goals aligned perfectly with the social housekeeping mission of the mainstream suffrage movement. The WTUL established a suffrage department in 1908 and urged working women and their male allies to attend suffrage rallies.

During the 1910s, some suffragists renewed demands for a federal amendment to the U.S. Constitution granting women the right to vote. In 1913, Alice Paul and Lucy Burns were appointed to the Congressional Committee of NAWSA. Paul and Burns soon alienated NAWSA with their militant tactics. Most controversial was

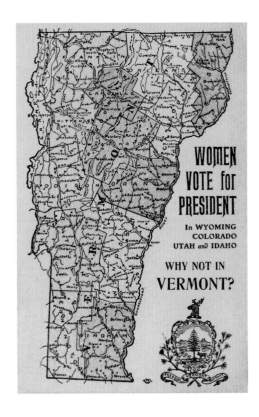

their proposal to campaign against Democratic candidates in the western states in order to pressure Congress and President Woodrow Wilson into supporting the suffrage amendment. Burns and Paul formed the Congressional Union, which became the National Woman's Party (NWP) in 1916. NAWSA expelled the Congressional Union from the Association in 1914.

Vermont did not have a chapter, but it is likely that the population of the state was too small to accommodate two suffrage organizations. Members of the state chapters of the NWP sent representatives to Washington to lobby Congress to pass the federal suffrage amendment and participated in the various parades and demonstrations organized by the NWP, including the pickets of the White House during 1917. Thirty suffragists from New England were charged with "obstructing traffic" and sentenced to prison where they endured deplorable living conditions and mistreatment by guards.

Katharine Martha Houghton Hepburn, president of the Connecticut Woman Suffrage Association (CWSA), praised the

Opposite: A postcard calling for suffrage in Vermont, 1908.
Above, top: Suffragists in Boston collect jewelry to raise funds
for their camapign, 1914. Above, bottom: Men and women
attend the opening day of the Congressional Union summer
headquarters in Newport, Rhode Island, 1914.

Above: Members of the Connecticut
Woman Suffrage Association.

"Although Connecticut and Vermont were the 37th and 38th states to ratify the amendment, these actions proved critical when the validity of the Tennessee and West Virginia votes were challenged in court"

NWP's dedication to the suffrage cause. In an interview with the *Hartford Courant*, Hepburn expressed her support for Catharine Flanagan, who was arrested in August 1917: "I admire Mrs. Flanagan very much for being willing to go to jail for her convictions. It is more than most people could conceive of doing for an ideal." This was markedly different from the position of NAWSA, which denounced the picketers as un-American and threw its support behind President Wilson and the war effort. When NAWSA refused to condemn the horrific treatment of suffragists in prison, several leaders of the CWSA, including Hepburn, resigned from their offices in protest.

The work of suffragists on the local and national level paid off. After President Wilson urged Congress in 1918 to support woman suffrage as a war measure, suffragists around the country lobbied intensively to persuade their representatives and senators to follow through and pass a suffrage amendment. On January 10, 1918, Congresswoman Jeannette Rankin of Montana introduced the 19th Amendment on the floor of the House of Representatives. The House passed the amendment the same day 274–136, just over the two-thirds majority required. The Senate voted the following day but fell two votes short of the necessary two-thirds. Although the majority of Republican senators voted in favor of the amendment, the Republican senators from Massachusetts— Henry Cabot Lodge and John Weeks—voted no. NAWSA and the NWP joined forces to target Weeks and three other senators who had voted against the amendment for defeat in the November 1918 election. The efforts of the Massachusetts Woman Suffrage Association contributed to the unseating of Weeks, who was replaced by Democrat David Walsh, a former governor and the first Democratic senator elected from Massachusetts in over a century. The following year, Senator Lodge attempted to delay a vote on the suffrage amendment on procedural grounds but failed. On June 4, 1919, the Senate passed the amendment, sending it to the states for ratification.

Four of the New England states contributed directly to ratifying the 19th Amendment. Massachusetts was the eighth state in the nation to do so, in 1919, followed by New Hampshire and Maine the same year, and Rhode Island in 1920. Although Connecticut and Vermont were the 37th and 38th states to ratify the amendment, these actions proved critical when the validity of the Tennessee and West Virginia votes were challenged in court. Plaintiff Oscar Leser sued the state of Maryland to prevent two women from voting in Baltimore, charging, among other things, that the state legislatures in Tennessee and West Virginia had violated their rules of procedure in adopting the 19th Amendment. In Leser v. Garnett, the U.S. Supreme Court declared this point was moot: since Connecticut and Vermont had ratified the amendment, the amendment had been ratified by enough states to become "valid to all intents and purposes as part of the Constitution of the United States."

Although New England suffragists had limited success in gaining votes for women in their respective states, their political skills were critical in the push for a federal amendment to the U.S. Constitution. Their story complicates the canonical history of woman suffrage that focuses on Seneca Falls. Several nationally prominent suffrage leaders hailed from the New England states, and the first two national women's rights conventions were held in Worcester, Massachusetts. From the mid-19th century through to 1920, New England suffragists fought tirelessly for votes for women on both the state and national level.

This article was originally commissioned by the National Conference of State Historic Preservation Officers in partnership with the United States National Park Service.

WOMAN SUFFRAGE IN THE MID-ATLANTIC

From grassroots activists to suffrage leaders, women from the Mid-Atlantic states were instrumental in the long battle for the ballot

By Christine L. Ridarsky

Women in the Mid-Atlantic states were at the forefront of the woman suffrage movement at its inception in the mid-19th century, and they provided much of the leadership that would ultimately ensure ratification of the 19th Amendment in 1920. A small band of mostly Quaker women, including Philadelphia's Lucretia Mott, along with Elizabeth Cady Stanton organized the first women's rights convention in Seneca Falls, New York, in 1848. Though scholars have debated the true significance of this largely regional event, these women inspired the national woman suffrage conventions that followed, held annually beginning in 1850—five in New York and one in Pennsylvania—which were arguably more influential in launching the women's movement prior to the Civil War. In the 20th century, a suffrage victory in New York and a push by Alice Paul and Lucy Burns for a national amendment finally helped make a woman suffrage amendment a reality.

Women's interest in securing their right to vote grew initially out of their experiences working for reform within antislavery and temperance circles, where their participation was limited by male leaders and social norms that prevented women from speaking publicly. Finding parallels between their own legal and social status and that of the enslaved, women's early efforts focused on achieving human and civil rights for Black men and all women. As a result, women in the Mid-Atlantic states worked together across race lines early in the movement. Margaretta Forten and Harriet Forten Purvis, daughters of Black abolitionists James and Charlotte Forten, helped organize the fifth National Woman's Rights Convention in Philadelphia in 1854, and Black women likely

"Women in the Mid-Atlantic states worked together across race lines early in the movement"

attended most, if not all, of the early women's rights conventions, though the minutes usually did not record their presence.

In addition to organizing the annual conventions, women's rights activism in the antebellum era included writing, lecturing, and petitioning legislators for change. In 1849, Amelia Bloomer started publishing *The Lily* in Seneca Falls, the first newspaper for women in the United States. Though it initially focused on temperance, Elizabeth Cady Stanton, writing under the alias "Sunflower," quickly pushed it into addressing broader women's rights themes.

Women largely suspended their women's rights activism during the Civil War, choosing instead to focus on supporting soldiers and assisting formerly enslaved people who were freed by President Lincoln's Emancipation Proclamation. At the war's end, however, women immediately resumed their efforts to secure rights for African Americans and women. In 1866, as the nation debated the meaning of citizenship in the wake of emancipation, Elizabeth Cady Stanton, now living in New York City, and Susan B. Anthony, of Rochester, New York, established the New York Equal Rights Association as well as the American Equal Rights Association (AERA), which agitated for suffrage "irrespective of race, color or sex." The AERA elected Mott its president, and Black and white activists continued to work side by side. Harriet Purvis served on the AERA's executive committee. Other state affiliates soon organized. Philadelphia activists founded the Pennsylvania Equal Rights Association in January 1867. In October, women in Vineland, New Jersey, organized the Vineland Equal Rights Association and sent a petition to the Republican state convention advocating for "Impartial Suffrage, irrespective of Sex or Color." New Jersey women also established one of the first U.S. organizations dedicated specifically to securing the vote for women: In November 1867 they founded the New Jersey Woman Suffrage Association (NJWSA) and elected Lucy

Stone, living in Orange, New Jersey, as president and her sister-in-law, Antoinette Brown Blackwell, of Somerville, vice president.

New York's 1867 constitutional convention provided an opportunity for the AERA to press its case for universal suffrage. Woman suffragists thought they had an ally in Suffrage Committee chairman Horace Greeley, who had supported women's voting rights as editor of the *New-York Tribune*. But, when Greeley submitted his report, he recommended amending the state constitution to give the vote to Black men but not women. Angered at the betrayal, Stanton and Anthony attacked the manhood of convention delegates who opposed woman suffrage. The tactic backfired; delegates voted 125 to 19 to support Greeley's position. Ultimately, the state's voters rejected the new constitution altogether and enfranchised neither group.

New Jersey women also challenged voting restrictions. The original New Jersey constitution had allowed women and Black men to vote, provided they met the minimum requirement for property ownership, and there is evidence that at least a small number of women cast ballots in the state's first decade. However, in a dubious legal maneuver, the legislature limited the vote to "free, white, male, citizens" in 1807; the state constitution was amended in 1844 to reflect this change. But after the Civil War women began to assert their right to vote again. In March 1868, Portia Kellogg Gage, a founder of the NJWSA, attempted to vote in the local election in Vineland but was turned away because she was not registered. In November, Gage and 171 other women, Black and white, attempted to vote in the federal election. When their ballots were refused, they set up their own table and their own special ballot box and proceeded to cast their votes—and they continued the practice for several years.

In 1869, debate over the 15th Amendment, which prohibited denial of the vote on the basis of race, fractured the AERA, and

Previous pages: Women from equal suffrage states demonstrate
for the vote in New York. Above: A gathering of prominent
Pennsylvanian abolitionists, including Lucretia Mott
(front row, second from right).

the era of cross-racial alliances largely came to an end. Abolitionist Wendell Phillips declared it the "Negro's hour," arguing that women needed to temporarily set aside their demands for the benefit of the Black man, but Stanton and Anthony refused. Instead, they formed the National Woman Suffrage Association (NWSA), focused on a national woman suffrage amendment. Lucy Stone and her husband, Henry Blackwell, set up the rival American Woman Suffrage Association (AWSA), which supported the 15th Amendment and turned to state campaigns to secure voting rights for women. The NJWSA quickly aligned with the AWSA, as did the new Pennsylvania Woman Suffrage Association, established in December 1869 with abolitionist Mary Grew of Philadelphia as president. The New York State Woman Suffrage Association, on the other hand, was organized nearly concurrent with the NWSA, and for 20 years they operated practically as one.

Almost immediately, suffragists focused on a federal approach adopted a strategy known as the New Departure.

They argued that women had a legal right to vote based on language in the 14th Amendment that defined citizens as "all persons born or naturalized in the United States." Contending that voting was one of the "privileges or immunities" of citizenship, women began to go to the polls. After Philadelphia election officials refused to accept Carrie Burnham's ballot in 1871, she became one of the first to use the courts to test the argument. She relied not only on the 14th Amendment but also on Pennsylvania law, which conferred voting rights on "freemen," a term she argued described status, not sex. The Pennsylvania Supreme Court disagreed, ruling against Burnham in 1873. In November 1872, Susan B. Anthony was one of several Rochester women to cast her ballot in the presidential election and then was arrested. Anthony was charged with the crime of voting illegally and found guilty by a federal court, though the judge decided the case on narrow grounds, leaving the constitutional question unsettled. The U.S. Supreme Court finally settled the matter of women's voting rights under the 14th Amendment in 1875 when it ruled in Minor v. Happersett that suffrage was not "one of the privileges or immunities of citizenship"; states, therefore, had the right to exclude women from the franchise.

Meanwhile, the AWSA and state suffrage societies focused on changing voting rights clauses in state constitutions. In 1873, Pennsylvania's constitutional convention acknowledged the requirements of the 15th Amendment when it replaced the words "white freeman" with "male citizens," but it failed to include women. New York, New Jersey, and Delaware did not update their constitutions during this period.

By 1876, the NWSA settled on a new strategy; it would seek an amendment to the U.S. Constitution barring states from using sex as a basis for disenfranchisement. A proposed 16th amendment, later named for Susan B. Anthony, was introduced before Congress in 1878; it was largely buried in committee and ultimately defeated in 1887. With the federal strategy seemingly at an impasse, the rival NWSA and AWSA called a truce and merged to form the National American Woman Suffrage Association (NAWSA) in 1890 with Anthony as its first president and headquarters in New York City.

Now under a single umbrella, state suffrage organizations adopted a common strategy of organizing local and county suffrage clubs to disperse the suffrage message more broadly. The state associations in New York, New Jersey, and Pennsylvania all began encouraging formation of local and county affiliates. By 1893, New York's suffrage association reported that 23 auxiliary county clubs had been established. Even women in Delaware began to organize. Under the leadership of Philadelphia's Rachel Foster Avery, a protégé of Susan B. Anthony, they established Delaware's first women's rights organization, the Wilmington Equal Suffrage Club, in November 1895.

With constitutional conventions scheduled in New York in 1894 and Delaware in 1896, suffragists directed resources at those states throughout the 1890s. New York suffragists took a decidedly different

THE WOMAN-SUFFRAGE MOVEMENT IN NEW YORK CITY.

tack than they had during the 1867 convention. Instead of "hanging about the convention" and lobbying delegates as they had in the earlier campaign, state president Jean Brooks Greenleaf determined that the best tactic was to organize a massive canvass to collect signatures on pro-suffrage petitions and calculate the value of taxable property owned by women. When the convention got underway in May 1894, suffragists presented petitions nearly every day for two weeks in support of striking the word "male" from the clause assigning voting rights. In August, the full convention debated the question over four days

Previous pages: Women pictured voting in New Jersey c. 1800
(left); a magazine cover featuring "society leaders securing
signatures" in New York, 1894 (right). Above: Women's rights
leader Alice Paul. Opposite: Susan B. Anthony (left) with
one of her protégés Rachel Foster Avery.

before voting 97 to 58 against woman suffrage. In Delaware, women finally organized a state association in 1896. Despite their efforts, the woman suffrage amendment failed in Delaware's convention in 1897; the following year the legislature passed a law allowing taxpaying women to vote in school elections. New Jersey couldn't even get that much; in 1897, voters defeated an amendment that would have allowed women to vote in school elections.

The merger of the two national suffrage organizations came at a time of increasing racial tensions marked by legalized segregation and violence against African Americans in the South and de facto segregation in the North. Black women found that they were no longer as welcome within mainstream suffrage organizations as they had once been and set about establishing their own clubs, usually with broader objectives than those of their white counterparts. In Rochester, Hester C. Jeffrey founded several organizations for African American women, including the philanthropic and suffrage-focused Susan B. Anthony Club. Jeffrey also continued to work alongside her friend Susan B. Anthony within the New York State Woman Suffrage Association and NAWSA. For Black women, the vote was about more than improving their own status; it was also about protecting the status of Black men who were being disenfranchised through educational tests and intimidation. Thus, few Black women's clubs were organized solely to advocate for suffrage, though many included it among the causes they supported.

As Black women built their own movement, white activism seemed to plateau. Mainstream suffragists in Mid-Atlantic states

turned their attention to educating women about the benefits of equality rather than lobbying for legislative reform. But that changed early in the 20th century as a new cadre of young leaders emerged. Anthony retired as NAWSA president in 1900 and died in 1906. Two of her acolytes led NAWSA over the next 20 years: Carrie Chapman Catt (1900–1905 and 1915–1920) and Anna Howard Shaw (1906–1914). Rachel Foster Avery reinvigorated the Pennsylvania movement when she was elected state president in 1908 and opened a headquarters in Philadelphia. Elizabeth Cady Stanton's daughter Harriot Stanton Blatch also took on the mantle of leadership during this period, establishing her Equality League of Self-Supporting Women, later the Women's Political Union, in New York City in 1907 with the goal of drawing working-class and immigrant women into what had been a predominantly middle-class Protestant movement.

Among the most influential of these new 20th-century leaders was Alice Paul, of Mount Laurel, New Jersey. Like Blatch, Paul had spent time in England learning the militant tactics of British suffragettes and believed that American suffragists needed to take a more radical approach in pressing for their rights. This included organizing public spectacles to attract attention to the cause. In 1912, the annual New York City suffrage parade, inaugurated by Blatch in 1910, drew 20,000 marchers and half a million onlookers. Paul and colleague Lucy Burns, of New York, demonstrated another method for attracting attention when, in 1911, they staged the first open-air campaign in the Keystone State. With the help of Caroline Katzenstein, secretary of the

Above and opposite: Suffragists staged major parades in New
York City in the 1910s that saw practiced legions of women,
wearing white, filling the streets.

Above: Silent Sentinels representing New York
picket the White House in the rain, 1917.

"'Silent Sentinels' held signs asking 'Kaiser Wilson' how much longer women had to wait for equal rights, comparing the president Woodrow Wilson to the German emperor"

Pennsylvania Woman Suffrage Association, they held 21 outdoor meetings across Philadelphia between July 25 and September 30.

By 1913, Paul and Burns had formed the Congressional Union (CU), which grew out of NAWSA's Congressional Committee. The young militants clashed with the organization's more conservative leaders over strategy. NAWSA concentrated on winning the vote in the states, while Paul and Burns had returned to Stanton and Anthony's focus on a federal amendment and argued that suffragists should hold the party in power (Democrats) publicly accountable. They recruited Mabel Vernon to become their first national organizer, sending her first to her home state of Delaware to organize a state branch of the CU there.

Beginning in 1909, Catt encouraged suffrage clubs to reorganize by legislative district in a manner similar to political parties. The strategy was put to a test in 1915 when voters in New York, New Jersey, and Pennsylvania each voted for a referendum on woman suffrage; all were defeated. But Catt's "Winning Plan" finally paid off when New York State's voters granted full suffrage to women in November 1917, making it the first state east of the Mississippi River to do so. Catt declared that "the victory is not New York's alone. It's the nation's." She felt sure that Congress would now be forced to pass a federal amendment. But, as the United States entered the First World War, NAWSA suspended most of its work. The National Woman's Party (NWP), however, which had grown out of the CU, refused to do so, choosing instead to use the war for freedom abroad to highlight the hypocrisy of women's disenfranchisement at home.

Beginning in January 1917, the NWP organized a series of protests outside the White House. "Silent Sentinels" held signs asking "Kaiser Wilson" how much longer women had to wait for equal rights, comparing the president Woodrow Wilson to the German emperor. By spring 1919, when the pickets ended, more than 500 women had been arrested; 168 of them spent time in jail, including many women from Mid-Atlantic states who were force-fed during hunger strikes at the District of Columbia Jail or the Occoquan (Virginia) Workhouse.

In June 1919, both Houses of Congress passed the 19th Amendment and sent it to the states for ratification. Thirty-six states needed to approve the measure. New York became the sixth state to ratify on June 16; Pennsylvanians approved the measure on June 24. New Jersey was slower to ratify but did so on February 10, 1920. By March, only one more state needed to ratify, and both NAWSA and the NWP looked to Delaware to put them over the top. But it wasn't to be. The state senate voted 11 to six for ratification, but in June the House refused to bring the measure to the floor, thereby killing it. Delaware wouldn't approve the amendment until March 1923, almost three years after the amendment took effect on August 26, 1920.

When Tennessee became the 36th state to ratify the 19th Amendment, women throughout the nation secured the right to vote and the campaign that began in upstate New York in the 1840s came to an end. Mid-Atlantic women—from Lucretia Mott and Harriet Purvis, to Elizabeth Cady Stanton and Susan B. Anthony, to Alice Paul and Lucy Burns, and so many more—had been instrumental, as leaders and foot soldiers, in every aspect of the 72-year battle for woman suffrage. It is hard to imagine the movement without them.

This article was originally commissioned by the National Conference of State Historic Preservation Officers in partnership with the United States National Park Service.

WOMAN SUFFRAGE IN THE SOUTHERN STATES

The struggle for woman suffrage in the South was bound up with the tensions of racial politics, but also delivered a decisive victory for equal rights

By Sarah H. Case

Although the woman suffrage movement emerged later and had fewer victories in the South than in the West and Northeast, southern women could claim responsibility for the decisive vote leading to the ratification of the 19th Amendment to the Constitution, declaring that voting rights could not be restricted "on account of sex." In the summer of 1920, the amendment had passed Congress and been ratified by 35 of the necessary 36 states, and all eyes turned to Tennessee. In August, the state Senate easily ratified the amendment, but the vote in the House resulted in a tense tie. Surprising his colleagues, a young representative from a district with strong anti-suffrage support named Harry T. Burn suddenly changed his vote in favor of ratification. With Burn's vote, Tennessee became the final state needed for ratification. When asked why he had changed his mind, Burn pointed to a letter from his mother in which she exhorted him to "vote for Suffrage and don't keep them in doubt ... be a good boy and help Mrs. Cat [Carrie Chapman Catt, leader of the National American Suffrage Association] with her 'Rats.'!"

This charming story of a loyal son, however, obscures the hard work of suffrage supporters that led to Burn's decisive vote as well as the continuing fierce opposition to the expansion of the franchise. The ratification campaign in the summer of 1920 summer was grueling, intense, and bitter and reflected ongoing tensions surrounding equal citizenship, gender, and race. As elsewhere in the nation, but perhaps even more profoundly in

THE AWAKENING.
She's awakened,
She is answering
To the Call of all
Mankind;
Then annul the Laws
That bind her,
And the Customs
That restrict her;
Deny Her Not
The greater service,
For the Child,
The Home, the State.

Copyright 1912, and Published by The Equal Suffrage League of Virginia.

Previous pages: Members of the Equal Suffrage League of Richmond, VA, 1914. Above: A card with a message supporting women's rights, published by the Equal Suffrage League of Virginia, 1912. Opposite: Carrie Chapman Catt.

the South, the question of woman suffrage was intimately entwined with racial politics shaped by the Civil War, Reconstruction, and its aftermath. The expansion of Black civil rights after the Civil War, with the 14th and 15th Amendments to the U.S. Constitution, and attempts to curtail those rights, set the context for debates over voting rights in the southern states for decades. These tensions helped shape the complex, difficult, and divisive fight for woman suffrage in the southern states.

Southern women, like their northern and western sisters, joined women's clubs and voluntary associations during the "age of association" of the 1830s. Two, Sarah and Angelina Grimké, daughters of a South Carolina slaveholder, were among the first American women to speak publicly on behalf of both abolition and women's rights; they did so, however, after leaving the South and moving to Philadelphia. In the 1840s and 1850s, elite white women in Virginia and elsewhere participated in political campaigns, often aligning themselves with the Whig Party, which tended to support benevolent reform measures that attracted women's support more robustly than did the Democratic Party of the era and even celebrated women's civic contributions. But although individual women favored voting rights, very little organized support of opening the franchise to women existed in the southern states in the antebellum period.

During Reconstruction, some southern women did seek to create suffrage organizations, founding branches of the American Woman Suffrage Association (AWSA) or the National Woman Suffrage Association (NWSA). The end of the Civil War and passage of three constitutional amendments, the 13th (ending slavery), 14th (promising equal birthright citizenship), and 15th (prohibiting racially based disenfranchisement), engendered a national conversation about civil rights, equality, and voting rights, one that many women sought to extend to include consideration of woman suffrage. Some southern Reconstruction-era woman suffrage organizations included Black and white women. But Reconstruction's end and the ascendency of overtly racist state governments bent on undoing its reforms discouraged these coalitions. By the turn of the century, southern states had created elaborate segregation and disenfranchisement measures, such as poll taxes, literacy tests, and grandfather clauses, and the Supreme Court had upheld them as constitutional. In the post-Reconstruction era, in which state governments institutionalized white supremacy, to link woman suffrage with Black civil and voting rights discredited both movements. The nascent southern woman suffrage movement lost influence and visibility, even as individual women remained committed to the cause.

Organizational activity increased after the AWSA and NWSA merged in 1890 as the National American Woman Suffrage

"In this racially hostile environment, Black women who sought equal civil and political rights knew that outspoken resistance to the status quo could be met by violence"

Association (NAWSA). NAWSA set a policy of founding local clubs across the nation, including in the South, and dedicated itself to recruiting southern women into its ranks. This strategy worked to an extent; women created NAWSA clubs across the region, but they tended to be overly dependent on the leadership of an individual, often a woman who had lived part of her life in the Northeast, and declined or collapsed after she left the organization. The lack of cultivation of grassroots support in the 1890s led to a decline in the southern suffrage movement in the following decade.

After 1910, energized partially by the expansion of the national movement under the leadership of Carrie Chapman Catt and the successes of referenda in western states, the southern movement gained new strength. There were reasons specific to the region for the increase of support as well. Southern suffragists tended to be members of the new urban middle class. Their fathers and husbands, and sometimes they themselves, took part in the industrializing economy, in positions that linked them to a national market or to urban centers, such as in small business, education, the law, and local banking. This distinguished them from the traditional southern elite tied to the plantation economy and industries that served them—textile manufacturing, railroads, and mining. Southern suffrage supporters often had an advanced education, sometimes a college education, and a few had attended northeastern women's colleges. Many worked for part of their lives in the new urban economy, often as teachers or in family businesses. As elsewhere, many of these women became involved in Progressive-Era reform, as settlement workers, clubwomen, and missionaries, responding to the new problems created by urbanization and industrialization and exercising skills they gained through education and employment.

For example, Atlanta, the archetypical "New South" city, grew from 9,554 people in 1860 to over 65,000 in 1890 to over 150,000 in 1910 and became a center for Black and white women's employment and social activism. It was not until after 1910 that the region produced a critical mass of "new women of the New South" as the economy industrialized and urbanized. Many of these women became interested in expanding education, abolishing child labor and the convict lease system, improving city services, and, through their support for reform, attracted to the suffrage cause.

Opposite: Four African American women pose
in front of a university building in Atlanta,
Georgia, around the turn of the century.

During the pivotal decade of the 1910s, southern women lent their support to woman suffrage organizations that varied widely in their political objectives and strategies. Most joined local groups associated with NAWSA such as the Equal Suffrage League of Virginia; a few affiliated themselves with Alice Paul's National Woman's Party (NWP), an organization single-mindedly focused on a national amendment. Smaller in number but influential was the uniquely southern states' rights suffrage movement. Headed by Kate Gordon of Louisiana, the southern states' rights suffragists opposed a federal amendment while pressuring state legislatures to enfranchise women—or, to be more accurate, white women. Gordon, who created the Era (or Equal Rights for All) Club in New Orleans in 1896, explicitly viewed state-level woman suffrage measures as a way to maintain white supremacy and a majority white electorate. Her visibility as head of the Era Club gained her the support of NAWSA and in 1903 the position of corresponding secretary of the organization. NAWSA leadership hoped that Gordon could help expand the movement in the southern states. But, over time, her unyielding support of the states' rights approach alienated her from the national movement.

In 1913, responding to the growing support for a national amendment, Gordon formed the Southern States Woman Suffrage Conference (SSWSC). The motto of its journal, "Make the Southern States White," underlined its view of the goal of enfranchising white women. Although at first envisioned and funded as a branch of NAWSA, Gordon's organization was increasingly at odds with the national group, and even an outright adversary. Most southern suffragists disagreed with Gordon's rejection of a national amendment and the national organization and found her attempt to defeat both counterproductive. In Louisiana, the division between SSWSC supporters and NAWSA members was acrimonious and destructive. Gordon refused to work with a NAWSA-affiliated group in 1918 to support a proposed state suffrage amendment that she favored; though passed by the legislature, it failed ratification by the electorate. This defeat stemmed from a variety of sources, including opposition from a powerful New Orleans political machine steadfastly opposed to reform movements of all kinds. But Gordon's hostility toward other suffrage supporters weakened the movement in Louisiana. She continued to oppose a national amendment, actively campaigning against the 19th Amendment, because it would enfranchise Black women. Many white southerners, like Gordon, feared that a national woman suffrage amendment would bring increased federal scrutiny of elections and enforcement of the 14th and 15th Amendments. Racial ideology was central to political struggles in the New South.

Gordon's outspoken support of woman suffrage as a way to ensure white supremacy was not typical of those who joined

MARY CHURCH TERRELL

1863–1954

By Debra Michals

Mary Eliza Church Terrell was a well-known African American activist who championed racial equality and women's suffrage in the late 19th and early 20th century. An Oberlin College graduate, Terrell was part of the rising Black middle and upper class who used their position to fight racial discrimination.

The daughter of former slaves, Terrell was born on September 23, 1863 in Memphis, Tennessee. Her father, Robert Reed Church, was a successful businessman who became one of the South's first African American millionaires. Her mother, Louisa Ayres Church, owned a hair salon. She had one brother. Terrell's parents divorced during her childhood. Their affluence and belief in the importance of education enabled Terrell to attend the Antioch College laboratory school in Ohio, and later Oberlin College, where she earned both Bachelor's and Master's degrees. Terrell spent two years teaching at Wilberforce College before moving to Washington, D.C., in 1887 to teach at the M Street Colored High School. There she met Robert Heberton Terrell, also a teacher, whom she married in 1891. The Terrells had one daughter and later adopted a second daughter.

Her activism was sparked in 1892, when an old friend, Thomas Moss, was lynched in Memphis by whites because his business competed with theirs. Terrell joined Ida B. Wells-Barnett in anti-lynching campaigns, but Terrell's life work focused on the notion of racial uplift, the belief that Blacks would help end racial discrimination by advancing themselves and other members of the race through education, work, and community activism. It was a strategy based on the power of equal opportunities to advance the race and her belief that, as one succeeds, the whole race would be elevated Her words—"Lifting as we climb"—became the motto of the National Association of Colored Women (NACW), the

group she helped found in 1896. She was NACW president from 1896 to 1901.

As NACW president, Terrell campaigned tirelessly among Black organizations and mainstream white organizations, writing and speaking extensively. She also actively embraced women's suffrage, which she saw as essential to elevating the status of Black women, and consequently, the entire race. She actively campaigned for Black women's suffrage. She even picketed the Wilson White House with members of the National Woman's Party in her zeal for woman suffrage. Terrell fought for woman suffrage and civil rights because she realized that she belonged "to the only group in this country that has two such huge obstacles to surmount... both sex and race."

In 1909, Terrell was among the founders and charter members of the National Association for the Advancement of Colored People. Then in 1910, she co-founded the College Alumnae Club, later renamed the National Association of University Women.

Following the passage of the 19th amendment, Terrell focused on broader civil rights. In 1940, she published her autobiography, *A Colored Woman in a White World*, outlining her experiences with discrimination. In 1948, Terrell became the first Black member of the American Association of University Women, after winning an anti-discrimination lawsuit. In 1950, at age 86, she challenged segregation in public places by suing the Thompson's Restaurant in Washington, D.C. when staff would not serve her. She was victorious when, in 1953, the Supreme Court ruled that the District's segregated eating facilities were unconstitutional, a major breakthrough in that era. Terrell died four years later in Highland Beach, Maryland.

This article appears courtesy of the National Women's History Museum.

groups affiliated with NAWSA or the NWP. More typical were arguments that Black women would be disenfranchised by the same measures that disenfranchised Black men. As a pamphlet from the Equal Suffrage League of Virginia asserted, "As these [state-level voting] laws restrict the negro man's vote, it stands to reason that they will also restrict the negro woman's vote." NAWSA and NWP affiliates sought to politely avoid the race question, denouncing neither Black disenfranchisement nor the overtly racist language of Gordon and her allies. White woman suffragists' lack of support for Black women's (and men's) voting rights points to their regrettable acceptance of Jim Crow in the southern states and in much of the nation.

In this racially hostile environment, Black women who sought equal civil and political rights knew that outspoken resistance to the status quo could be met by violence. Yet African American women born in the South had a profound influence on the suffrage movement, often after they left the region. Ida B. Wells-Barnett, born in 1892 in Holly Springs, Mississippi,

advocated for civil rights, women's rights including suffrage, and an end to lynching from her adopted home of Chicago, where she settled after her life was threatened in Memphis. In Chicago, she founded the Women's Era Club and later the Alpha Suffrage Club of Chicago, the first Black woman's club dedicated to voting rights for women. Despite the indifference or even hostility she faced from white suffrage activists, she continued to push for enfranchisement of Black women. Taking part in the significant 1913 parade in Washington, D.C., sponsored by NAWSA, Wells refused to march in a Blacks-only section and instead joined the rest of the Illinois delegation.

Some Black women advocated for suffrage while remaining in the South. Mary Church Terrell, born in Memphis, Tennessee, graduated from Oberlin College and spent most of her career in Washington, D.C. A writer and educator, she headed an active suffrage movement in that city and associated herself with the Republican Party. In urban areas, such as Atlanta, Black female progressives viewed suffrage for all as essential for securing civil

Above: Ida B. Wells-Barnett.

rights. Black women in Nashville supported suffrage from a variety of secular and church organizations. After Tennessee women won the right to vote in municipal elections in 1919, Black and white clubwomen of that city created a coalition designed to increase the political influence of both. Making a class- and gender-based alliance, Nashville women worked to enact educational and social service reform, as well as Black representation in municipal services. This alliance was remarkable and unusual; typically white suffrage supporters avoided association with Black women and attempted to downplay the accusations of anti-suffrage activists that woman suffrage would increase Black women's political influence.

Indeed, anti-suffragists played on racial anxieties in their attempt to resist woman suffrage in the South. Georgia, the first state to vote against ratification of the 19th Amendment, had a particularly visible "anti" movement. In 1914, they formed the Georgia Association Opposed to Woman Suffrage (GAOWS), the first southern branch of the National Association Opposed to Woman Suffrage, founded in New York City in response to the growing power of the movement in the Northeast. As was true for anti-suffragists elsewhere, female opponents to suffrage in the South feared that the vote would "desex" women, destroy the home, and lessen, rather than strengthen, women's power and influence. As leading Georgia anti Mildred Lewis Rutherford declared in 1912, "if there is a power that is placed in any hands, it is the power that is placed in the hands of the southern woman in her home... That power is great enough to direct legislative bodies—and that, too, without demanding the ballot."

Additionally, southern antis feared that a federal woman suffrage amendment would violate the racial order, since it would bring increased, and unwelcome, scrutiny to southern elections. Anti-suffrage propaganda often pointed to the "horrors" of

The Federal Suffrage Amendment
WILL NEVER BE RATIFIED
IF THE PEOPLE OF TENNESSEE
GUARD THEIR RIGHTS

DO YOUR BIT, ORGANIZE MASS MEETINGS,
Circulate Petitions, and we will UPHOLD
the Constitutional Rights of the People.

Reconstruction, especially Black voting power, as a cautionary tale against extending the franchise. Antis also worried that the intimidation techniques used against Black men would not work against women. As a Virginia newspaper declared, "We have managed the men, but could we manage the women? It is a different proposition. We believe that most of the women would qualify and we further believe that they would persuade many of the men to qualify; and pay their poll taxes for them if need be." Southern antis pointed to Black women's educational and employment gains by the 1890s, asserting that Black

Above: An anti-suffrage broadside calling on the people of Tennessee to "guard their rights." Opposite: A group of women gather to register as new voters in Richmond, VA, as part of a League of Women Voters drive, 1920.

women outpaced Black men in literacy and in determination to pay their poll tax even if it they would "go hungry." Antis believed that whites needed total control over voting (not just a majority of votes) by state-level restrictions to maintain political dominance.

Antis proved influential and formidable. In 1920 only Texas and Arkansas had full voting rights for (white) women. Tennessee allowed voting in presidential elections and citywide elections. A few states, including Kentucky, Mississippi, and Louisiana, allowed women to vote in some school elections, and women voted in some cities in Florida on municipal matters. Of the southern states that ratified the 19th Amendment, all—Kentucky, Texas, Arkansas, and Tennessee—had some degree of state-level female enfranchisement. After the ratification of the 19th Amendment, many southern women—especially Black women, but also some white women—found themselves disenfranchised by poll taxes and other measures. Despite the success of the federal amendment, antidemocratic forces in state and local politics continued to limit the ability of southern women to exercise the right to vote.

At the turn of the 20th century, as southern legislators sought to limit the franchise for African American men, many white southerners were loath to support any expansion of voting rights. Whereas antis tended to openly advocate support for racial inequality, white suffrage supporters approached the issue in different ways, with some viewing white women's enfranchisement as a way to ensure white supremacy, others downplaying the issue, and a small number forming coalitions with Black women. Southern African American women viewed woman suffrage as part of the struggle for civil rights and racial equality. In the early 20th-century South, the debate over woman suffrage was inextricably linked with contemporary views on race, Black disenfranchisement, and white supremacy.

This article was originally commissioned by the National Conference of State Historic Preservation Officers in partnership with the United States National Park Service.

CHAPTER FIVE

A CAUSE WITHOUT BORDERS

THE INTERNATIONAL HISTORY OF THE U.S. SUFFRAGE MOVEMENT

Activists and movements outside the United States, as well as a broad range of international goals, were critical to organizing for that right deemed so quintessentially American— the right to vote

By Katherine M. Marino

The history of the U.S. woman suffrage movement is usually told as a national one. It begins with the 1848 Seneca Falls convention; follows numerous state campaigns, court battles, and petitions to Congress; and culminates in the marches and protests that led to the 19th Amendment. This narrative, however, overlooks how profoundly international the struggle was from the start. Suffragists from the United States and other parts of the world collaborated across national borders. They wrote to each other; shared strategies and encouragement; and spearheaded international organizations, conferences, and publications that in turn spread information and ideas. Many suffragists were internationalists, understanding the right to vote as a global goal.

Enlightenment concepts, socialism, and the abolitionist movement helped U.S. suffragists universalize women's rights long before Seneca Falls. They drew their inspiration not only from the American Revolution, but from the French and Haitian Revolutions, and later from the Mexican and Russian Revolutions. Many were immigrants who brought ideas from their homelands. Others capitalized on the Spanish-American War and the First World War to underscore contradictions between the United States' growing global power and its denial of woman suffrage. A number of women of color used the international stage to challenge U.S. claims to democracy, not only in terms of women's rights but also in terms of racism in the United States and in the suffrage movement itself. The complex international connections and strategies that suffragists cultivated reveal tensions in feminist organizing that reverberated in later movements and are instructive today.

Previous pages: U.S. suffragists and international guests gather in
Washington, D.C., 1888, including Susan B. Anthony (front row,
second from left), Elizabeth Cady Stanton (front row, third from
right), and Matilda Joslyn Gage (front row, second from right).
Above: The World Anti-Slavery Convention in London, 1840.

"Stanton's idea to include the right to vote in the Declaration of Sentiments was directly inspired by calls for universal suffrage made by British Chartists"

These multiple, and sometimes conflicting, international strands worked in synergy, bolstering the suffrage cause and expanding the women's rights agenda. The resources that women shared with each other across national borders allowed suffrage movements to overcome political marginalization and hostility in their own countries. A radical challenge to power, the U.S. movement for women's voting rights required transnational support to thrive.

Although the American Revolution and Mary Wollstonecraft's *Vindication of the Rights of Woman* (1792), which circulated in the United States, activated discussion of women's rights, it was the transatlantic crucible of abolitionism that truly galvanized the U.S. women's rights movement. The antislavery movement, which Frederick Douglass called "peculiarly woman's cause," provided broad ideals of "liberty" as well as key political strategies that suffragists would use for the next 50 years—the mass petition, public speaking, and the boycott. Transatlantic networks of organizations, conferences, and publications drove abolitionism. Women in the United States looked to their British sisters, who in 1826 made the first formal demand for an immediate rather than gradual end to slavery.

Boston reformer and African American abolitionist Maria Stewart, one of the first U.S. women to publicly call for women's rights before a mixed-race and mixed-sex audience, embraced a diasporic vision of freedom when she asked in 1832, "How long shall the fair daughters of Africa be compelled to bury their minds and talents beneath a load of iron pots and kettles?" Her vision of rights for African American women, specifically, in the face of economic marginalization, segregation, and slavery, drew upon universal rights that she found expressed not only in the U.S. Constitution and Declaration of Independence but in the French *Declaration of the Rights of Man* and the Haitian Revolution, the largest slave uprising, from 1791 to 1804.

The hostility that Stewart and other female abolitionists faced for overstepping boundaries of female propriety by speaking out in public threw into sharp relief that, as abolitionist Angelina Grimké put it, "the manumission of the slave and the elevation of the woman" should be indivisible goals. At the first Anti-Slavery Convention of American Women in 1837, an interracial group of 200 women called for women's rights. When Elizabeth Cady Stanton, Lucretia Mott, and other female delegates were excluded from the 1840 World Antislavery Congress in London, Stanton hatched the idea for a separate women's rights convention.

The resulting 1848 Seneca Falls convention and its demands for women's rights were only possible because of abolitionists' groundwork and the broad meanings of emancipation flourishing in the United States and in Europe, where revolutions had broken out that year. Stanton's idea to include the right to vote in the convention's Declaration of Sentiments was directly inspired by calls for universal suffrage made by British Chartists, the first mass working-class movement in England. Quaker minister and abolitionist Lucretia

Mott explicitly connected the Declaration to the 1848 abolition of slavery in the French West Indies, opposition to the U.S. war with Mexico, and Native American rights. She and Stanton also found models in the matrilineal communities of the Seneca people, in which women held political power. The right to vote proved to be the convention's most controversial demand, and abolitionist Frederick Douglass was one of its most avid proponents.

The right to vote became key to the many U.S. women's rights conventions that Seneca Falls set into motion, inspiring and drawing on the support of women in Europe and elsewhere, including immigrant women in the United States. In 1851, from Paris jail cells, revolutionary women's rights activists cheered U.S. women's activism. In March 1852, German immigrant and socialist Mathilde Anneke started the first women's rights journal in the United States published by a woman, the *Deutsche Frauen-Zeitung*. After the Prussian victory over Germany she had fled to the United States, where she became a friend of Stanton and Susan B. Anthony. Polish-born immigrant and abolitionist Ernestine Rose expressed her global vision for suffrage in 1851: "We are not contending for the rights of women in New England, or of old England, but of the world."

Such ideas resonated with the African American activist Sarah Parker Remond, whose life reflects the overlapping transnational abolitionist and woman suffrage movements. In 1832, she helped found the first female antislavery group in Salem, Massachusetts. In 1859, while on an antislavery speaking tour in England,

Remond reported, "I have been received here as a sister by white women for the first time in my life... I have received a sympathy I never was offered before." For Remond, transnational connections became a concrete way to escape racism in the United States. She settled permanently in Italy, where she became a physician. In 1866, Remond affixed her name to John Stuart Mill's petition to the British Parliament for woman suffrage.

Transnational connections initiated by the 19th-century abolitionist movement only grew in the following decades. After construction of the first transatlantic telegraph lines in the 1860s, communications, travel, and transnational print culture helped produce the first international organizations for women's rights that drew significantly on U.S. women: the World's Woman's Christian Temperance Union (WWCTU), founded in 1883 by U.S. temperance leader Frances Willard; the International Council of Women (ICW), founded in 1888 by Stanton and Anthony; the International Woman Suffrage Alliance (IWSA, later renamed the International Alliance of Women), founded in 1904 and presided over by Carrie Chapman Catt (then-president of the National American Woman Suffrage Association); and Women's International League for Peace and Freedom (WILPF), founded by U.S. social settlement worker Jane Addams in 1915.

Alongside each organization's particular focus—international arbitration, universal disarmament, temperance, married women's civil rights, anti-trafficking of women, equal pay for equal work, among others—a global goal of women's political equality drove

Opposite, left: German immigrant and socialist Mathilde Anneke.
Opposite, right: Polish-born abolitionist Ernestine Rose.
Above: Temperance leader Frances Willard.

Above: Members of the Woman's Christian
Temperance Union, c. 1909.

"Lucretia Mott explicitly connected the Declaration to the 1848 abolition of slavery in the French West Indies, opposition to the U.S. war with Mexico, and Native American rights"

them. These organizations connected women across the lines of nation, culture, and language and had overlapping memberships. They hosted international conferences, and they helped spearhead publications such as the IACW's *Jus Suffragii* and the ICW's *Bulletin*, which shared information about suffrage organizing in Asia, Latin America, Europe, and other parts of the world.

Of the four, the WCTU inspired the most dramatic grassroots suffrage activism, becoming the largest women's organization in the world, with over 40 national affiliates. An outgrowth of the U.S. Woman's Christian Temperance Union (1874), the WCTU argued that women could use their vote to promote temperance and end men's alcohol-infused violence. The organization transformed the goal of woman suffrage into a legible and compelling one for large numbers of women. Spearheading the first organized suffrage efforts in the white British colonies of South Africa, New Zealand, and South Australia, the WCTU was responsible for the world's first national suffrage victory in New Zealand in 1893, and in Australia in 1902.

Although these groups spoke of "global sisterhood," their memberships were predominantly Anglo-American and European,

and their publications usually only published in French, English, and German, in spite of demands to expand beyond these languages from women in Spanish-speaking countries and other parts of the world. These international groups generally marginalized or excluded, and in the WCTU's case segregated, U.S. women of color.

These groups often reflected what historians have called "imperial feminism"—a belief that white, Western women will "uplift" women in "uncivilized" parts of the world. This logic went hand in hand with some suffrage efforts. WCTU missionaries in Hawai'i who sought to secure woman suffrage there in the 1890s allied with white U.S. business and military interests who were establishing imperial control over the island. Suffragists also demanded the vote in the United States' imperial acquisitions from the 1898 Spanish-American War—the Philippines, Puerto Rico, and Cuba—both as part of a civilizing mission and to force discussion of a federal suffrage amendment in the United States.

Meanwhile, while celebrating early suffrage victories within the western United States in the same period, most white suffragists overlooked the fact that these states denied the right to vote to many Asian American, Mexican American, and Native American women.

African American suffragists powerfully critiqued Anglo-American dominance on the international stage and within the U.S. suffrage movement as they made important contributions to it. They also continued to connect global ideals of "freedom" with local women's rights issues, expanding the international agenda to address such goals as universal suffrage for men and women, anti-lynching, and education. Abolitionist Frances Ellen Watkins Harper, a pivotal African American civil rights and women's rights leader, spoke at the 1888 founding of the ICW and oversaw the formation of many "colored WCTU" groups that contributed to school suffrage victories in several states in the 1890s. On a speaking tour in England, the anti-lynching activist Ida B. Wells brought global attention to WCTU president Frances Willard's failure to defend African American men lynched on false rape accusations. Wells went on to found the most vital African American woman suffrage group in the country, the Alpha Suffrage Club, in Chicago, and at the 1913 suffrage march on Washington, she refused to march in a section reserved for African American women. In 1904, Mary Church Terrell, the first president of the National Association of Colored Women, spoke in fluent German at the ICW meeting in Berlin, pointing out that a global women's rights agenda must include attention to Black women's unequal access to many rights, including education and employment. Newspapers in Germany, France, Norway, and Austria lauded her speech.

Above: German socialist Clara Zetkin. Right: Delegates from Norway, Finland, and Great Britain march through the streets of New York City.

At the end of the 19th century, a more modern and militant suffrage internationalism emerged. A growing embrace of the term "feminism"—implying a movement that demanded women's full autonomy—along with working women's strong public presence, international socialism, and the Russian Revolution, contributed to the idea of a new womanhood breaking free from old constraints.

International socialism had long upheld universal, direct, and equal suffrage as a demand, but German socialist firebrand Clara Zetkin revived the goal, spearheading the inclusion of woman suffrage in the 1889 Second International in Paris. This gathering of socialist and labor parties from 20 countries in turn fostered vigorous women's movements in Germany, France, and elsewhere in Europe. In Finland, socialist feminists and the Social Democratic Party were critical to the country's, also Europe's first, woman suffrage victory in 1906.

Socialism, and the growing numbers of working women it inspired, breathed new life into the U.S. suffrage movement. In 1909, women workers in New York demanded women's right to vote, launching what became International Women's Day. Over the next six years, working women exploded in labor militancy, viewing the vote as a tool against unjust working conditions and for what Polish-born labor organizer and suffragist Rose Schneiderman called "bread and roses." The 1911 Triangle Shirtwaist Factory fire that claimed the lives of 145 workers, most of whom were young, immigrant women, made suffrage more urgent. Collaborations with middle-class reformers helped spread many of the tactics that suffragists later employed on a wider scale: mass meetings, marches, and open-air street speaking.

Immigrants and women from throughout the Americas were key to these efforts, and to connecting suffrage to broad social justice goals. In cigar factories in Tampa, Florida, the Puerto Rican

anti-imperialist, anarchist, and feminist Luisa Capetillo inspired African American, Cuban American, and Italian American women workers with calls for woman suffrage, and for free love, workers' rights, and vegetarianism. From Texas, Mexican-born feminist Teresa Villarreal, who had fled the dictatorship of Porfirio Díaz, supported the Mexican Revolution, the Socialist Party, and woman suffrage, publishing with her sister Andrea that state's first feminist newspaper, *La Mujer Moderna* (The Modern Woman) and starting the publication *El Obrero* (The Worker). In 1911, after the First Mexican Congress in Laredo, Texas, journalist Jovita Idár praised woman suffrage in *La Crónica* (The Chronicle), connecting it to her longstanding demands for Mexican American civil rights.

Socialist, working-class suffrage militancy in England also galvanized the British Women's Social and Political Union

Opposite: The cover of a pamphlet for the International Woman Suffrage Alliance Congress in London, 1909. Above: British activist Emmeline Pankhurst (center) with U.S. suffragist Lucy Burns (left).

Above: Suffrage activists prepare to picket the White House
with a sign meant to draw the attention of visiting Russian
delegates to their cause.

"International pressure helped compel Wilson's announcement of support for suffrage, as he promoted the United States as a beacon of democracy"

(WSPU), founded in 1903 by Emmeline Pankhurst. This group became the driving force in the British movement for nearly two decades, influencing militant suffrage activism around the world, including in China. After the U.S. suffragist Alice Paul, one of Pankhurst's followers, was arrested several times in the U.K. in 1909, she helped organize the 1913 suffrage march in Washington, D.C., and founded the Congressional Union for Woman Suffrage, later renamed the National Woman's Party (NWP), that focused on a federal constitutional suffrage amendment. Its sash of purple, white, and yellow was modeled on the British purple, white, and green one, and its confrontational suffrage strategies of civil disobedience and picketing government buildings were inspired in large part by WSPU activism.

The First World War, and a wave of suffrage legislation in Europe, further accelerated the U.S. suffrage movement. In the five years after 1914, suffrage passed in Denmark, Iceland, Russia, Canada, Austria, Germany, Poland, and Britain. Although the NWP had already been picketing the White House for several months, it was only when they embarrassed President Woodrow Wilson in front of a visiting Russian delegation, whose wartime cooperation he was trying to secure, that the first six suffragists were arrested. These women, held on charges of obstructing traffic, were followed by a long line of U.S. women imprisoned for suffrage activism. The violence they faced on the picket line (for holding signs saying "Kaiser Wilson" amid rabid anti-German sentiment) and in jail, with forced feedings during hunger strikes, became

international news. International pressure helped compel Wilson's January 1918 announcement of support for suffrage, as he promoted the United States as a beacon of democracy. By this time, the House had already passed the suffrage amendment (the Senate would still vote against it), but Wilson's endorsement was significant to U.S. and international public opinion. In Uruguay, suffragists utilized Wilson's support to push their legislators toward suffrage.

Two more years of federal and state lobbying and organizing led to ratification of the 19th Amendment in August 1920. For Crystal Eastman, a pacifist, enthusiast of the Russian Revolution, and cofounder of the American Civil Liberties Union (ACLU), this accomplishment represented not an end, but a new beginning— one with internationalist significance: "Now [feminists] can say what they are really after," she announced, "and what they are after, in common with all the rest of the struggling world, is freedom."

Struggles for women's voting rights did not end with ratification of the 19th Amendment, which failed to eliminate the residency requirements, poll taxes, and literacy tests in the South that denied most African American men and women the vote. The majority of African American women would not be able to exercise this right until the 1965 Voting Rights Act. For many, lack of rights in the United States drove new transnational activism. In the 1920s and '30s, African American women collaborated with women from Africa, the Caribbean, and around the globe in the International Council of Women of the Darker Races (1922). They also took part in in Pan-Africanist and leftist organizing that connected demands for women's

political autonomy with those for antiracism, anticolonialism, and Black nationalism, specifically viewing Black women's self-determination as critical to broad and transformative social justice.

U.S. women's involvement in Pan-American feminism was also an outgrowth of the U.S. suffrage movement. In 1928, U.S. and Cuban feminists created the Inter-American Commission of Women, the first intergovernmental organization in the world. Initially led by NWP suffrage veteran Doris Stevens, the commission forced an international treaty for women's civil and political equal rights into Pan-American and League of Nations congresses. A heterogeneous group of Latin American feminists, however, also recognized continuing efforts of U.S. women to dominate the movement and developed their own anti-imperialist Pan-Hispanic feminism that demanded the vote. They asserted their own leadership over Pan-American feminism and used it to call for *derechos humanos* (human rights), which implied women's political, civil, social, and economic rights alongside anti-imperialism and anti-fascism. At the 1945 San Francisco meeting that created the United Nations, Latin American female delegates, led by Brazilian feminist Bertha Lutz, drew on this movement to push women's rights into the UN Charter and proposed what became the UN Commission on the Status of Women. In the wake of these events, numerous Latin American countries passed woman suffrage.

The transnational legacies of the suffrage movement are evident in U.S. women's ongoing quests for full citizenship today. Then as now, fights for women's rights are connected to global movements for human rights—for immigrant, racial, labor, and feminist justice. The internationalist history of the woman suffrage movement shows us that activists and movements outside the United States, and a broad range of diverse, international goals, were critical to organizing for that right deemed so quintessentially American—the right to vote. It reminds us how much we in the United States have to learn from feminist struggles around the world.

This article was originally commissioned by the National Conference of State Historic Preservation Officers in partnership with the United States National Park Service.

Opposite: Crystal Eastman. Above: Bertha Lutz
speaks at a conference on the UN Charter.

Above: British activist Emmeline Pankhurst
delivers a speech to a crowd in New York on
an earlier visit to the United States, c. 1911.

EMMELINE PANKHURST'S "FREEDOM OR DEATH" SPEECH

A leading British women's rights activist, Pankhurst delivered
this speech in Hartford, Connecticut on November 13, 1913,
while on a fundraising tour of the United States

"I do not come here as an advocate, because whatever position the suffrage movement may occupy in the United States of America, in England it has passed beyond the realm of advocacy and it has entered into the sphere of practical politics. It has become the subject of revolution and civil war, and so tonight I am not here to advocate woman suffrage. American suffragists can do that very well for themselves.

I am here as a soldier who has temporarily left the field of battle in order to explain—it seems strange it should have to be explained—what civil war is like when civil war is waged by women. I am not only here as a soldier temporarily absent from the field at battle; I am here—and that, I think, is the strangest part of my coming—I am here as a person who, according to the law courts of my country, it has been decided, is of no value to the community at all; and I am adjudged because of my life to be a dangerous person, under sentence of penal servitude in a convict prison.

It is not at all difficult if revolutionaries come to you from Russia, if they come to you from China, or from any other part of the world, if they are men. But since I am a woman it is necessary to explain why women have adopted revolutionary methods in order to win the rights of citizenship. We women, in trying to make our case clear, always have to make as part of our argument, and urge upon men in our audience the fact—a very simple fact—that women are human beings.

Suppose the men of Hartford had a grievance, and they laid that grievance before their legislature, and the legislature obstinately refused to listen to them, or to remove their grievance, what would be the proper, and the constitutional, and the practical way of getting their grievance removed? Well, it is perfectly obvious. At the next general election the men of Hartford would turn out that legislature and elect a new one.

But let the men of Hartford imagine that they were not in the position of being voters at all, that they were governed without their consent being obtained, that the legislature turned an absolutely deaf ear to their demands; what would the men of Hartford do then? They couldn't vote the legislature out. They would have to choose; they would have to make a choice of two evils: they would either have to submit indefinitely to an unjust state of affairs, or they would have to rise up and adopt some of the antiquated means by which men in the past got their grievances remedied.

Your forefathers decided that they must have representation for taxation, many, many years ago. When they felt they couldn't wait any longer, when they laid all the arguments before an obstinate British government that they could think of, and when their arguments were absolutely disregarded, when every other means had failed, they began by the tea party at Boston, and they went on until they had won the independence of the United States of America.

It is about eight years since the word militant was first used to describe what we were doing. It was not militant at all, except that it provoked militancy on the part of those who were opposed to it. When women asked questions in political meetings and failed to get answers, they were not doing anything militant. In Great Britain it is a custom, a time-honored one, to ask questions of candidates for parliament and ask questions of members of the government. No man was ever put out of a public meeting for asking a question. The first people who were put out of a political meeting for asking questions were women; they were brutally ill-used; they found themselves in jail before 24 hours had expired.

We were called militant, and we were quite willing to accept the name. We were determined to press this question of the enfranchisement of women to the point where we were no longer to be ignored by the politicians.

"The influence of those who have got power commands a great deal of attention; but the wrongs and the grievances of those people who have no power at all are apt to be absolutely ignored"

—Emmeline Pankhurst

You have two babies very hungry and wanting to be fed. One baby is a patient baby, and waits indefinitely until its mother is ready to feed it. The other baby is an impatient baby and cries lustily, screams and kicks, and makes everybody unpleasant until it is fed. Well, we know perfectly well which baby is attended to first. That is the whole history of politics. You have to make more noise than anybody else, you have to make yourself more obtrusive than anybody else, you have to fill all the papers more than anybody else, in fact you have to be there all the time and see that they do not snow you under.

When you have warfare things happen; people suffer; the non-combatants suffer as well as the combatants. And so it happens in civil war. When your forefathers threw the tea into Boston Harbor, a good many women had to go without their tea. It has always seemed to me an extraordinary thing that you did not follow it up by throwing the whiskey overboard; you sacrificed the women; and there is a good deal of warfare for which men take a great deal of glorification which has involved more practical sacrifice on women than it has on any man. It always has been so. The grievances of those who have got power, the influence of those who have got power commands a great deal of attention; but the wrongs and the grievances of those people who have no power at all are apt to be absolutely ignored. That is the history of humanity right from the beginning.

Well, in our civil war people have suffered, but you cannot make omelettes without breaking eggs; you cannot have civil war without damage to something. The great thing is to see that no more damage is done than is absolutely necessary, that you do just as much as will arouse enough feeling to bring about peace, to bring about an honorable peace for the combatants; and that is what we have been doing.

We entirely prevented stockbrokers in London from telegraphing to stockbrokers in Glasgow and vice versa: for one whole day telegraphic communication was entirely stopped. I am not going to tell you how it was done. I am not going to tell you how the women got to the mains and cut the wires; but it was done. It was done, and it was proved to the authorities that weak women, suffrage women, as we are supposed to be, had enough ingenuity to create a situation of that kind. Now, I ask you, if women can do that, is there any limit to what we can do except the limit we put upon ourselves?

If you are dealing with an industrial revolution, if you get the men and women of one class rising up against the men and women of another class, you can locate the difficulty; if there is a great industrial strike, you know exactly where the violence is and how the warfare is going to be waged; but in our war against the government you can't locate it. We wear no mark; we belong to every class; we permeate every class of the community from the highest to the lowest; and so you see in the woman's civil war the dear men of my country are discovering it is absolutely impossible to deal with it: you cannot locate it, and you cannot stop it.

'Put them in prison,' they said, 'that will stop it.' But it didn't stop it at all: instead of the women giving it up, more women did it, and more and more and more women did it until there were 300 women at a time, who had not broken a single law, only 'made a nuisance of themselves' as the politicians say.

Then they began to legislate. The British government has passed more stringent laws to deal with this agitation than it ever found necessary during all the history of political agitation in my country. They were able to deal with the revolutionaries of the Chartists' time; they were able to deal with the trades union agitation; they were able to deal with the revolutionaries later on when the Reform Acts were passed: but the ordinary law has not sufficed to curb insurgent women. They had to dip back into the Middle Ages to find a means of repressing the women in revolt.

They have said to us, government rests upon force, the women haven't force, so they must submit. Well, we are showing them that government does not rest upon force at all: it rests upon consent. As long as women consent to be unjustly governed, they can be, but directly women say: 'We withhold our consent, we will not be governed any longer so long as that government is unjust.' Not by the forces of civil war can you govern the very weakest woman. You can kill that woman, but she escapes you then; you cannot govern her. No power on earth can govern a human being, however feeble, who withholds his or her consent.

When they put us in prison at first, simply for taking petitions, we submitted; we allowed them to dress us in prison clothes; we allowed them to put us in solitary confinement; we allowed them to put us amongst the most degraded of criminals; we learned of some of the appalling evils of our so-called civilization that we could not have learned in any other way. It was valuable experience, and we were glad to get it.

I have seen men smile when they heard the words 'hunger strike,' and yet I think there are very few men today who would be prepared to adopt a 'hunger strike' for any cause. It is only people who feel an intolerable sense of oppression who would adopt a means of that kind. It means you refuse food until you are at death's door, and then the authorities have to choose between letting you die, and letting you go; and then they let the women go.

Now, that went on so long that the government felt that they were unable to cope. It was that, to the shame of the British government, they set the example to authorities all over the world of feeding sane, resisting human beings by force. There may be doctors in this meeting: if so, they know it is one thing to feed by force an insane person; but it is quite another thing to feed a sane, resisting human being who resists with every nerve and with every fibre of her body the indignity and the outrage of forcible feeding. Now, that was done in England, and the government thought they had crushed us. But they found that it did not quell the agitation, that more and more women came in and even passed that terrible ordeal, and they were obliged to let them go.

Then came the legislation—the 'Cat and Mouse Act.' The home secretary said: 'Give me the power to let these women go when they are at death's door, and leave them at liberty under license until they have recovered their health again and then bring them back.' It was passed to repress the agitation, to make the women yield—because that is what it has really come to, ladies and gentlemen. It has come to a battle between the women and the government as to who shall yield first, whether they will yield and give us the vote, or whether we will give up our agitation.

Well, they little know what women are. Women are very slow to rouse, but once they are aroused, once they are determined, nothing on earth and nothing in heaven will make women give way; it is impossible. And so this 'Cat and Mouse Act,' which is being used against women today, has failed. There are women lying at death's door, recovering enough strength to undergo operations who have not given in and won't give in, and who will be prepared, as soon as they get up from their sick beds, to go on as before. There are women who are being carried from their sick beds on stretchers into meetings. They are too weak to speak, but they go amongst their fellow workers just to show that their spirits are unquenched, and that their spirit is alive, and they mean to go on as long as life lasts.

Now, I want to say to you who think women cannot succeed, we have brought the government of England to this position, that it has to face this alternative: either women are to be killed or women are to have the vote. I ask American men in this meeting, what would you say if in your state you were faced with that alternative, that you must either kill them or give them their citizenship? Well, there is only one answer to that alternative, there is only one way out—you must give those women the vote.

You won your freedom in America when you had the revolution, by bloodshed, by sacrificing human life. You won the civil war by the sacrifice of human life when you decided to emancipate the negro. You have left it to women in your land, the men of all civilized countries have left it to women, to work out their own salvation. That is the way in which we women of England are doing. Human life for us is sacred, but we say if any life is to be sacrificed it shall be ours; we won't do it ourselves, but we will put the enemy in the position where they will have to choose between giving us freedom or giving us death.

So here am I. I come in the intervals of prison appearance. I come after having been four times imprisoned under the 'Cat and Mouse Act,' probably going back to be rearrested as soon as I set my foot on British soil. I come to ask you to help to win this fight. If we win it, this hardest of all fights, then, to be sure, in the future it is going to be made easier for women all over the world to win their fight when their time comes."

CHAPTER SIX

AFTER
THE 19TH

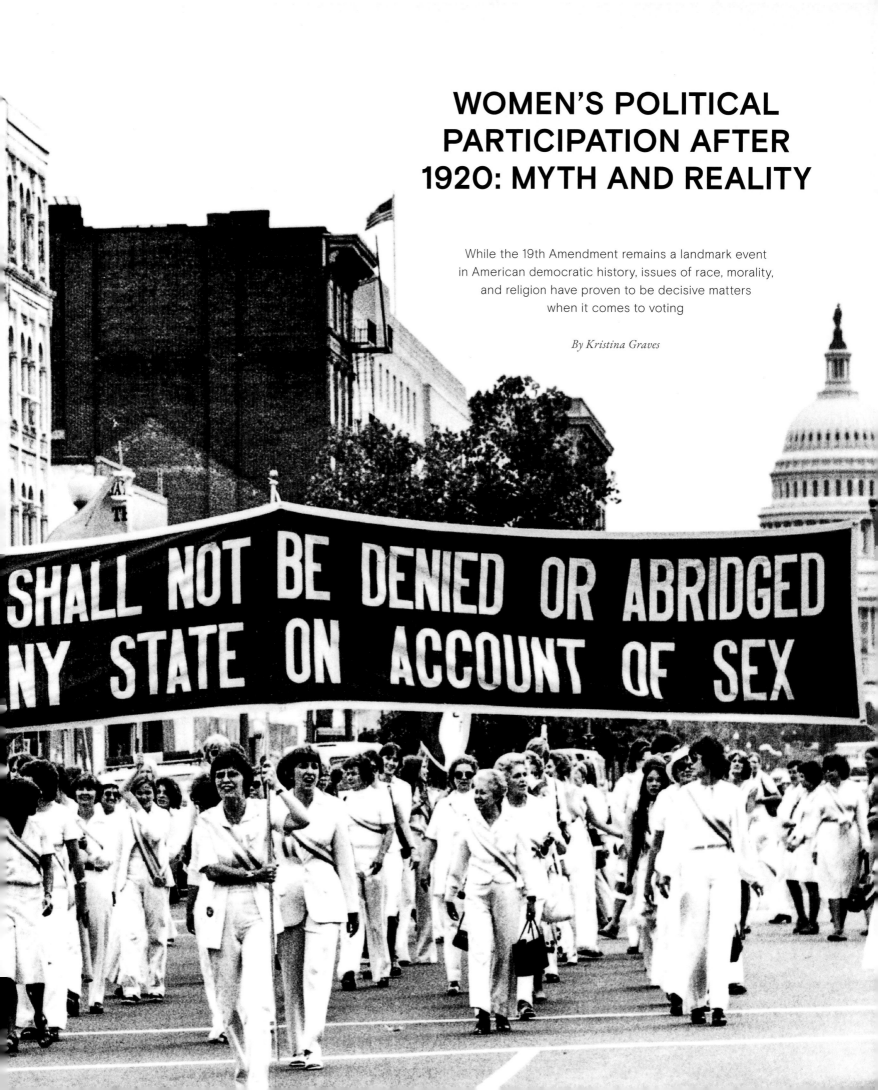

WOMEN'S POLITICAL PARTICIPATION AFTER 1920: MYTH AND REALITY

While the 19th Amendment remains a landmark event in American democratic history, issues of race, morality, and religion have proven to be decisive matters when it comes to voting

By Kristina Graves

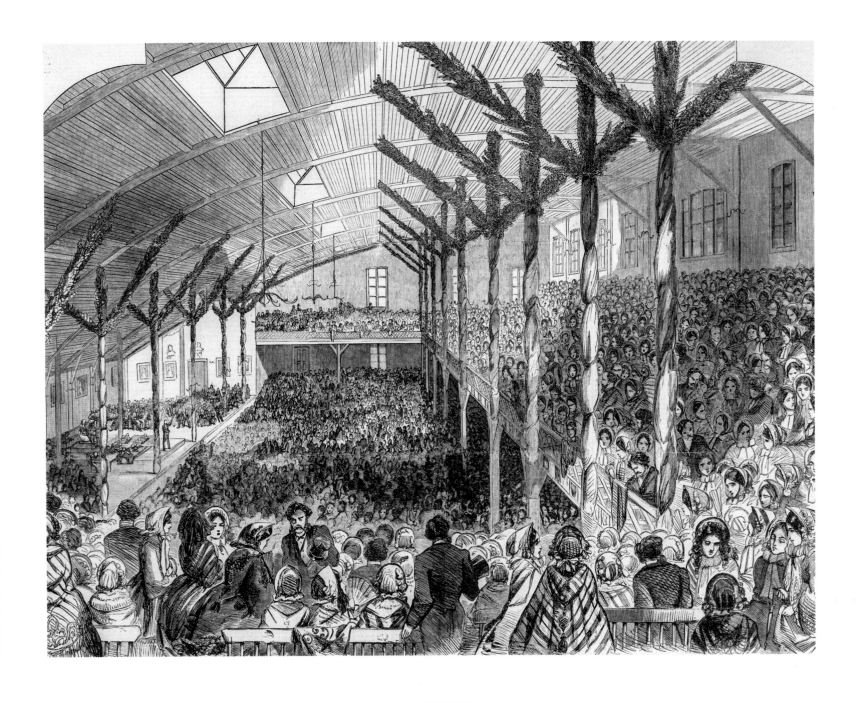

Previous pages: Supporters march in Washington, D.C. to demand
passage of the Equal Rights Amendment, 1977. Above: Men and
women attend a Republican convention, 1860.

In a 1912 letter written to British suffragist Millicent Garrett Fawcett, President Theodore Roosevelt remarked that he was "amused" that women in suffrage states voted similar to men and that their votes contributed to his defeat for a third presidential term. Though Roosevelt was an avid supporter of women's suffrage, he believed that women's involvement would have no significant impact in American politics, a belief that many Progressive era Americans did not share. Roosevelt wrote to Fawcett six years before American women gained the right to vote under the 19th Amendment, but his words contradicted what many suffragists argued: that women's involvement in voting and politics would create broad changes that would create a better, stronger America.

In American history, the 19th Amendment represents the end of a long-fought 72-year campaign for women's voting rights. The popular narrative of this watershed is that women were not politically active prior to 1920. This version of history often ignores the reality that American women have aligned and acted according to political ideology since the days of the American Revolution. Furthermore, the assumption that all women did not have the right to vote because there was no federal amendment is a false one. Several western states granted full voting rights to women prior to 1920, such as Wyoming, Colorado, Idaho, Utah, California, Nevada, Arizona, Oregon, and Washington. Southern states did not grant women voting rights, but some Midwestern and Eastern states allowed women to vote in local or state elections. Not only did women vote in key states, they also participated in national party politics. During the antebellum period, women were key players in the Free-Soiler, Liberty, and Republican Parties and, during the Gilded Age, women participated in the political "machinery" to expand their opportunities and access to the public sphere.

Historian Christine Stansell states that the 19th Amendment was the "single greatest act of mass enfranchisement" in American history. Despite this, the 1920 watershed is a problematic one. One, it did not enable Black women to vote in the South. It would take several decades before Black women specifically, and women

of color generally, would achieve full voting rights in the United States. Two, it did not drastically increase the number of women voters in elections. Finally, it did not create a "gender gap" capable of significantly influencing American elections. Prior to the passage of the 19th Amendment, suffragists argued that women's voting rights would benefit society. Suffragists like Carrie Chapman Catt, president of the National American Woman Suffrage Association, suggested that women voters would clean up society on issues like temperance, ending white slavery, child labor laws, and government corruption. Furthermore, some suffragists argued that granting white women the right to vote would act as a preventative measure against groups considered inferior, such as African Americans in the South; Native Americans, Chinese, and Mormons in the West; and Western and Eastern European immigrants in the North.

In reality, the 19th Amendment, and women by the same standard, had very little impact on the voting landscape of America in the years following the ratification of the federal amendment. The generation immediately following the First World War was so apolitical that some former suffragists did not even vote. Voter apathy among women was so prevalent that magazines ran articles titled "Is Woman Suffrage a Failure" and "Woman Suffrage Declared a Failure." In a survey conducted in 1927, it was determined that only 35 to 40 percent of eligible women voters participated in the presidential elections of 1920. In the same survey, it was stated that women followed the political example of their husbands and fathers when deciding whether or not to vote in the election. However, Illinois was the only state that recorded the presidential vote according to sex. This makes it difficult for historians to determine exactly how many American women voted in the 1920 and 1924 presidential elections.

While it is difficult to determine specific numbers of gendered voting, historians have identified trends that influenced the first nationally voting generation of women. One of the main reasons for voter apathy among women was that men did not easily relinquish political power to women. A good example of this is two southern states' (Mississippi and Georgia) response to the 19th Amendment.

"Women proved to be more divided on issues than previously anticipated, particularly on matters of protective legislation and racial issues"

The political leadership of both states defied the newly ratified amendment in a deliberate act of voter suppression by refusing to update the deadline for registering newly enfranchised women. Political party leadership also made it difficult for many women to participate in the process and only acknowledged women as a voting group when it was convenient or necessary for election success.

After the passage of the 19th Amendment and the failure of party leadership to acknowledge women's issues as legitimate issues, many women's organizations embraced non-partisanship as their official platform. Such was the case with the National American Woman Suffrage Association (NAWSA) and later the League of Women Voters (LWV) which, both under the leadership of Carrie Chapman Catt, embraced candidates from a wide array of political parties. On an individual level, women continued to vote according to partisan preferences. Generally speaking, women in the North and West tended to vote for the Republican Party because it was the party with the most distinct ties to the women's suffrage movement. In the South, white women overwhelmingly favored the Democratic Party despite the fact that the leadership never supported women's voting rights. Women were not solely responsible for the successful election of Warren G. Harding as president in 1920, but they did contribute to an overall Republican landslide in other races at the local, state, and national levels of government.

Discouragement of women's involvement was not limited to voting but also running for political office. One of the main promises that suffragists made was that women would become more involved in the political machinery and help to clean out corruption. In reality, women were seldom elected to positions of political power. Often, this was because women tended to embrace concepts of pacifism, feminism, and gender equality, which made them controversial candidates. Political party leadership only supported women candidates when it benefited the party as a whole and actively discouraged women from running for political office. These tactics were effective and long-lasting. In 1925, out of 7,500 state legislature seats, women only held 150. By 1930, there were only 13 women elected to Congress, but half of them were temporarily filling vacant seats. Women did not begin voting in record numbers and form an increasingly Democratic voting bloc until the 1980s. This was in response to the women's liberation movement far more than the suffrage movement. It would not be until 1992 that women gained a significant number of seats in Congress. With each subsequent election, more and more female candidates are elected to serve at the local, state, and national levels of government.

The gender gap that was predicted by suffragists never happened. Women proved to be more divided on issues than previously anticipated, particularly on matters of protective legislation and racial issues. A good example of this is the debate over the Equal Rights Amendment (ERA) during the 1920s because women were divided on the language of the proposed amendment. Militant suffragists like Alice Paul, who authored the amendment, and the National Woman's Party supported gender equality, while other women like Carrie Chapman Catt and the League of Women Voters, established from the National American Woman Suffrage

Opposite: Prospective Black voters wait to register in Mississippi,
1966. Above: Members of the League of Women Voters register
a group of female voters, c. 1923.

Above: Delegates of the League of Women Voters prepare to
present a "mile of signatures" to President Coolidge as part of the
drive for international peace, 1923. Opposite: Female members
of the National Association for the Advancement of Colored
People promote their organization.

Association in 1920, supported the protective labor laws for women and were fearful that the ERA would erode this legislation. Similarly, racial issues split the women's vote along color lines, particularly in the American South. Issues of white womanhood, religious fundamentalism, and fears of miscegenation complicated the outcome of the vote for white women. The 1920s witnessed the rebirth of the Ku Klux Klan and white women comprised four million members in the organization, furthering the group's commitment to racial purity and radical conservatism with efforts designed to disenfranchise the South's Black population en masse.

Then, as is the case now, women did not vote for candidates just because of their gender and some refused to vote for another woman out of personal disagreements with the individual. Furthermore, just as women had been some of the more vocal opponents to women's voting rights, women voters did not always vote in line with the feminist platform. Women disagreed on issues of birth control, pre-marital sex, and fashion and those differences translated into differences in the voting booth. The "New Woman" of the Progressive era and the younger "flapper" generation were stark contrasts in American womanhood. The shift in values from citizen as voter to citizen as consumer had a major impact on women after the First World War and contributed greatly to women's apparent apathy towards the vote. In contrast to what suffragists argued, women were not more inclined to participate in political discourse now that it was legal for them to do so.

The 19th Amendment was a watershed moment for American women and was the largest example of enfranchisement in the nation's history. However, it did not become the broad stroke of equality for which suffragists advocated. For Black women in the South, gerrymandering and Jim Crow would prevent access to the vote, and it would be another 45 years before African Americans would be able to make use of their legal voting rights. This was also true of other women of color: Latinas, Asian Americans, and Native Americans in the West faced discrimination in voting laws similar to African Americans in the South. The groups that would have benefited the most from enfranchisement under the 19th Amendment were the least able to access their rights legally for a significant portion of the 20th century.

It is for this reason that the 19th Amendment has a mixed legacy. For one, it enfranchised, legally, a large percentage of American women. In reality, many women were still unable, or unwilling, to vote. After a 1927 research study examining women's voting patterns, the League of Women Voters responded to the data by claiming that "women are the worst offenders" when it came to non-voting. According to the Pew Research Center, the gender gap promised by suffragists began to rise in the late 20th century with the women's liberation movement. However, as recently as the 2016 presidential election, the data also shows that white women and Black women continue to be divided in their votes. The majority of white women voted for President Trump, while Black women were solidly voting for Hillary Clinton.

While the 19th Amendment will continue to be an important event studied in history classes at the secondary and collegiate level, it is critical that we examine the amendment for what it actually did versus what suffragists argued it would accomplish. Women continued to be partisan and apolitical, just as before the passage of the amendment. Issues of race, morality, and religion influenced women's voting behaviors. Despite the amendment and promises of a female-centered future, men overwhelmingly continued to hold a tight grip on the American political system in the years to come. The women's liberation movement of the 1970s and 1980s would be the generation to attempt increasing women's political presence. Nevertheless, women in America continue to this day to be split between Black and white, liberal and conservative, young and old. The reality of the 19th Amendment is that the law demonstrates the complicated political history of American women, one that is deeply divided and still developing.

This article appears courtesy of the National Women's History Museum.

LEGISLATING HISTORY

In the years since the 19th Amendment was ratified, hundreds of women have assumed congressional seats and have, over the decades, progressively exerted influence in every aspect of governance

Three hundred forty-five women have served in Congress since the first female member took her seat in 1917. Their progression through leadership ranks was slow but sure. In many ways, their integration into government has reflected women's entry into public life.

Jeannette Rankin became the first woman elected to Congress. A Republican, she won her election on August 29, 1916 to occupy one of Montana's two at-large seats, and she entered Congress three years before all women in the United States had the right to vote. Rankin presented her credentials and claimed her seat on April 2, 1917. "I may be the first woman member of Congress," she observed, "but I won't be the last."

Rankin worked as a professional lobbyist for the National American Woman Suffrage Association. Her organizing efforts yielded Montana women the right to vote in 1914. Candidate Rankin promised to address social welfare issues and advocate for a constitutional amendment to grant voting rights to women. Rankin warned constituents that she opposed U.S. involvement in the First World War. And when the time came, she voted against it. Montana's voters turned her out of office after one term. She returned for a second term more than two decades later in 1941. "No one will pay any attention to me this time," Rankin proclaimed after her victory. "There is nothing unusual about a woman being elected."

Four women took seats in Congress in 1921. One of them, Mae Ella Nolan of California, became the first woman to chair a congressional committee. America's first female senator, Rebecca Felton, served for just 24 hours after Georgia's governor appointed her to fill the remainder of a term.

Alice Robertson of Oklahoma became the second woman elected to the House of Representatives during a regular election. Robertson was also the first woman to preside over a session of the House. Ironically, Robertson opposed woman's suffrage, yet she was assigned to the Committee on Woman Suffrage. Her reputation for supporting veterans helped her into office, but her opposition to the World War I Veterans Bonus Bill led to her departure after one term.

The first generation of congresswomen arrived without experience in elected office. However, many came of age during the Progressive Era. They fought for women's voting rights, public health, and against child labor. Though lacking official experience, they knew politics. Ruth Hanna McCormick served as the head of the Republican Women's National Executive committee before taking her House seat in 1929. McCormick went on to become the first woman to manage a presidential campaign. In 1940 she led Thomas E. Dewey's campaign for the Republican nomination.

Women members demonstrated early on that they would not agree on every issue. For example, Prohibition was enacted under pressure from the largely female temperance movement. By the 1930s, rising public sentiment demanded its repeal. Female congresswomen split over the question in 1933. Some cited moral grounds to keep alcohol illegal. Others voted for repeal to stimulate the flagging economy.

The Great Depression and support for or against New Deal policies proved to be the most significant factor for women retaining their seats in the 1930s. Roosevelt's majorities swept Republican women out and Democratic women in. Senator Hattie Caraway and Representatives Caroline O'Day and Mary Norton each chaired committees in 1939. All were Democrats.

Thirty-six women entered Congress from 1935 to 1954. They arrived with more experience than their predecessors, and several rose to influence. They took seats on prestigious committees including Agriculture, Armed Services, Banking and Currency, and Judiciary. Five served on the Foreign Affairs Committee, a key post both before and after the U.S. entered the Second World War. Their leadership came during a tumultuous period that included expanding government social programs, a world war, and the start of the Cold War.

First elected to the House in 1925, Edith Nourse Rogers served 18 terms until her death in 1961. A volunteer nursing assistant during the First World War, she spent a lifetime advocating for veterans. She introduced the funding that created the veterans' hospital system and she also secured pensions for army nurses. After U.S. entry into the Second World War, Rogers introduced a bill creating the Women's Army Auxiliary Corps. The WAAC measure allowed up to 150,000 women to volunteer for military service. In 1942, a new law granted women official military status in the Army. Soon after, women joined other uniformed services including the Navy (WAVEs), Air Force (WASPs), and Coast Guard (SPARs). In 1948, Margaret Chase Smith's Women's Armed Services Integration Act permanently included women in the military.

Previous pages: Jeannette Rankin, the first woman elected to
Congress. Opposite: The first female senator Rebecca Felton
(seated center), 1922. Above: Representative Alice Robertson.

"Thirty six women entered Congress from 1935 to 1954. They arrived with more experience than their predecessors, and several rose to influence"

Women legislators during the post-war period focused less on traditional women's issues than their predecessors. Many minimized gender distinction, insisting that they represented all of their constituents, not just women. Following the war, the U.S. set an expansive foreign policy agenda with the involvement of key congresswomen. Emily Taft Douglas, a Democrat from Illinois, advocated for the establishment of a post-war United Nations. Chase Going Woodhouse, a Democrat representing Connecticut, pushed for the Bretton Woods Agreements, creating the World Bank and International Monetary Fund. Edna Kelly, head of the European Affairs Subcommittee on the Foreign Affairs panel, backed creation of the North Atlantic Treaty Organization (NATO).

Margaret Chase Smith developed a reputation for independence. During the height of Senator Joseph McCarthy's "red scare," she vocally denounced him in her "Declaration of Conscience" address. Although she did not mention McCarthy by name, her meaning was unmistakable. She also took her colleagues to task for condoning the permissive context in which McCarthyism was allowed to flourish.

The United States experienced great social upheaval between 1955 and 1976 as marginalized groups protested inequities and challenged the government to legislate equality. The 39 women who entered Congress during this period were challenging in their own ways. They were less deferential to tradition and prioritized action over fitting in. Many were reformers who championed causes including civil rights and women's rights and supported Vietnam War protesters.

In 1964, Patsy Takemoto Mink, from Hawaii, became the first woman of color and first Asian American woman elected to Congress. Mink championed women's issues, including passage of the Women's Education Equity Act and co-sponsorship of Title IX—the civil rights law that prohibits sex-based discrimination

Opposite, top: Representatives Caroline O'Day, Edith Nourse Rogers, Mary Norton, Nan Honeyman, and Virginia Jenckes, and Senator Hattie Caraway, 1938. Opposite, bottom: Margaret Chase Smith, the first woman to serve in both houses of Congress. Above: Congresswoman Patsy Takemoto Mink moves into her new office.

in any school or other education program that receives federal money. Mink's principled stance against the Vietnam War set her at odds with her military-dependent district. "It was such a horrible thought to have this war that it really made no difference to me that I had a military constituency," she recalled, years later. "It was a case of living up to my own views and my own conscience... There was no way in which I could compromise my views on how I felt about it."

Shirley Chisholm was the first African American woman elected to Congress. Representing the Bedford–Stuyvesant neighborhood in Brooklyn, New York, Chisholm was known as "Fighting Shirley" for her passionate advocacy for her poor and minority constituents. Chisholm made gender a campaign issue in her successful 1968 election. "There were Negro men in office here before I came in five years ago, but they didn't deliver."

Taking a cue from the Civil Rights movement, a women's liberation movement began in the 1960s. The movement included a series of protests and campaigns aimed at securing women full legal, economic, vocational, educational, and social rights and opportunities for women, equal to those of men. Bella Abzug emerged as a symbol of the women's rights movement. Elected to the House in 1971, she ran on an antiwar and pro-feminist platform. She wrote the first version of the Equal Credit Opportunity Act, which prohibited discrimination against women by banks in lending. She also introduced groundbreaking legislation aimed at increasing the rights of lesbians and gays. Abzug's political

aide Marilyn Marcosson recollected, "Bella was like the congresswoman for every woman in the world." Women's progress entering Congress in the 1970s mirrored women's larger efforts to break into professional fields. The majority of new congresswomen elected after 1976 proved themselves first in state legislatures. Several had held state executive office positions or been mayors of large cities. Some had federal experience ranging from U.S. ambassador to cabinet secretary. Their committee assignments expanded to include the Budget, Finance, Commerce, Foreign Relations, and Intelligence Committees. Though they had more power than any prior generation of congresswomen, they recognized their shared perspectives as women. And the Congresswomen's Caucus convened its first meeting on April 19, 1977.

An increasing number of women entered office with young families in tow. They faced the challenge of balancing a political career with family life. Yvonne Brathwaite Burke, who served from 1972 to 1979 representing California's 37th and 28th Districts in the House of Representatives, was the first sitting member of Congress to give birth in office when she gave birth to a daughter in 1973. Burke was both celebrated and reviled in the press. "If you ran for Congress at that time and you were a woman, everything about you was always open to the press," she remembered. "Your life was an open book. It was unusual for a woman who was in business or an elective office to talk about having family and being able to carry out their duties. I, personally, have always felt that women have a right to choose what they want to do."

Opposite: Shirley Chisholm speaks at the Democratic
National Convention, 1972. Above: Ileana Ros-Lehtinen,
the first Hispanic woman elected to Congress, and her
daughter Patricia.

RUTH HANNA McCORMICK

1880–1944

By Jeanette Patrick

Ruth Hanna McCormick Simms was a Republican United States Representative from Illinois who served from 1929 to 1931. Before running for office herself, for three decades Hanna McCormick had political experience working in the office of her father, Senator Marcus Alonzo Hanna, and campaigning for her husband, Representative and Senator Medill McCormick. Hanna McCormick was a leader in the suffrage movement and worked to ensure that the newly enfranchised women would support Republicans in elections. Her partisan activities set her apart from many other suffragists. Hanna McCormick was also the first woman elected to a statewide office, the first to be nominated by a major party to the Senate, and the first to manage a presidential nomination campaign.

Hanna McCormick was born on March 27, 1880 in Cleveland, Ohio. She attended elite private schools. When she was 16 her father was elected to the U.S Senate. After she graduated from high school, Hanna McCormick joined him in Washington, D.C. where she worked as his

personal secretary. When her father was not able to attend debates in the Senate, Hanna McCormick would sit in the gallery taking notes for him. During these sessions, she learned legislative procedure and political technique. She married Medill McCormick, heir to the *Chicago Tribune*, on June 10, 1903.

The couple moved to Chicago where Medill worked as the *Chicago Tribune* publisher for eight years. During their years in Chicago, Hanna McCormick worked towards many progressive reform activities, was part of the Settlement House Movement, and raised three children, Katrina, Medill, and Ruth. Hanna McCormick was also active in the pure foods movement and, when she was unable to find clean milk for her children, she opened a dairy and breeding farm. Hanna McCormick then sold the clean, safe milk to the community.

From 1913 until the ratification of the 19th Amendment in 1920 Hanna McCormick was active in the suffrage movement. Hanna McCormick's husband was elected to the Illinois legislature, and she worked as a lobbyist to ensure passage of the Illinois Equal Suffrage Act in 1913. She also succeeded Alice Paul as the chair of the Congressional Committee of the National American Woman Suffrage Association in 1913. Hanna McCormick's goal in working towards suffrage was to bring women into the Republican Party. The Republican Party was pushing for major reforms during the Progressive Era and Hanna McCormick believed female voters would support these ideals. Hanna McCormick was also a supporter of Prohibition. To help her better organize women to vote Republican, in 1918 Hanna McCormick was appointed to direct the newly created Republican Women's National Executive Committee.

When women won the right to vote in 1920, Hanna McCormick involved herself even more in party politics, and became the first National Committeewoman from Illinois. After Hanna McCormick's husband failed to be renominated for his Senate seat in 1924, he committed suicide in February of 1925. Hanna McCormick attributed her husband's lost election to a lack of women voters. So she spent the next four years creating a network of Republican Party women's clubs, establishing clubs in 90 of Illinois' 102 counties.

Throughout her political career Hanna McCormick ran on a platform to keep the United States out of foreign wars. While she was not a pacifist she did not think it benefited the country to be involved in Europe's problems. Hanna McCormick was elected U.S. Representative At-Large from Illinois in 1928. Her election is credited to the grassroots base of women she had built up over the previous years. She was appointed to the House Committee on Naval Affairs, becoming the first woman to serve on the committee.

After a successful term in the House of Representatives Hanna McCormick ran for the Senate. She was nominated by the Republican Party, and became the first woman nominated for the Senate by a major party. Hanna McCormick's nomination was again credited to the network of women she had created. Hanna McCormick did not win the Senate election of 1930 for a variety of reasons. Her Democratic opponent agreed with her signature stance on non-intervention in European wars. Another woman, Lottie O'Neill angered by Hanna McCormick's pledge to support the results of the Illinois referendum on the repeal of Prohibition, ran as an independent and siphoned off women voters who supported the continuation of Prohibition. Hanna McCormick was further undermined by revelations of her large campaign expenditures, which damaged her in the first years of the Great Depression. Ultimately, the poor economy was the biggest factor in her defeat.

Hanna McCormick married Albert Gallatin Simms in 1932 and moved with him to Albuquerque, New Mexico. He had also been a Representative during the 71st Congress, and their marriage marked the first time two concurrent Members had married. In New Mexico, McCormick Simms founded a girls' school in 1934, and continued to manage two newspapers and a radio station back in Illinois. In 1940, she sold her Illinois dairy farm and bought a 250,000-acre Colorado cattle and sheep ranch.

In 1940, McCormick Simms became the first woman to manage a presidential campaign when she worked on Thomas Dewey's campaign against Franklin D. Roosevelt. Dewey was only 37 and lacked political experience, but McCormick Simms used her many years of experience to help run his bid for president. McCormick Simms campaigned hard. During speaking tours, she often gave multiple speeches a day and traveled overnight to ensure the most opportunities to meet with voters in each region. However, Dewey did not win the nomination and the campaign ended after the convention.

McCormick Simms spent much of the next four years on her ranch in Colorado. She also spent time offering Dewey political advice on his term as governor and his next presidential campaign. In October 1944, while riding a horse on her ranch the horse fell and McCormick Simms broke her shoulder. Not long after leaving the hospital McCormick Simms was diagnosed with pancreatitis. On December 4, her pancreas ruptured and on December 31 McCormick Simms died.

This article appears courtesy of the National Women's History Museum.

By the 1980s, Ileana Ros-Lehtinen, who was born in Havana, Cuba and moved to the U.S. with her family at age 7, was the first Hispanic woman elected to Congress. She was first elected in 1989 during a special election and went on to serve three decades representing Florida's 18th and 27th districts for the Republican Party. She served as the chair of the Committee on Foreign Affairs in the 112th Congress. Ros-Lehtinen sponsored legislation awarding the Congressional Gold Medal to the Women Airforce Service Pilots (WASP). The WASP was established during the Second World War, and from 1942 to 1943, more than a thousand women joined, flying 60 million miles of non-combat military missions.

Carol Moseley-Braun was the first African American woman elected to the Senate, serving one term from 1992 to 1999. Moseley-Braun, who had held local offices in Chicago, was motivated to run by the spectacle of the U.S. Supreme Court confirmation hearings for Clarence Thomas and the treatment of his accuser Anita Hill. She was one of four women Senators elected in 1992.

The 1992 election shifted U.S. politics. More women ran for office in that year than ever before in U.S. history, the first to be nicknamed "the Year of the Woman." Four of the 11 women Senate candidates won their races, as did 47 of the

record 106 women running for the House. After the election, women made up 11 percent of Congressional membership, a historic high point.

A changing political landscape catapulted more women into office. As the Cold War ended, the nation's attention turned inward. Voters worried over the prolonged economic recession, failing schools, and rising healthcare costs, as well as environmental issues and the AIDS crisis. Popular perceptions that women were better on domestic issues combined with increased fundraising among women's political action groups, such as NOW, Emily's List, and the Women's Campaign Fund, to sweep women into office.

Deborah Pryce was one of the few Republican women elected to the House in 1992. She rose through leadership to become the first woman ever to serve as the Republican Conference Chair, which she did in the 108th and 109th Congresses (2005–07 and 2007–09).

The 1992 elections inaugurated a decade of gains for women in Congress in both their number and seniority. These gains were capped by the election of Representative Nancy Pelosi as Speaker of the House in 2007. She became the first woman to serve as Speaker—the third position in presidential succession, after the Vice President—and has continued to lead the House Democrats ever since.

However, the achievements of women in 1992 were outstripped by those in the 2018 elections. A record-breaking 103 women were elected or re-elected to the House of Representatives for the 116th Congress, also earning 2018 the tag "Year of the Woman." The year included many firsts: Ilhan Omar and Rashida Tlaib became the first Muslim women to be elected to either house of Congress; Angie Craig became the first lesbian mother to be elected; Sharice Davids and Deb Haaland became the first Native American women elected; and Alexandria Ocasio-Cortez, aged 29 in 2018, became the youngest woman ever elected.

In 2021, there are 144 women in Congress, representing 26.9 percent of the seats. This is a historic high but is still a relatively small percentage internationally, with the U.S. currently standing at 70th on one worldwide table of female representation in national parliaments.

Yet it is undeniable that women in the U.S. Congress have steadily risen in number and up the leadership ranks. Over the past 104 years, 345 women have assumed congressional seats. They legislated on behalf of their principles and constituents. They exerted influence in every aspect of governance. From the first to the most recent, these women demonstrated that a woman's place is not only in the House... but also in the Senate.

This article appears courtesy of the National Women's History Museum.

Previous pages: Carol Moseley-Braun, the first African American woman elected to the Senate. Above: The first woman Speaker of the House, Nancy Pelosi.

KAMALA HARRIS

1964–

By Emma Rothberg

On January 20, 2021, Kamala D. Harris became the first woman, the first African American woman, the first Indian-American, the first person of Asian-American descent, and the first graduate of an HBCU (Historically Black College and University) to be sworn in as Vice President of the United States of America. As she said in her election acceptance speech, she "may be the first, but [she] will not be the last." Kamala Harris has spent her life breaking glass ceilings.

Born on October 20, 1964 in Oakland, California, Harris is the daughter of immigrants. Her father was born in Jamaica and her mother was born in India. After her parents divorced, Harris and her younger sister Maya were raised by their mother, Shyamala Gopalan Harris. Harris recalls she "had a stroller-eye view of the Civil Rights movement" as she went with her mother to marches. These early experiences inspired her to make it her life's work to fight against injustice.

While growing up in Oakland, she was immersed in both Indian and African American culture. Her mother took Harris to spend time with her grandparents in India during the summer but also made sure her girls were connected to their African American roots. Harris noted in her autobiography, "My mother understood very well that she was raising two black daughters… She knew that her adopted homeland would see Maya and me as black girls and she was determined to make sure we would grow into confident, proud black women."

After high school, Harris attended Howard University, a HBCU in Washington, D.C. She then received her law degree from the University of California Hastings College of the Law in San Francisco and began her career in the Alameda County District Attorney's Office. In 2003, Harris was elected as the District Attorney of the City and County of San Francisco.

As a lawyer, Harris immediately began breaking glass ceilings. In 2010, Harris was elected as the first African American and first woman to serve as California's Attorney General. While Attorney General, she married lawyer Doug Emhoff and became stepmother—or "Momala," as they named her—to his two children. In 2016, she was elected as a Senator for California, becoming only the second African American woman to ever be elected to the Senate in U.S. history. When speaking to *The Washington Post* in 2019, Harris spoke about how politicians should not have to fit into boxes because of the color of their skin or their background, saying, "My point was: I am who I am. I'm good with it. You might need to figure it out, but I'm fine with it."

While in the Senate, Harris served on two powerful committees: the Intelligence Committee and the Judiciary Committee. As the committees dealt with important issues—such as the investigation into Russian influence and meddling in the 2016 election and judicial appointments to the Supreme Court—Harris became known as a sharp, aggressive questioner who could unnerve opposing witnesses.

In 2019, Harris launched her campaign for President of the United States. While she did not win the Democratic primary, she proved that she was capable of taking on an even larger leadership role in the United States. Because of her commitment to fighting injustice, her eloquence, and capabilities for leadership and governance, the Democratic Party's Presidential candidate Joseph R. Biden chose Harris as his running mate. This pick made Harris the fourth woman on a major party's national ticket and the second African American on a presidential ticket.

On the evening of November 7, 2020, standing on an outdoor stage in Wilmington, Delaware, Harris—wearing a suit in suffrage white—spoke to a crowd of cheering Americans about the work women have done, and continue to do, in the United States. "When [my mother] came here from India at the age of 19, maybe she didn't quite imagine this moment," said Harris. "But she believed so deeply in an America where a moment like this is possible. So, I'm thinking about her and about the generations of women—Black women, Asian, White, Latina, and Native American women throughout our nation's history who have paved the way for this moment tonight. Women who fought and sacrificed so much for equality, liberty, and justice for all, including the Black women, who are too often overlooked, but so often prove that they are the backbone of our democracy… But while I may be the first woman in this office, I won't be the last. Because every little girl watching tonight sees that this is a country of possibilities. And to the children of our country, regardless of your gender, our country has sent you a clear message: Dream with ambition, lead with conviction, and see yourself in a way that others might not see you, simply because they've never seen it before."

This article appears courtesy of the National Women's History Museum.

TRACING THE ROOTS OF WOMEN ON WALL STREET

The history of female achievement in the world of finance predates most of the industry's founding institutions, but women have always had to fight for recognition —a struggle that continues to this day

By Sheri J. Caplan

A buttonwood tree that once stood in lower Manhattan symbolizes the formal beginning of what would later become the New York Stock Exchange. There, in 1792, 24 men met below its branches and signed an agreement that established a new market for a more orderly system of buying and selling securities. No women numbered among them.

Even then, however, many women were participating in the formation of the young nation's capital structure. They did so in various ways. Some invested in government securities and bank shares—Abigail Adams, for example, secured large gains through her financial activities. Moreover, women comprised 61 percent of investors in the 1759–60 Pennsylvania Indian Commission Loan, and they represented 11 percent of stockholders of the Insurance Company of North America between 1792 and 1799.

Women also took part in the colonial economy by directly engaging in commerce, despite certain legal restrictions. As early as the 1600s, many women who were single or widowed managed small businesses as "she-merchants" and "deputy husbands." During the American Revolution, personal necessity and patriotic duty encouraged women to take a more active role in managing financial matters. Women helped raise funds for the Continental Army and took care of their families' farms and businesses while their husbands fought in the war. These responsibilities raised their confidence, broadened their abilities, and gave them a sense of empowerment—even if short-lived. Their experience foreshadowed what would become a recurrent theme underscoring the historical relationship between American women and finance: political or personal necessity may foster financial empowerment, but it is not always warmly welcomed, easily endured, ultimately appreciated, or long lasting.

As the country entered the 19th century, it was still believed that a woman's place was in the home. While women remained entrenched in their domestic duties, the country's financial

217

infrastructure matured. The invention of the telegraph in 1844, the rise of industrialization, and federal spending during the Civil War lavished riches on Wall Street and gave way to the Gilded Age. By then, the term "Wall Street" had become symbolic of the nation's securities market, which attracted both male and female investors. The era also provided the backdrop for a few women to pursue professional financial paths as they sought their share of the Gilded Age's riches.

Victoria Woodhull and Hetty Green are two of the better-known women in financial history. Woodhull, also the first woman to run for U.S. president, and her sister Tennessee Claflin had made the acquaintance of the business magnate Commodore Vanderbilt. The sisters aimed to get rich, and Woodhull wanted to fund her political aspirations. They opened the first female-owned brokerage in the heart of lower Manhattan in 1870. More keen on courting publicity than analyzing earnings, their firm lasted only a few years, and they were largely dismissed as a joke.

Hetty Green, dubbed "The Witch of Wall Street," is usually regarded as little more than a wealthy heiress and a miserly eccentric. Typically shrouded in a black veil and shabby attire, her fashion choices and dour nature did nothing to help her image. But her knowledge of money matters, which she gleaned at a young age by immersing herself in the financial news of the day, later enabled her to vastly increase her fortune through shrewd investments. The unfortunate nickname bestowed upon her by the public has concealed her keen financial mind and participation in key financial dealings of the times.

Another woman of the same era goes for the most part unnoticed. The daughter of a former slave, Maggie Walker grew up in Richmond, Virginia, and recognized as a young woman the importance of financial literacy and empowerment, particularly for Black women. She founded the St. Luke Penny Savings Bank in 1903. Her professional legacy, although not based in Manhattan or primarily in securities, endures to a much greater extent than that of her otherwise better-known counterparts. The entity that she founded lasted into the 21st century as the country's longest continually owned and operated African American bank.

The business dealings of these women helped to draw the attention of other women to finance and raised public scrutiny of whether a woman "belonged" on Wall Street, but did not give rise to an influx of women financial leaders. Not until wartime did American women make further significant headway in finance.

The First World War provided the watershed moment at which more women were introduced to finance—again, personal necessity and patriotic duty coincided to make this happen. In this case, it was the women who powered the Liberty Bond sales during the First World War who deserve much of the credit. They focused public attention on the skills and prowess of women and broadened the financial vocabulary of the volunteers and the public at large.

Soon, many of the women who had once worked on the bond drives became the first women to enter the expanding commercial banking workforce. Although professional networking is often thought of as a modern-day development, the first organizations for women in finance originated in 1921 with the beginnings

Previous pages: The Fearless Girl statue confronts the New York
Stock Exchange. Opposite: Victoria Woodhull, who co-founded
a brokerage firm with her sister in 1870 and went on to run for
U.S. president two years later—the first woman to do so.
Above: Female employees gather after another busy day
at the New York Stock Exchange, 1944.

of the Association of Bank Women and the formation of the
Women's Bond Club. According to rumor, a woman even sought
membership on the New York Stock Exchange in 1927, 40 years
before female membership became a reality.

Women made inroads, particularly in commercial banking,
during the interwar years. Isabel Benham became the first female
railroad analyst in 1934 and embarked on a successful career that
spanned six decades. Mary Roebling became the first woman
president of a major commercial bank, Trenton Trust, in 1937.

When the Second World War came, a familiar story unfolded.
Women answered the country's call to duty and even filled empty
posts on the trading floor of the New York Stock Exchange, but were
booted out when the war ended and men returned home.

In the ensuing decades, however, both a booming economy
and a growing acceptance of women's professional roles helped
power further progress. From the 1950s through the 1970s,
both Wall Street and American women staked their positions

Above: Helen Hanzelin becomes the first woman to work on
the trading floor of the New York Stock Exchange in 1943.
Opposite: Muriel Siebert, pictured in 1985, was the first
woman to purchase a seat on the exchange in 1967.

amid a changing landscape. A few intrepid leaders broke new ground at the crossroads. Of particular note are Mary Roebling, who became the first woman governor of the American Stock Exchange in 1958, and Julia Montgomery Walsh and Phyllis Peterson, who in 1965 became the first women members there. In 1967, Muriel Siebert became the first woman to purchase a seat on the New York Stock Exchange.

By the late 1960s, the investor base had become increasingly democratized, and the WASPish preserve of Wall Street had consequently begun to fade. Women pursued their careers against the backdrop of the women's liberation movement and other calls for societal change. Nevertheless, Wall Street could still be characterized in 1970 as "a feminist organizer's Waterloo [because of] the tendency for its female minority elite to grin and bear the system."

When the economy boomed in the 1980s, Wall Street gained a measure of popular fascination. For the first time, women numbered among its stars. Elaine Garzarelli, who predicted the 1987 market crash, and Abby Joseph Cohen, who foresaw a prolonged economic expansion and bull market run during the 1990s, became household names. Other women, however, faced inhospitable workplaces. Beginning in 1996, the first gender-based class-action lawsuits were brought against major Wall Street firms and focused public attention on the way some women were treated in the financial industry. For the first time, women in finance had gone from quietly seeking to advance their personal careers to becoming more vocal and challenging the status quo.

By the turn of the 21st century, an amalgam of political, legal, economic, and cultural advances raised female professional aspirations. Wall Street women now embarked on engineering their own careers, forging strong identities, and advocating for a greater examination of gender-based inequities in the financial industry. Overtly hostile workplaces largely disappeared, and firms stepped up their attempts to increase workforce diversity and encourage significant mentoring.

In the public sector, many of the leading regulators of the financial-services industry have been women in recent years. However, the corner suites of Wall Street firms remain lonely places for women. They remain underrepresented at senior ranks and endure a significant pay gap within the industry. In the aftermath of the 2008 financial downturn, they shouldered a disproportionate share of industry layoffs even though pundits questioned whether the crisis would have occurred at all had they occupied more positions of power.

The roots of women on Wall Street run deep. Recognizing female accomplishments in finance may further accelerate their ascent by inspiring others, dispelling outdated notions of female inadequacy in this realm, and emphasizing the importance of financial literacy for everyone.

This article appears courtesy of the National Women's History Museum.

LEADING WITH AN INCLUSIVE ETHOS

Deloitte is committed to fostering an
inclusive culture where everyone feels that
they can connect, belong, and grow

"Diversity is like being asked to the party, inclusion is being asked to dance," explains Terri Cooper, the Chief Inclusion Officer at Deloitte, as she discusses the company's journey.

Deloitte has been helping shape corporate America's inclusion landscape since 1993, when it became the first professional services organization to establish women's and diversity initiatives. Since then, Deloitte has been named on numerous best-of lists for diversity and inclusion, and continues to innovate. It launched Inclusion Councils, which connect professionals from different identities and backgrounds to engage on topics that matter to them. It hosted an inaugural Inclusion Summit for 800 of its professionals to learn from one another and develop skills to be an inclusive leader. Deloitte also produces leading research that provides insights and informs conversations for their clients and the marketplace.

The organization and its employees are proud of their achievements but don't want to stop there in their efforts to cultivate an inclusive culture. "Professionals are encouraged to demonstrate inclusive behaviors and act as allies to one another," says Cooper. "Deloitte has six traits of inclusive leadership – commitment, curiosity, collaboration, cognizance of bias, cultural intelligence, and courage – and all of these have been embedded throughout the organization."

Deloitte's recent research, *The State Of Inclusion 2019*, looked into bias in the workplace and showed that, while 77 percent of people felt their workplace was inclusive, 64 percent felt they had experienced bias in the past year. Such biases are often subtle and indirect, but they can have an impact on morale and productivity. To advance inclusion, Deloitte is focused on small daily interactions in order to find ways to inspire and model inclusive behavior.

"We found that 92 percent of people consider themselves allies, meaning that they want to support those who are different to them," says Cooper. "So we are looking to find ways for people to connect. Our Inclusion Councils are one way that we have been able to facilitate that. We also talk to them about the leadership we want people to bring to their team and are very open about our expectations."

That's because inclusion matters. Not just in social and ethical terms, but also to ensure that a company achieves its potential. Numerous studies have shown that demographic diversity generates higher levels of creativity, reduces risk, and improves financial performance. "If you have a room of people who look the same and come from the same background, they can have a very limited lens to view things through," says Cooper. "Having a host of people from different backgrounds, who are actively engaged, enables an organization to achieve significant innovation."

Being a professional services firm, Deloitte's professionals are in the office and at the client sites. "We try to create an inclusive environment in both of those places," says Cooper. "One thing we have learned in the past 25 years is that you have to stay laser-focused. You can't assume this will maintain its own momentum, and you don't take your foot off the pedal. It's not ingrained in your thinking unless you are acting on it on a daily basis."
www.deloitte.com

A PURPOSE YOU CAN BANK ON

BMO's mission to benefit the worlds of business and community alike has always informed the bank's promotion of equality

"I've worked in energy, telecoms and a number of different industries, and although the commitment of diversity and inclusion was strong through those past experiences, I must say that BMO stands out," says Tracie Morris, U.S. Chief Human Resources Officer at BMO Financial Group. "BMO has taken diversity and inclusion a step further through its efforts to provide intentional pathways of growth and development for women."

BMO was founded some 200 years ago in Montreal, Canada, and the bank has always prided itself on establishing strong relationships with employees and customers alike in the knowledge that diversity and inclusion help it better reflect the needs, goals, and perspectives of different communities.

Now North America's eighth largest bank by assets, BMO serves more than 12 million customers, providing personal and commercial banking, wealth management, and investment services. It has operations across Canada, the US, and select global markets in Europe, Asia, the Middle East, and South America, and in its 2019 financial year the company earned a net income of $5.76 billion on revenues of $22.77 billion—both up by 6 percent on 2018 figures.

BMO fosters a workplace culture in which all of its 45,000 employees feel included and empowered. In 1957, BMO employee Mary Pollock made the news by becoming the first woman in Canadian banking history to be appointed to a management position, and today more than half of its US and Canada employees are female. The bank is also making good progress to maintain and exceed its target of 40-50 percent representation of women in senior leadership roles, with 40 percent of its current executive-level managers being women.

This focus on equality applies to its customers and clients as well as its employees. Gender inequality creates barriers to economic success, which is why the company runs BMO for Women, a scheme that provides financing for women-owned businesses, creates innovative educational platforms, and sponsors organizations that support women entrepreneurs.

To ensure that access to capital and credit isn't a stumbling block for female entrepreneurs, in 2014 BMO set a goal to loan $2 billion to women-owned businesses by November 2017. In 2018, it went one better and released $3 billion in credit available to women business owners across Canada over a three-year period. One beneficiary of the scheme was Véronique Lecaul, co-founder of the Vancouver-based biotechnology company AbCellera. BMO played a meaningful role in helping the business build a custom lab facility. The company has since expanded to more than 75 employees and now has its eyes set on becoming a multi-billion-dollar Canadian biotech firm.

It's an ethos that extends into BMO's customer outreach. The bank champions a "purpose to boldly grow the good in business and life"—a commitment that informs its efforts to promote an inclusive society and economic prosperity for women, both in the workplace and in the community. To help close the financial literacy gap for women, for instance, BMO has developed training programs for its client-facing employees on how to support female customers and address their specific pressures and concerns. It has also created a series of podcasts called Her Money, Her Way to inform women about a wide array of finance-related topics. Looking ahead, BMO plans to focus further on what it can do for women in the communities that it serves to ensure that more join the bank ready for positions of leadership. As Morris explains: "From interns to senior leaders, we want more women to be attracted to BMO as their employer of choice."
www.bmo.com

ESSENTIAL INTELLIGENCE

Specializing in financial information and analytics,
S&P Global believes that business can only gain from
having diverse voices at every level of management

S&P Global is rooted in financial information and analytics, providing the market intelligence that allows companies, governments, and individuals to make decisions with conviction. With so much data at its fingertips, the company is uniquely placed to understand the importance of workplace diversity, something that has been embedded in S&P Global's own practices under CEO Doug Peterson. "Leaders across the globe recognize that we benefit from having diversity of voices around the table," says Annette O'Hanlon, the Chief Corporate Responsibility and Diversity Officer. "We know that different perspectives bring new ideas to the discussion and help find solutions. As our culture has evolved, we continue to advance our diversity, equity, and inclusion (DEI) practices, signalling to the rest of the company and the outside world that DEI is important and valued. This permeates throughout the company."

The self-reinforcing nature of successful diversity policies can be seen in the series of economic and business reports created by S&P Global researchers and economists for its international audience. These have titles such as "The Financial Future Is Female" and "When Women Lead, Firms Win," and are comprehensive studies analyzing the benefits of diversity, grouped under its #ChangePays campaign (the launch of which, with S&P Global's U.S. Chief Economist Beth Ann Bovino, is pictured opposite). "Through this work, we've established partnerships with local and national organizations, such as the Progressive Policy Institute's Mosaic Project, to publish research and share our insights around women's impact on economic growth," said Darlene Rosenkoetter, Global Head of Government Affairs & Public Policy. "We continue to celebrate the changes we are seeing in government, with more women in primary leadership roles than ever before, and to engage with policymakers to promote the best practices we've illuminated through our research."

A recent report— "Something's Gotta Give"—looked in particular at the impacts of Covid-19 on family-leave policies and women workers. In these areas, S&P Global had already made considerable in-roads. Its "people first" HR philosophy had seen it introduce a number of forward-thinking policies such as extended parental leave and unlimited compassionate leave, which resonated with young people trying to balance life and work.

During Covid-19, S&P Global's existing employee networks were a considerable help for people needing support and a sense of united purpose. "We have our ERGs—employee-resource groups—for all of our affinity groupings and some of these have been in place for many years, the oldest being our women's network," says O'Hanlon. "The membership of these groups has grown and, even virtually, they provide a real connectivity for the organization. We facilitated a series of events, panel discussions, and speaker series with internal and external leaders on racial justice and gender. These were heartfelt, courageous conversations, and we benefited from having them, especially in this remote-working environment, as people felt supported, cared for, and listened to."

S&P Global is working to advance a focus on ESG (environmental, social, and governance), including the diversity of the workforce. With a global lens, and regional and country nuances, advancing DEI is a priority. "As you can imagine for a company that deals in data insight, we monitor and track so much of this information that we have continual feedback to use as we enhance and improve," says O'Hanlon. "We are proud of the progress we have made, but we understand our responsibility to continue our efforts. This work is of the utmost importance, and DEI is central to our values and our commitment to employees. We are committed to creating an inclusive workplace where our people feel a sense of belonging and can grow and thrive."
www.spglobal.com

THE WOMEN OF NASA

Women have played an essential role in the functions of NASA for almost a century, as exemplified by the administration's many female trailblazers

The beginnings of NASA can be traced back to 1915 with the creation of the National Advisory Committee for Aeronautics (NACA), which started as an advisory committee to the president. In 1920, the NACA expanded with its first research and testing facility, the Langley Aeronautical Laboratory, in Hampton, Virginia. It continued to grow and boomed during the Second World War, testing new aircraft, including supersonic flight. After the Soviet Union launched the first artificial satellite, Sputnik 1, in 1957, the US feared they would fall behind in technology. The following year, the NACA became the National Aeronautics and Space Administration, otherwise known as NASA.

Women have been an integral part of the NACA and subsequently NASA operations since 1922. They have played important roles, such as mathematician, computer, astronaut, engineer, and supervisors, have made lasting impacts, and helped land a man on the moon. As of 2012, women made up one third of all employees, including 30 percent of supervisors and 20 percent of engineers. And as of 2017, 37 percent of new hires were female and 50 percent of the newest class of astronauts were women. While these numbers may sound small, this is a significant increase in female employees at NASA compared to the previous few decades.

In 1935, the first group of female "human computers" were hired. Before electronic computers, all mathematical equations and computations would be done by hand by people, often known as human computers. With the advent of the Second World War, many male employees at NACA left to fight overseas. More and more women were needed to fill their roles, and soon African American women were hired to help with the shortfall.

These African American women were sent to a segregated computing section known as the West Area Computing Unit (which featured at the center of the 2016 movie *Hidden Figures*). In April 1942, a memo was passed around stating that, "The engineers admit themselves that the girl computers do the work more rapidly and accurately than they could." The women computers were becoming increasingly valuable and doing incredible work along the way.

The first woman hired by the NACA was Pearl Young in 1922. She was originally hired to the Instrument Research Division, which "designed, constructed, calibrated, and repaired virtually all instrumentation carried on aircraft." She quickly became an integral part of the organization and revolutionized the way technical manuals and papers were written and dispersed. By the time Young retired from NASA in 1961, she had served as the Chief Technical Editor for close to 20 years. In that role, "she insisted that all reports be checked and rechecked for consistency, logical analysis, and absolute accuracy."

Opposite: Mary Jackson, who became NASA's first Black woman engineer in 1958, pictured at the Langley Research Center in 1977.

"You tell me when you want it and where you want it to land, and I'll do it backwards and tell you where to take off"

—Katherine Johnson

Kitty O'Brien Joyner joined the NACA in 1939 as an electrical engineer after she graduated from the University of Virginia (UVA). She was the first woman to graduate from the engineering program at UVA and the first female engineer at the NACA. Joyner spent her career working in and managing wind tunnels and supersonic flight research.

Vera Huckel started work at the NACA in 1939. At the time, very few women worked as computers. By 1945 she was a section head in charge of up to 17 women. Through the years she also worked as mathematician, aerospace engineer, and supervisory mathematician.

Huckel's main area of work was in the Dynamic Loads Division. There, she was one of the only female computers. She worked with the mathematics and testing of sonic booms in supersonic flight. Often, she would travel to the deserts in the western United States and work out the mathematics of the test flights. If she was not able to travel, the numbers and test results would be sent to her in Virginia, where she was the only one trusted to do the math. Additionally, Huckel wrote the first program for the first electronic computer at NASA.

Dorothy Vaughan worked previously as a math teacher but heard that the NACA was recruiting and jumped at the chance in 1943. In 1949, she became the first African American manager at the NACA as section head of the West Area Computing Unit. When NASA was created in 1958, Vaughan joined the Integrated Analysis and Computation Division, and became an expert at the computing language FORTRAN. She even taught male engineers how to use the computers.

Kathryn Peddrew also joined the NACA in 1943. She was originally hired as a chemist but when the NACA found out she was African American they sent her to join the West Area Computing Unit. Peddrew spent over 40 years working for the NACA/NASA, mainly in the Instrument Research Division.

Mary Jackson began working at the NACA and the West Area Computing Unit in 1951. By 1953, she had joined a group working on the Supersonic Pressure Tunnel. While there, Jackson was encouraged to enter a training program run by UVA in order to become an engineer. She had to gain permission from the City of Hampton, Virginia to take the class because classes were segregated at the time.

In 1958, Jackson became NASA's first African American female engineer. She spent her career working on supersonic research, finally retiring in 1985 after 34 years with the administration.

In 1953, Katherine Johnson joined the NACA. She worked for the West Area Computing Unit for a short while before joining the Maneuver Loads Branch of the Flight Research Division.

Opposite, top: Human computers at work at the Langley Research Center, 1955. Opposite, bottom: Electrical engineer Kitty Joyner, 1952.

There she analyzed data from flight tests. In 1960, she became the first woman in the division to receive author credit on a paper titled "Determination of Azimuth Angle at Burnout for Placing a Satellite over a Selected Earth Position."

Her work was directly related to the space program as she analyzed flight trajectory and landing for multiple flights including Alan Shepard's Freedom 7 and John Glenn's Friendship 7. In the early days of electronic computing, she would double check the equations done by the electronic computer. Many astronauts, including John Glenn, relied on her for correct calculations. As Johnson said, "You tell me when you want it and where you want it to land, and I'll do it backwards and tell you where to take off. That was my forte." Johnson was crucial in calculating the mathematics for the lunar landing and in the rendezvous of the command module and the lunar module.

Johnson retired in 1986 after more than 30 years with the organization. She has received many awards and honors throughout and after her career, including the Presidential Medal of Freedom in 2015; having a building named after her at the Langley Research Center (Katherine G. Johnson Computational Research Facility) in 2016; and having a movie produced and book written about her accomplishments.

These women, and many more, changed the way NASA was run and the way women in mathematics were viewed. At one time, women weren't considered to have the aptitude to be engineers at NASA, but these women proved the men wrong and went on to great things. They taught men how to use electronic computers and put a man on the moon. They proved that women engineers and mathematicians are not to be underestimated and continue to inspire the next generation of girls and boys.

This article appears courtesy of the National Women's History Museum.

Opposite: NASA engineer Mary Jackson at work in
1980. Above: NASA mathematician Katherine Johnson,
whose calculations were vital to the success of the
Friendship 7 mission in 1962.

MOTHERS OF INVENTION

Minesoft operates a giant database of patent
information and makes web-based products
for intellectual property research

When Minesoft's founder Ann Chapman first looked into the history of female innovators in science, she was appalled to discover that for decades women were simply not allowed to register patents. That had to be done by a male relative or colleague. "At Minesoft we gather together all the patents filed all over the world in searchable databases," she says. "When I looked at the landscape of patents to see when the first women inventors began to appear, I was amazed to find women weren't allowed to own patents in their own name. That includes many famous female inventors. Things only really started to change after women won the right to vote."

Minesoft's database of 140 million searchable patents is growing all the time—by 50,000 per week from China alone. Female innovators are now far better represented. "Historically, we can see that women often invent things associated with improving women's lives," says Chapman. "Tools for household cleaning like washing machines, tumble dryers, and even various kinds of brooms and dustpans. Even today, female innovators are improving the home, health, and education."

Most recently these include ingenious, low-cost inventions for use in developing countries. Stanford University alumna Jane Chen and product designer Honey Bajaj's came up with the Embrace Warmer: a blanket that keeps premature or underweight babies warm outside of hospital. Harvard graduate Jessica O. Matthews' Sockket is a soccer ball that converts mechanical energy generated by play into electricity that can then be used to power lights or recharge batteries. Ex-Harvard entrepreneur Elizabeth Sharpf and her team invented a low-cost sanitary pad made from agricultural by-products such as banana tree fibers that are plentiful in countries like Rwanda.

Minesoft helps advance such innovation by making its databases available to underdeveloped countries at accessible rates. "That means that they can get access to this critical information on inventions," says Chapman, "which they can adapt to their environments. We spread innovation around the world through our own database products, which handle huge amounts of data much faster than was possible when we came into the industry. We can analyze hundreds of thousands of patents in seconds. If you are looking to develop something, you have to be able to refer to the history of that field; and we offer access to a huge body of existing innovation going back hundreds of years."

The rise of women innovators is tied to education as well as emancipation. Chapman cites the importance of science or engineering degrees as a prerequisite to becoming a patent attorney, which partly explains why women are under-represented.

"You find far fewer women in this field; and that's partly because there still aren't as many girls doing science in school and beyond as there are boys," says Chapman. "Those early decisions make such a difference and it's only now that girls are being encouraged widely to pursue science and engineering. But 35 years ago when I started, I was often the only woman in the room; and that is changing. There are more and more women in this field, coming through different routes. At Minesoft, I want to ensure we provide opportunities for young women and mentor them. My generation had to really fight for our position, so we want to give them the support they need in what is still a man's world."

www.minesoft.com

A WORLD LEADER IN WOMEN'S ISSUES

Through initiatives such as the Office of Global Women's Issues,
the U.S. Department of State has long worked to promote
women's equality at home and abroad

With its establishment in 1789, the agency now known as the Department of State became the first federal agency in the United States. It works on behalf of the American people to promote and demonstrate democratic values and advance a free, peaceful, and prosperous world. For more than a century the Department of State has played a significant role in promoting women's equality at home and around the world. In fact, it was the 43rd Secretary of State—Bainbridge Colby—who certified the 19th Amendment as part of the United States Constitution in 1920.

Women have played, and continue to play, a significant role in advancing the State Department's mission to lead America's foreign policy through diplomatic engagement and advocacy. In 1922, Lucile Atcherson became the first woman to join the Department of State's Foreign Service. Thousands of women have followed in Lucile's footsteps, and women now account for more than 46 percent of the department's workforce.

In 1995, the U.S. Department of State created a special office dedicated to women's empowerment, now known as the Secretary's Office of Global Women's Issues. The office, currently led by an Ambassador-at-Large for Global Women's Issues, spearheads the State Department's efforts to promote women's full and meaningful political, economic, and social participation in society.

Since 2007, the U.S. Secretary of State has celebrated International Women's Day by recognizing extraordinary women from around the world with the International Women of Courage Award. More than 130 women from over 70 countries have been honored for their advocacy of the promotion and protection of human rights, often at great personal risk. In 2017, the United States became the first country to pass comprehensive, national legislation enshrining the principles of United Nations Security Council Resolution 1325 on women, peace, and security to enfranchise women politically around the world.

From the women, peace, and security agenda to cross-cutting issues such as stopping gender-based violence, promoting women's leadership, and combating violent extremism, the Office of Global Women's Issues works to integrate women's empowerment into every element of the Department of State's mission and diplomacy around the world.

The Department of State has resolved to remain steadfast in its commitment to women's empowerment over the next 100 years. While women have made massive strides over the past century, there is still much to achieve to ensure women everywhere are viewed as full and equal members of society, and the State Department is committed to leading international advocacy for women's equality and empowerment around the world.

Opposite: Lucile Atcherson, the first woman to join the
ranks of the Department of State's diplomatic service
in 1922. Above: A recipient holds her International
Women of Courage Award.

THE CHOICE OF A NEW GENERATION

For more than 60 years, PepsiCo has led the way in diversity and inclusion—and the company is using its scope and influence to bring this progressive ethos to the international market that it serves

PepsiCo has always understood the importance of diversity. This is, after all, the first major American corporation to create an all African-American salesforce, to appoint an African-American vice-president, and one of the first that elected a woman to the board in the 1950s. Today, the company's diversity award is named after one of those pioneers—one-time VP of special markets Harvey Russell, a former salesman who rose through the ranks—as PepsiCo continues a drive for diversity that has already lasted five decades.

"We want to represent our consumers through our workforce," says Tina Bigalke, PepsiCo's Global Chief Diversity and Engagement Officer. "In 2016 we set these ambitious goals to achieve gender balance—parity and pay—in our ranks by 2025. We have made steady progress since then. We are currently at 41 percent female managers, and there is less than a 1 percent pay gap between men and women, and between employees of different races."

The global pandemic since 2020 has been challenging for the entire economy. "In particular, COVID-19 highlighted the inequities in our society," says Bigalke. "For our North American employees who are parents, we've provided educational support, virtual tutoring, and dependent care reimbursements. But we've also seen how the pandemic disproportionately affected Black and Hispanic communities, and we needed to step back and determine how corporate America can help to overcome this."

Part of that is ensuring that diversity is embedded in PepsiCo's practices. "As we bring in diverse talent, we're on this journey of ensuring that our employees move through that talent life cycle," says Bigalke. "However, we also want to use our scale and scope to address the diverse communities we serve." As well as improving Black representation at senior levels, PepsiCo has committed to invest more than $845 million over five years to uplift Black and Hispanic communities and businesses, and increase U.S. Black and Hispanic managerial representation at PepsiCo.

As an international brand, PepsiCo has also been active in using its scope and influence to support farmers in the developing world. "For us, women in agriculture are a significant focus," says Bigalke. "They face extraordinary hardships and typically don't have the access to capital that male farmers do. In 2020, we entered into a new, $20 million initiative with USAID to support women across our agricultural supply chain; something that drives business results, while strengthening the communities where we live and work, creating a more sustainable food system."

PepsiCo has also committed to providing 12,000 hours of mentoring to help Million Women Mentors, an initiative to spark the interest and confidence of women and girls to pursue STEM (science, technology, engineering, and math) careers. "It's all part of our aim to promote female voices," says Bigalke. "For instance, our premium water brand, LIFEWTR, has championed women in the arts, using bold designs from female artists around the world on its labels." Another PepsiCo brand, Stacy's Pita Chips, created Stacy's Rise Project, to connect and empower women business owners.

Bigalke has a 20-year history in human resources and sees HR as crucial for advancing a pipeline of diverse talent. "Study after study has explained the results of how diverse teams can improve innovation, growth, and market share," she says. "And there are also demographic shifts around the world that necessitate a company strategy that is able to bring in and encourage different types of voices to be heard, valued, and respected."

www.pepsico.com
www.pepsico.com/about/diversity-and-engagement

Above: Members of the Women Airforce Service Pilots, which
was established in August 1943. Opposite: A recruitment poster
encouraging women to join the Women's Army Corps, c. 1943.

BREAKING THE SERVICES' BARRIERS

The Defense Department Advisory Committee on Women
in the Services has been supporting women in the U.S. Armed
Forces since it was set up in 1951, but the history of women
in the military dates back well before then

Women's service has been integral to the success of the U.S. military. Hundreds of years before women were allowed to serve, they aided the fight by ensuring troops were fed and clothed. The U.S. military's reliance on women as nurses and the wartime need for additional support opened the door for women's permanent place in the military and, despite restrictions on their service and roles over the years, women have continued to succeed and break barriers.

Most notably, long before women were granted the right to vote in the U.S., they were serving in our nation's military. Women's service in the military helped propel the suffrage movement forward and convinced many Americans, including President Woodrow Wilson and members of Congress, that women deserved the right to vote.

During the American Revolution, women provided support to the battlefield by serving as nurses, cooks, laundresses, seamstresses, and water bearers. Some women served as saboteurs and spies who aided American troops by garnering important information, relaying messages, or carrying contraband. During the Civil War, nurses provided medical care to both Union and Confederate troops. Several hundred women disguised themselves as men to serve on the battlefield. Although women had no official role in the U.S. military, their service was vital to these war efforts. Women's continued success serving as nurses, in particular during the Spanish-American War, led to the establishment of the Army Nurse Corps in 1901 and the Navy Nurse Corps in 1908.

In 1917, the Navy opened enlistment for women to perform clerical work. However, women also served as mechanics, truck drivers, camouflage designers, cryptographers, telephone operators, and translators. In 1918, the Secretary of the Navy allowed women to enlist in the Marine Corps for the first time. The size and scope of women's roles greatly expanded during the First World War. More than 35,000 women served during this time, and nearly 400 women were killed in action. The scope of women's service to the nation during this conflict foreshadowed their involvement in the Second World War and the formation of the Defense Advisory Committee on Women in the Services (DACOWITS).

During the Second World War, the need for women's service expanded beyond nursing and clerical work with the establishment of the Women's Army Auxiliary Corps (later the Women's Army Corps), the Women Airforce Service Pilots, the Navy's Women Accepted for Volunteer Emergency Service, the Marine Corps Women's Reserve, and the Coast Guard Women's Reserve. Following the conclusion of the Second World War, President Truman drastically changed the U.S. military by signing the Women's Armed Services Integration Act in 1948, granting women permanent status in both the regular and Reserve forces.

"Long before women were granted the right to vote in the U.S., they were serving in our nation's military"

During the Korean War, the DACOWITS was established by the Secretary of Defense to advise on the recruitment of women into the U.S. military. By the start of the war, approximately 22,000 women were serving in the U.S. military, and by the end of the war a total of 120,000 women served. During the course of the Vietnam War, approximately 7,000 servicewomen served in Southeast Asia.

Modifications to the Women's Armed Services Integration Act in 1967 lifted restrictions, which allowed women to reach more senior officer ranks. In 1973, the U.S. military became an All-Volunteer Force. This significant change to the structure of the military necessitated a greater need for the recruitment of and reliance on women because there were not enough qualified male volunteers. The 1970s also opened the door for women to access additional training and professional development opportunities, the Reserve Officers' Training Corps, and the Military Service Academies.

During the 1980s and 1990s, women continued to gain access to new career fields, which included positions surrounding combat missions and serving on combatant ships. The Persian Gulf War had the largest wartime deployment of women in the history of the U.S. military up until that point, with more than 41,000 women serving in Kuwait. In 1993, the Secretary of Defense lifted restrictions to allow women to fly combat aircraft. The following year, women were permitted to serve on most Navy combatant ships. Throughout the 1990s, women continued to fill mission-critical roles in military engagements, including Operation Desert Storm.

U.S. involvement in Operation Enduring Freedom and Operation Iraqi Freedom changed the way women interacted with direct combat because of the erasure of the traditional battlefield and the wide range of roles women served. Women accounted for greater than 10 percent of the more than 2.7 million service members who deployed to Iraq and Afghanistan from 2001 to 2014. Women's contributions during this time required the U.S. military to reassess the definition of direct ground combat.

The 2010s saw historic expansions in women's opportunities to formally serve in combat. In 2010, the Navy announced it would begin allowing women to serve on nuclear submarines. In 2013, the Department of Defense lifted the ban on women participating in the ground services. As a result of this policy change, military occupations could remain closed to women only by exception and only if approved. That same year, the first Marine Lioness team (the precursor to female engagement teams) formed and deployed to Iraq and Afghanistan. In 2015, the Secretary of Defense announced women would be permitted to apply for all combat units and positions without exception starting in 2016.

As of 2015, women represented approximately 9 percent of the U.S. veteran population, and as of 2019, they represented 17 percent of the U.S. military. Indeed, women have served in some of the most senior roles in the military services—as four-star generals, the commander of a combatant command, and as the acting commanding general of the United States Army Forces Command, among others.

While substantial progress has been made toward gender integration, there is still more to be done. Congress and the Department of Defense continue to make headway to promote and realize full gender integration within the military services, which now include the newly created U.S. Space Force. With the introduction of this new branch, the U.S. military has a rare opportunity to create a gender-inclusive and integrated service at its inception.

As one of the oldest Department of Defense federal advisory committees, DACOWITS continues to provide advice and recommendations on matters and policies relating to the recruitment, retention, employment, integration, well-being, and treatment of servicewomen in the Armed Forces. Since 1951, the Committee has submitted over 1,000 recommendations to the Secretary of Defense for consideration. As of 2019, approximately 98 percent have been either fully or partially adopted by the Department.

Above: Now retired from service, Ann E. Dunwoody was
the first woman to achieve the rank of four-star general
in U.S. military history on November 14, 2008.

THE RIGHTS TO EDUCATION

An agency of the Department of Education, the Office for Civil Rights defends the right of access to education and helps support educational excellence

Created in 1966, the Office for Civil Rights (OCR) is a sub-agency of the U.S. Department of Education that is principally focused on enforcing civil rights laws prohibiting schools from engaging in discrimination on the basis of race, color, national origin, sex, disability, age, or membership in patriotic youth organizations. OCR's mission is to ensure equal access to education and to promote educational excellence through vigorous enforcement of civil rights in the nation's schools.

The office is one of the largest federal civil rights agencies in the United States, with a staff of approximately 560 attorneys, investigators, and other members. The agency can be found in 12 regional offices and in its headquarters in Washington, D.C.

OCR serves student populations facing discrimination and the advocates and institutions promoting systemic solutions to civil rights problems. An important responsibility is resolving complaints of discrimination. Agency-initiated cases—typically called compliance reviews—permit the office to target resources on compliance problems that appear particularly acute. OCR also provides technical assistance to help institutions achieve voluntary compliance with the civil rights laws that it enforces. An important part of this technical assistance is partnerships designed to develop creative approaches to preventing and addressing discrimination.

OCR enforces several federal civil-rights laws that prohibit discrimination in programs or activities that receive federal financial assistance from the Department of Education. Discrimination on the basis of race, color, and national origin is prohibited by Title VI of the Civil Rights Act of 1964; sex discrimination is prohibited by Title IX of the Education Amendments of 1972; discrimination on the basis of disability is prohibited by Section 504 of the Rehabilitation Act of 1973; and age discrimination is prohibited by the Age Discrimination Act of 1975.

These civil rights laws, enforced by OCR, extend to all state education agencies, elementary and secondary school systems, colleges and universities, vocational schools, proprietary schools, state vocational rehabilitation agencies, libraries, and museums that receive U.S. Department of Education funds. Areas covered may include, but are not limited to: admissions, recruitment, financial aid, academic programs, student treatment and services, counseling and guidance, discipline, classroom assignment, grading, vocational education, recreation, physical education, athletics, housing, and employment. OCR also has responsibilities under Title II of the Americans with Disabilities Act of 1990 (prohibiting disability discrimination by public entities, whether or not they receive federal financial assistance).

A complaint of discrimination can be filed by anyone who believes that an education institution that receives federal financial assistance has discriminated against someone on the basis of race, color, national origin, sex, disability, or age. The person or organization filing the complaint need not be a victim of the alleged discrimination, but may complain on behalf of another person or group.

Most of OCR's activities are conducted by its 12 enforcement offices throughout the country. These enforcement offices are organized into four divisions carrying out OCR's core work—preventing, identifying, ending, and remedying discrimination against America's students.

Above: Dr. Bernice Sandler, who died in 2019, was integral
to the creation and passage of the Title IX legislation
that the Office for Civil Rights enforces in educational
establishments and programs across the country.

ON A MISSION TO EDUCATE

Brigham Young University in Utah has been blazing
a trail for equality for more than a century

Some statements resonate through history and remain as relevant today as when first expressed. This is very much the case with Emmeline B. Wells's declaration: "I believe in women, especially thinking women." "This quote sums up an ethos that played a large part in shaping the suffrage movement in Utah," says Aaron Sorenson, Media Relations Manager at Brigham Young University (BYU).

Wells (pictured opposite, top left) was a close friend of national suffragist Susan B. Anthony (pictured overleaf, center) and devoted nearly 30 years of her life towards the suffrage movement in the state of Utah. She was one of the state's very first female voters and was instrumental in founding the Woman Suffrage Association of Utah in 1889.

"In 1912, Wells became the first Utah woman to receive an honorary degree from Brigham Young University, which today is one of the largest private religious universities in the United States," says Sorenson. "Originally established in 1875, BYU is sponsored by The Church of Jesus Christ of Latter-day Saints and located in the state of Utah. Wells, along with many other thinking women who helped shape BYU in its early days were the same women and leaders who influenced the suffrage movement in Utah and won the vote for women long before the 19th Amendment had ever been passed."

Latter-day Saints communities in present-day Utah were settled by pioneers who blazed trails across the United States in search of religious freedom, and their pioneering spirit carried over into politics. Utah was the second territory in the United States to grant suffrage to its female populace and, on February 14 1870, Utah women, many of them with ties to BYU, became the first to vote in a United States election under an equal suffrage law. Reports of women's suffrage being discussed on campus were recorded in

The White and Blue, an early student newspaper at BYU, which ran from 1897 to 1921.

"One of these early suffragists was BYU faculty member Zina Young Williams Card," says Sandra Rogers, International Vice President. "She earned international recognition due to being one of the first women to work in the woman's suffrage movement from the state of Utah. She visited the eastern United States as an ambassador, speaking out for her religious beliefs and women's rights, and she and Wells attended the convention of the National Woman Suffrage Association held in Washington, D.C., in 1879. Also, during that year, Card became the first Dean of Women at BYU and was later appointed to its Board of Trustees in 1918."

When the U.S. federal government used anti-polygamy legislation to rescind Utah's female suffrage in 1887, the Relief Society, a women's organization with The Church of Jesus Christ of Latter-day Saints, provided a ready-made framework for distributing information and initiating action. Those women worked with national suffragists to see their right to vote restored. Utah became the 45th state on January 4, 1896, and suffrage was included in the state constitution.

"Twenty-four years before women throughout the United States would gain voting rights, Utah's women had already won the vote twice," says Rogers. "National suffragists celebrated Utah statehood and there were now three states in the country with equal suffrage for men and women."

Between 1870 and 1920, Utah women could vote, but many other women throughout the United States could not. Utah's pioneer female voters, along with a new generation of enfranchised women, worked to help women across the country enjoy the right to vote. Another influential woman was Susa Young Gates (pictured opposite, top right; and bottom fifth from left), a daughter of The Church of Jesus Christ of Latter-day

Saints' president Brigham Young. She studied at BYU where she eventually founded the music department as a faculty member at the school. From 1891 to 1933, she was a member of the Board of Regents of BYU and, during that time, she also represented Utah at national and international suffrage conventions. "My conviction is that women should have the ballot in every land and clime," she declared. On October 3, 1919, Utah became the 17th state to ratify the proposed amendment, a topic discussed for more than 15 years in BYU's student newspaper.

"Alice Louise Reynolds was the first woman to teach college-level classes at BYU," says Sorenson. "She was also an active Democrat who served as a delegate to the party's national convention and various clubs and groups specifically for women, including the National American Woman Suffrage Association. As a delegate to the National Democratic Convention, Reynolds made a speech in 1920 seconding the nomination for William Gibbs McAdoo for President of the United States. Before, during, and after that time, Reynolds taught English at BYU and served for 19 years as the chairperson on a committee to establish the university's first library. Today, a conference room in BYU's library is named after her."

On November 2, 1920, more than 8 million women across the United States voted in elections for the first time. The *Salt Lake Telegram* reported: "Despite the fact that Utah women have had the right to vote for years, the enthusiasm displayed at the polls revealed the true joyful spirit of the woman voter which is in evidence throughout the nation today."

"That joyful and influential spirit is still part of BYU today," says Rogers. "These women not only helped build up a university and promote suffrage for women in the state of Utah but also left a legacy of thinking women who can still help influence change on a large scale."

www.byu.edu

THINKING BIG IN THE BIG APPLE

One of America's most prestigious universities, NYU
is staying ahead of the curve with an interdisciplinary
approach and a truly diverse global outlook

Although it was founded more than 200 years ago, New York University (NYU) remains at the heart of one of the world's most vibrant cities. As an institution it has always been extremely forward looking and today NYU is an incredibly diverse global university that continues to embody "the city as a classroom"—and not only New York, but cities across the world.

"New York is part of our nerve center," says Lisa Coleman, NYU's Senior Vice President for Global Inclusion and Strategic Innovation. "And, with additional locations in diverse and dynamic cities globally, we are able to immerse students and emerging leaders in local and global interdisciplinary learning, teaching, scholarship, and introduce new research focused on inclusion, innovation, global difference, and global connections."

NYU sends more students abroad and hosts more international students than any other university in the U.S. With two portal degree-granting campuses in Abu Dhabi and Shanghai, 11 global academic centers, research programs in over 25 countries, and more than 50,000 students representing every state in the U.S. and over 133 countries, it provides unparalleled opportunities for global scholarship, teaching, and research.

Since 2000, NYU academics have won five Nobel Prizes and five Pulitzers; 29 have been elected to the National Academy of Sciences and the National Academy of Engineering. Pulitzer prizewinners include Eliza Griswold, from NYU's Arthur L. Carter Journalism Institute (ALCJI), who won the 2019 general nonfiction prize, while Sharon Olds, a faculty member in the Creative Writing Program, won the 2013 Poetry Prize. Nobel laureates include Professor Paul Romer (from NYU's Stern School of Business), who won the 2018 economics prize; while author and journalist Ta-Nehisi Paul Coates (ALCJI) and photographer and curator Deborah Willis (from NYU's Tisch School of the Arts) are recipients of the John D. and Catherine T. MacArthur Foundation Fellowship "Genius" Award.

NYU's outstanding graduates have succeeded across a range of professions, and are celebrated by the university. Ali Stroker, a graduate of NYU's Tisch Drama Department, is the first actress in a wheelchair to appear on Broadway and win a Tony Award. Her success is just one example of NYU's extremely talented alums who are making contributions to society and changing the world.

"Part of NYU's success is its focus on trans/interdisciplinary research and teaching, global diversity, entrepreneurship,

and innovation," says Dr Coleman, "and its particular synthesis of the arts, humanities, engineering, and sciences." NYU's new MakerSpace (Brooklyn) integrates the schools and departments of arts, business, engineering, education, media, and technology; also highlighted in the recently opened NYU-Los Angeles.

Throughout 2020, the university's NYUWomxn100 program will focus on 100 years of varied and complicated histories and representations of women. Well over half of NYU's current leadership team are women, including the Chief Academic Officer, Provost Katherine Fleming. The 2023 graduating class of NYU-Tandon School of Engineering is 46 percent female, roughly double the average for U.S. engineering schools, and its dean, Jelena Kovacevic, is the first woman to lead the school since its founding in 1854.

Part of learning and working at NYU is gaining understanding of how to navigate diverse global and local contexts that Dr Coleman describes as "innovative, messy, and sometimes conflictual." "We experiment with new forms of science, technology, artistry, business, learning, pedagogy, and research," she says. "We enable community members to develop the skillsets to navigate the present, and innovate for our globally interconnected futures."
www.nyu.edu

SHE IS THE FUTURE

For 138 years, the Academy of Our Lady of Peace in San Diego has taught young women to value diversity, equity, and inclusion with a focus on innovation and leadership

Housed in what used to be the Villa Montemar estate in San Diego, the Academy of Our Lady of Peace (OLP) sits atop a hill underneath the perennially blue California sky. As the oldest continually operating women's educational institution in Southern California and the only all-girls' school in San Diego, its mission is the same today as it has been for 138 years.

"The school was established by the Sisters of St. Joseph of Carondelet in 1882," says Dr. Lauren Lek, the Head of School and the first layperson to hold the position. "It was a time when women's education was not at the forefront of people's thoughts. These pioneering Sisters were very entrepreneurial and certainly ahead of their time, real role models for the girls they educated."

Today, OLP takes in 750 students from 82 ZIP codes across San Diego County and from the cross-border region of Mexico. Twenty percent have familial ties to the school, some going back four generations. OLP is blessed by these familial ties such as the ones from generous patrons, Bob and Cheryl Kevane, whose granddaughters (pictured opposite, top left), current students Francesca (left, from the Class of 2022) and Cameron La Marca (right, also Class of 2022) and their aunt Patricia Kevane (who holds the title of Miss OLP from the Class of 1970). The school is fee-paying with robust tuition assistance offerings to ensure access to an OLP education is equitable. OLP girls come from a variety of religious, racial, and social backgrounds and, while they are expected to be part of the school's Catholic community, the school's "Dear Neighbor" philosophy provides an inclusive ethos.

"In France, when the Sisters began in 1650 following the Hundred Years' War," says Dr. Lek, "their intention was to serve the 'dear neighbor without distinction,' according to the needs of society. That idea—of inclusivity and unifying love—persists within the school community and as part of the curriculum from interfaith prayer services, to supporting students with learning differences to co-curricular programs."

Pupils excel in the visual and performing arts and the school has a proactive STEM (science, technology, engineering, math) program, with the result that 40 percent of graduates go on to study STEM fields in college: a remarkable statistic when compared to the national co-ed average of 16 percent. Many

OLP alumnae also excel in the fields of political science and international diplomacy, something that Dr. Lek believes is a result of the school's large number of cross-border students and its commitment to social justice.

"Whether they are in research or innovation, our alumnae are consistently seen working to move humanity forward and making a difference day in and day out," she says. "They are conscientious, caring women who never cease to amaze me. What's remarkable about our school is the feeling of sisterhood. Our girls build each other up, empower, and help one another." Taking into account the holistic picture of the girl is a priority for Dr. Lek, including the pressures on women brought by modern life, which the founding Sisters could not have envisaged.

As for the future, Dr. Lek says she will ensure that OLP remains at the forefront of innovative academic practices to equip the next generation of women to lead and invest in societal needs. "I want every girl to know that whatever discipline she wants to pursue there is a pathway for that. Our world needs her voice to be heard."

www.aolp.org

THINKING ALLOWED

The Emma Willard School, an independent high school for girls
in upstate New York, has fostered intellectual curiosity among its
students for more than two centuries

"When I was visiting as a candidate to lead this school, the most thought-provoking part of my interview process was the questions from the students," says Jenny Rao, Head of School at Emma Willard School in Troy, near Albany in upstate New York. "To this day, three years later, they are the ones who challenge and inspire me the most."

Rao was so impressed by these inquiring and fiercely intelligent teenagers that she ended up putting students' questions center stage in a weekly tradition now known as "Rao Rumbles." Pupils submit questions on everything from the trivial to the profound and the whole school, including inquiring students, gathers on a Friday to hear and discuss the answers.

Students have asked about everything—from Rao's definition of "success" to whether she ever feels less than her happy, vivacious self. One girl wanted to know if it was okay that she didn't have her life already sketched out; another if she had ever grieved someone's death. And Rao's answers are always honest. "We want to model what we expect from our girls," she says. "And that might mean vulnerability, authenticity, and asking questions to which there are sometimes no clear answers. I think in doing so we are not only setting the fabric for incredible learning but also setting the scene for courageous whole hearts that will serve, shake, and shape the world in magnificent ways."

Indeed, it is the development of courage and tenacity that lies at the heart of what this historic girls' boarding school—frequently referred to simply as "Emma"—seeks to do. It all started 206 years ago when women's rights advocate Emma Hart Willard opened a small school for girls in her home in Middlebury, Vermont, offering them a robust education comparable to that of their brothers. After an impressive fundraising campaign, she eventually moved the school to Mount Ida, Troy.

"The very way we were founded continues to define the spirit of this place," says Rao. "Back in 1814, Emma Willard herself was a woman ahead of her time. The education of women was not a popular idea, so she had to fight very hard to get the means to have that idea supported. This school was founded on making history and that continues to propel us forward."

This spirit is reflected in the fact that the school has turned out some impressive alumnae, including many famous names. Elizabeth Cady Stanton, the campaigner for women's suffrage, and the actress and activist Jane Fonda both now belong to the prestigious National Women's Hall of Fame, as does Emma Willard herself.

The glorious collegiate gothic architecture of the 137-acre school campus—constructed in 1910—is popular with film makers (*Scent Of A Woman* and *The Emperor's Club* are among the movies that were partly filmed there) but also key to the school's appreciation of its own history. "When you enter Emma Willard School you immediately get the feeling that you're part of something bigger than yourself," says Rao. "There's a unique spirit simply and solely because of the architecture and the buildings."

This reflects a "serious intent of purpose" among the girls, towards their studies, social justice, and to the big questions of the day, says Rao. But the pupils are well-rounded too. "You'll see our students being adolescent girls and doing similar and light-hearted things that girls should and will do," she says. "But they also think deeply and intellectually and with a full heart about the most pressing problems of the world."
www.emmawillard.org

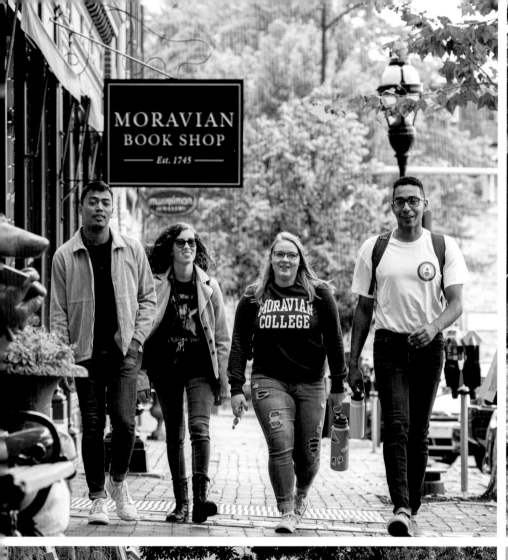

INNOVATE TO EDUCATE

Moravian College's progressive approach is deeply rooted in the trailblazing attitudes of Pennsylvania's pioneering settlers

If she were living as a young lady today, Countess Benigna von Zinzendorf would be regarded as somewhat precocious, in the best possible way. In 1742, at the age of just 16, she founded a school in Germantown, PA—the first in the US to educate girls—at the behest of her father, Count Nikolaus von Zinzendorf of Saxony. At the time, this was a revolutionary concept, promoted by the recently arrived Protestant Moravian settlers who believed in education for all, regardless of gender, financial, or social status.

Over the centuries, the girls' school has evolved into what is now Moravian College, a picturesque private college based in the historic town of Bethlehem, Pennsylvania. Now co-educational, it offers a thoroughly modern curriculum with a mix of liberal arts, sciences, and professional programs. But, 278 years after it was established, those founding principles and rich history still infuse everything the college does. A statue of John Amos Comenius—the philosopher and pedagogue who is widely regarded as the founder of modern, inclusive education—stands in its leafy grounds as a reminder of those values.

"The Moravians who founded the college had this unique idea of education for all, which included men and women, no matter their social status," says Bryon Grigsby, College President. "They felt that you couldn't have an educated society without women being educated, because they were the ones who were going to be the primary teachers of the children."

Indeed, everything at modern-day Moravian College is geared around leveling the playing field. Roughly 25 percent of its students are the first in their family to go to college, and Moravian even set up the first honor society in America dedicated to celebrating those students. On a more practical level, all freshmen are handed a MacBook Pro and an iPad in their first term—which swiftly removes any digital divide between richer and poorer students. Around $40 million is also handed out each year in financial aid.

In addition to offering these practical lifelines, the college is especially proud of its overall warm, welcoming atmosphere, designed to ensure that anybody and everybody can thrive. The modest size of Moravian College—it has just over 2,000 undergraduates and 445 graduate students—makes it a friendly place to study. "There is a strong sense of community," says Grigsby. "People always feel welcome, and there are strong relationships between students and faculty.

Accordingly, students aren't sitting in crowded lecture theaters with 600 others, but in classrooms, working closely with their professors. "This nurturing style enables students to discover where they want to go," says Grigsby. "Even students who come to Moravian not knowing what they want to do discover their passions, and they gain the practical experience to take those passions and build their careers."

Going hand-in-hand with this sense of care and support is an emphasis on community service. Every year on the college's Heritage Day, students celebrate the history of the institution and carry out good works in the community. Students also have the chance to follow the Peace Corps Preparation Program, and Moravian's annual "In Focus" scheme encourages them to take courses exploring big social issues such as poverty and inequality.

Indeed, as the college strives to promote inclusivity, community, and a well-rounded education, it's easy to imagine that John Amos Comenius himself would be proud. *www.moravian.edu*

INVESTED
IN INCLUSION

Set up in the aftermath of the 2008 financial crisis,
the Office of Minority and Women Inclusion is an office of the
U.S. Treasury that supports businesses owned by women and
minorities, and promotes diversity in the boardroom

Part of the U.S. Department of the Treasury's Office of the Comptroller of the Currency (OCC), the Office of Minority and Women Inclusion (OMWI) was established in January 2011 following the implementation of a federal law—drafted by Congressman Barney Frank and Senator Chris Dodd—that overhauled financial regulation in the aftermath of the 2008 financial crash.

The Dodd–Frank Wall Street Reform and Consumer Protection Act of 2010 made changes that affected all federal financial regulatory agencies. Section 342 of the act issued an instruction that each office of the Treasury "shall develop and implement standards and procedures to ensure, to the maximum extent possible, the fair inclusion and utilization of minorities, women, and minority-owned and women-owned businesses in all business and activities of the agency at all levels, including in procurement, insurance, and all types of contracts." The Treasury's Washington D.C. headquarters was one of eight financial agencies and 12 Federal Reserve banks to create Offices of Minority and Women Inclusion.

OMWI is responsible for all matters relating to diversity in management, employment, and business activities, excluding the enforcement of statutes, regulations, or executive orders pertaining to civil rights. The office is required to develop standards for equal employment opportunity and the racial, ethnic, and gender diversity of the workforce. In addition to workforce diversity, OMWI is charged with seeking increased participation of minority-owned and women-owned businesses in the programs and contracts of the agency. It is also responsible for establishing procedures to determine if agency contractors and their subcontractors have made good faith efforts to include minorities and women in their workforce.

Under the leadership of Joyce Cofield—who has been Executive Director in the 10 years since the office's launch—the OMWI's Diversity and Inclusion Team has developed several standards. It has aimed to increase the participation of minority-owned and women-owned businesses in the OCC's programs and contracts, including standards for coordinating technical assistance to such businesses. It promotes equal employment opportunity and the racial, ethnic, and gender diversity of the workforce and senior management of the OCC. It assesses the diversity policies and practices of the national

banks, federal savings associations, and federal branches and agencies of foreign banks that are regulated by the OCC.

The office also provides technical assistance to minority- and women-owned businesses, including hosting and presenting information at educational events and conferences. Its Campus Recruiting Program facilitates effective outreach and sourcing efforts by targeting professional organizations, job fairs, and conferences. The OMWI's summer hires and intern programs are designed to attract minority, female, and disabled high-school and college students for a variety of positions, using the agency's National Diversity Internship Program and the federal Pathways Program.

There is strong support for the conclusion that diversity in both leadership and the workforce is essential for maximizing mission effectiveness and impact. Research demonstrates that organizations with a diverse workforce, especially within the senior management ranks, outperform their peers over time. Diverse organizations have proven to be more capable than their counterparts in attracting top talent, developing stronger relationships with customers and stakeholders, improving decision-making and innovation, and increasing employee engagement and satisfaction. Incorporating a diversity of thought and perspectives into an organization's approach to solving problems and furthering its mission helps that organization achieve better outcomes.

In addition to these diversity-driven advantages in performance, federal law directs all federal agencies to seek to achieve a workforce drawn from all segments of society, to ensure equal employment opportunity, and to integrate diversity and inclusion as a key component of their human-resources strategies. Federal law specifically requires federal financial regulatory agencies to develop standards for workforce diversity, and to take specific affirmative steps to seek diversity at all levels of the agency's workforce in a manner consistent with applicable law.

Diversity alone, however, is not sufficient to achieve these performance advantages. The power of diversity is greatly amplified in organizations that value differences and cultivate and empower diversity of thought within the organization. A culture of inclusion is not only essential to equitable and fair practices, but, when coupled with diversity, inclusion enhances mission effectiveness and innovation.

Above: The Office of Minority and Women
Inclusion's Exective Director Joyce Cofield.

ACCENT ON EQUALITY

Equality, diversity, and inclusion are more than
just essential elements of the workplace culture
at Accenture—they are also critical to
the company's success

Accenture, a leading global professional services company, began its journey towards equality in 1995 with its first inclusion and diversity strategy. Today, its ambition to become the most diverse company in the world is championed by Julie Sweet, Accenture's CEO, who in 2019 became only the 15th female CEO of a Fortune 500 company. "Inclusion and diversity is critical for what we do," says Sweet. "It enables us to be innovative and solve problems for our people, our clients and our communities every day."

What Accenture says and does is important because the company has a huge reach—more than half a million employees in 200 cities in 50 countries, serving 6,000 clients across 40 industries. The company wants each and every one of its people to be able to bring their true selves to work, recognizing that equality and diversity help create a culture of innovation and collaboration that helps everyone advance and thrive.

To realize that culture, Accenture consistently and publicly sets bold workforce goals and measures its progress toward reaching them. For example, to advance equality, the company is currently working toward a 50/50 gender split and 30 percent women managing directors globally by 2025 (it reached its previous goal of 25 percent in 2020). These goals have helped produce impressive results—since 2014, the number of women at Accenture has doubled, and women now make up 45 percent of its global workforce and more than a third of the company's board.

In addition to gender, areas of focus include ethnic and racial diversity—for which the company has also set and published workforce goals—mental health and wellness, disability inclusion, gender identity and expression, and sexual orientation. For the past three consecutive years, the Refinitiv Inclusion and Diversity Index placed Accenture at the top of its list of publicly traded companies with the most diverse and inclusive workplaces.

That recognition is due in part to Accenture's strategy— approaching inclusion and diversity with the same discipline it applies to every business priority. "It starts with the CEO and making sure there is rigor in terms of requiring goals, execution plans, and measurement," says Sweet. "We publish our goals because we want people to know we are serious and willing to hold ourselves accountable."

The company believes its diversity and its commitment to inclusion and equality are a powerful multiplier of innovation and growth, a differentiator in attracting the best talent, and a key driver of its success. Accenture research has shown that in the most equal and diverse cultures, employees' innovation mindset—their willingness and ability to innovate—is 11 times greater than in the least-equal and diverse cultures.

"We are committed to working collaboratively with other companies, government leaders, and the non-profit sector to make more change in the communities where we work and live," says Sweet. "You can only have a culture of equality if you start with the belief that diversity matters—and that it's not only the right thing to do, but an important part of your business."

www.accenture.com/equality

A PLACE FOR EVERYONE

Recognizing the value of inclusion and belonging
is key to real progress, explains veteran corporate leader
and distinguished speaker Amanda McMillian

"Sometimes international colleagues chuckle when I use the word 'y'all'," says Amanda McMillian, former Executive Vice President and General Counsel of Anadarko Petroleum. "My retort? It's gender neutral!" It's an anecdote which epitomizes this proud eighth-generation Texan, who has risen to the top of a notoriously male industry while making it her mission to achieve equality in the workplace.

Her own career has, she says, been blessed by several champions, most of whom were men, who were strongly supportive of her as a woman. "When I was pregnant with both of my children, my bosses encouraged me to take as much parental leave as I wanted," says McMillian. "I have always felt valued. I've worked with executive teams who understood that having a more inclusive workplace mattered."

But she acknowledges that both the law and energy sectors have historically been plagued by systemic inequality. "When I graduated from law school in 1998, we had just about reached gender parity in terms of graduates, but only about 15 percent of equity partners were women and a much smaller percentage were women of color. Two decades later, this has only increased by a few points. It's shocking. Society's attention to diversity, inclusion, belonging, and equity have been dramatically heightened by recent events. We must accelerate the pace of change and shine new light on the strengths that diversity, inclusion, and belonging bring to any organization."

For McMillian, the best way to encourage corporations to do this is to make the business case. "Thankfully, that's easy to do," she says. "Countless studies demonstrate that more inclusive workplaces produce better decisions and positively impact the bottom line. The process is as important as the outcomes, so measuring inclusive behaviour is essential. You can make all the slickly produced videos in the world, but that's not going to help at the end of the day."

She explains that diversity isn't just about making sure you have more women or people of color on your team, but rather ensuring that you are providing real opportunity for everyone. "Belonging is about being able to bring your authentic self to work every day," she says. "It's about being comfortable sharing ideas and actively engaging with your co-workers to help your organization succeed. So if, to quote diversity advocate Vernā Myers, diversity is being invited to the party, and inclusion is being asked to dance, perhaps belonging is being comfortable showing your best moves on the dance floor."

McMillian advocates giving employers actionable tools they can use to make a difference, such as demonstrating engagement in inclusive behaviours. "That can be everything from not scheduling a meeting at 7.30 a.m. because someone's taking their kids to school, to providing a safe space for uncomfortable conversations about where an organization is struggling with inclusion and belonging. It's all about building and maintaining a culture—which takes time."

Since Anadarko was acquired by Occidental Petroleum last year, McMillian enjoyed a period of "interim retirement," taking on public-speaking engagements, acting as chair of the Presidential Search Committee for her alma mater Southwestern University, and spending time with her family. In April 2020 she was appointed as President and CEO of United Way of Greater Houston, a non-profit which helps struggling people in Houston to achieve financial stability and assists with disaster relief. "I've always strived to make a difference in my community," she says. "My greatest achievement is that I've been able to help others succeed. Imagine what we could accomplish as a society if we could achieve truly inclusive cultures across organizations."

www.directwomen.org/alumna/amanda-m-mcmillian

A STEAK IN THE FUTURE

Texas Roadhouse is a family-friendly
restaurant known for its hand-cut steaks,
made-from-scratch food, and legendary service

"We are a people company that happens to sell steak," says Kent Taylor. He's talking about Texas Roadhouse, the casual-dining company that Taylor founded in 1993, and of which he remains the CEO. Based in Louisville, Kentucky, it now owns and operates nearly 600 restaurants in 49 U.S. states and nine foreign countries.

Long before opening his first restaurant, Taylor's people-first philosophy was shaped by both his mother, Marilyn, and Dottie Mahon, the owner of a seafood restaurant, who hired 15-year-old Taylor to be a busboy. "My mother raised my brother and I to love everyone, period," says Taylor. "We looked for the good in people. Dottie Mahon showed me the importance of creating a culture of caring for your employees. She introduced me to the food-service industry, where I have remained for more than 40 years."

From early on, female leaders were critical decisionmakers for Texas Roadhouse. Vice President of Purchasing Debbie Hayden started her career with Texas Roadhouse in 1998 and has had a seat at the table ever since. It's leaders like Hayden who have inspired other employees to exemplify Texas Roadhouse's core values, which Taylor describes as "passion, partnership, integrity, and fun... with purpose."

Today, Texas Roadhouse employs nearly 78,000 people—known affectionately as "Roadies"—of whom over 55 percent are women. The emphasis on equality and diversity means employees feel like family and recent accolades highlight the company's inclusive culture, including being named one of America's Best Employers for Diversity and one of America's Best Employers for Women by *Forbes* magazine.

Texas Roadhouse has long recognized its duty and responsibility to be a "people first" organization – a company driven by what is best for its employees and for the communities they serve. Recognition, professional development, and growth opportunities are major focuses in both operations and at the company's Support Center.

Part of taking care of their employees means being there during times of hardship. Dee Shaughnessy, a long-time Roadie and Director of Care & Concern, created Andy's Outreach Fund to do just that. She started the fund in 2005, and it has since given out $13 million. Ninety-five percent of the profits from the company's Logan, Utah restaurant go to Andy's Outreach and any staff member can apply to receive aid from the fund.

"We take care of our people and celebrate our wins," says Gina Tobin, Texas Roadhouse VP of Training. Her Texas Roadhouse journey began 24 years ago as a Managing Partner of a restaurant and she now oversees the Training Department for the $2 billion company. Tobin was one of the first operators to be awarded Managing Partner of the Year in 1998, which is the company's highest honor. "Leadership roles at Texas Roadhouse have always been available to any individual," says Tobin. "Women who performed at a high level, showed initiative, and have embraced our company culture have every avenue open to them."

In response to the gender imbalance and the barriers to advancement that are often prevalent in the food-service industry, Texas Roadhouse set out to redefine restaurant standards by setting their own benchmarks for success. Since its inception, Texas Roadhouse's "Women's Leadership Series" invites groups of emerging leaders and managers to share their unique work experiences, provide opportunities for mentorship and skill development, and to discuss challenges women face in the workplace.

"Seeing people like yourself being successful helps you gain confidence that if you work hard, you can become a leader," says CFO, Tonya Robinson. "Female leadership is not the exception at Texas Roadhouse, it's the rule."

Texas Roadhouse also runs a business development group, which organizes regular meetings to give Managing Partners from operations the chance to talk to leaders from each department at the Support Center. Last year, a group of female managers was invited to the Support Center to share their unique experiences as women in management and to detail what particular work–life challenges they face.

Texas Roadhouse has developed a culture which it believes is right for the restaurant and for the hospitality industry as a whole. Since 2012, the company has been a supporter and partner of the national organization, Women's Foodservice Forum (WFF). WFF is the food industry's thought leader on gender equity, helping organizations identify the levers that actually drive change and create work environments where women thrive, and organizations reap the rewards of a gender-diverse workforce. Texas Roadhouse has been a proud champion of their work and meets annually under their umbrella to convene with other industry leaders to ensure they are aligning the work of gender equity with others in their industry.

Managing Partner Amber Agnew of Palm Bay, Florida has had the opportunity to participate in the "Women's Leadership Series," business development meetings, and WFF during her 22 years with the company. "Having grown up in the restaurant business, Texas Roadhouse has changed my life," she says. "I started as a server, was a Corporate Trainer, Service Manager, Kitchen Manager, and now a Managing Partner. It's incredible to see so many female Managing Partners and Kitchen Managers represented at every meeting I go to." These events and the Texas Roadhouse culture create a sense of camaraderie to encourage all Roadies to set goals and have big dreams, no matter their gender.

Roadies around the world and from all walks of life come together every day in the name of legendary food to provide a unique guest experience that can only be found at a place where employees love their jobs. From female leaders to professional development, Texas Roadhouse prides itself on being one of the best workplaces in town. The company believes there are opportunities in the future to continue their commitment to diversity and inclusion but knows treating people right has been the focus since day one.
www.texasroadhouse.com

Above, top: Demonstrators gather following the Triangle Shirtwaist
Factory fire of 1911, which prompted calls for safer working
conditions. Above, bottom: The Women's Bureau is helping to
increase the number of women in apprenticeship programs.

WORKING FOR WOMEN

Founded in the same year that the 19th Amendment
was ratified, the Women's Bureau is an agency within the
Department of Labor dedicated to the economic prosperity
and well-being of women in the workplace

By Dr. Laurie Todd-Smith

In 1920, Old Glory boasted only 48 stars, the country was two years removed from the First World War, and it was the year of the 19th Amendment, which recognized women's right to vote. In that same year, Congress passed a law establishing the first government institution in the United States dedicated solely to the economic prosperity and well-being of women in the workplace, the Women's Bureau.

At the time, the public may have considered a Women's Bureau or even women's suffrage a radical idea, but decades of brave women entering public life had already permanently altered American culture. In just a decade, from 1910 to 1920, the number of women in the workforce increased from 5 million to 8 million. In an era when the Triangle Shirtwaist Factory fire—where 123 women and girls lost their lives—was still fresh in the American psyche, it was evident that women deserved and were entitled to representation.

With Mary Anderson as its first leader, the Women's Bureau charged forward representing women in industry and labor. In its first decade, the Women's Bureau conducted 87 studies about women in the workforce, including 16 state studies on women working in textile mills. According to *Women's Bureau Bulletin* No. 63, published in 1929, women were nearly three times as likely to miss work because of home duties as men were.

A century on from its founding, the Women's Bureau continues to study and address the challenges facing women. Today, those challenges include: What is the long-term impact of a pandemic on women workers? And how does access to childcare affect women's careers?

The government has made tremendous strides in recent years with paid leave, implementing both the First Step Act in December 2019, which provides up to 12 weeks of paid leave for many federal employees, and the Families First Coronavirus Response Act, which provides government-subsidized paid leave for many private- and public-sector workers during the pandemic.

The Women's Bureau is studying the impact of these policies on women in the workforce, as well as employer-designed paid-leave programs, to see how they compare.

The bureau is finalizing a National Database of Childcare Costs (NDCC), examining county-level costs across the United States plus demographic and economic data to assess how childcare prices are associated with county-level employment and earnings. Currently, only 11 percent of employers offer childcare benefits, and many parents have a $3,000 per child tax exemption on childcare, which is significantly less than the cost.

Additionally, the Women's Bureau is overseeing a variety of projects and grant programs complementing priorities such as expanding apprenticeship and combating the opioid crisis. To support these initiatives, the bureau administers the Women in Apprenticeship and Nontraditional Occupations (WANTO) grants to increase the number of women participating in pre-apprenticeship and apprenticeship programs, and the Re-Employment, Support, and Training for the Opioid Related Epidemic (RESTORE) grants, which help women affected by the opioid crisis to re-enter the workforce.

Although current public-health measures have prevented the Women's Bureau from celebrating its centennial with public ceremonies, its work continues. As state governments reopen their economies, the Women's Bureau will focus its studies on childcare access and regulatory reforms that can help women return to the workforce. This work is just as important as ever.

To face the challenges ahead, the bureau draws inspiration from the tenacity and creativity of working women over the past century. With renewed determination, the Women's Bureau is committed to supporting new and expanded opportunities for women, and ensuring they have what they need to succeed in the workplace.
Dr. Laurie Todd-Smith is a former Director of the U.S. Department of Labor's Women's Bureau.

A HEALTHY APPROACH TO ACCESS

With a diverse management team that gives women a place
at the table, Memorial Hermann in Houston is a health system
that inspires pride from staff and community

Women have played a prominent role in Memorial Hermann Health System from its earliest days. The organization's history goes back to 1907, when Ida J. Rudisill sold an 18-bed sanitorium in downtown Houston to a Baptist minister who wanted to establish a charitable hospital whose doors were open to everyone, regardless of race, religion, or ability to pay.

Rudisill stayed on and became superintendent of nursing and the unofficial manager of the hospital. Meanwhile Lillian Wilson, fresh out of nursing school, joined the following year and swiftly worked her way up to the rank of nursing director and then director of the hospital—a position she held until her retirement in 1947.

Fast forward some seven decades, and the same degree of gender balance can be found in today's Memorial Hermann, which is now one of the largest not-for-profit health systems in Texas. "From its earliest days, Memorial Hermann has been a place for women to succeed," says Erin Asprec, Executive Vice President and Chief Operating Officer. "We promote from within. Since I came to Memorial Hermann in 2002, I've been able to serve in several leadership roles—including as CEO of more than one hospital campus. And I'm not the only woman at the table; I work with other women in leadership every day."

Women make up 74.6 percent of Memorial Hermann's workforce. Among those at the highest levels of management—vice president and above—the health system is 65.9 percent women. Among those at the manager level and above, it's 70.1 percent female.

The strong representation of women in leadership isn't an accident. In 2015, Asprec spearheaded the creation of Women Leaders of Memorial Hermann, an organization that provides women who work in the Memorial Hermann system with a strong network of mentors and champions to help them succeed in their careers. The group now has more than 600 members, all with a mission to create a culture of excellence within the organization and in service to the community.

But, whether male or female, what unites Memorial Hermann's 28,000-strong workforce is a shared vision to create healthier communities, now and for generations to come. With 17 hospitals including 11 acute care facilities and more than 250 care delivery sites scattered across the Greater Houston area, Memorial Hermann has about 2.3 million patient encounters each year. An encounter can mean anything from an urgent care visit to a hospital stay.

"Creating healthier communities means treating people who come through our doors," says Asprec, "but it also means helping people across Greater Houston be healthier so they can avoid needing hospital care in the first place. That's a bold goal for a health system to set, but it's important to us that we serve the community that owns us."

The Greater Houston area has a population of nearly 7 million and the city of Houston is the most diverse in the country, which means that Memorial Hermann treats patients who have roots in every corner of the globe and people at every level of society. While its hospitals provide a broad range of treatments, emergency trauma care is a specialty. It has one of the busiest Level I trauma centers in the United States.

Memorial Hermann is proud of its trademarked Life Flight critical air ambulance service. Its helicopters travel to

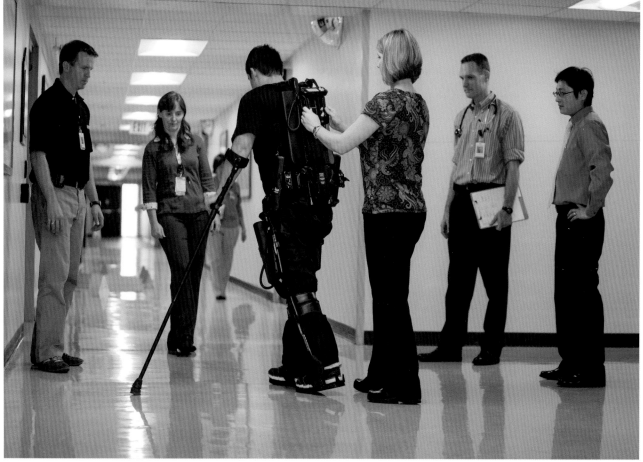

pick up critically ill and injured patients within a 150-mile radius. Flight nurses and paramedics on board give life-saving care while the helicopter brings patients to one of Memorial Hermann's hospitals. Life Flight crews perform around 3,000 such missions each year—which means multiple flights every day and night.

The system also includes a nationally recognized rehabilitation hospital, TIRR Memorial Hermann. There, patients who have experienced a life-altering injury or illness—whether due to a motor vehicle collision or an amputation, cancer, or a stroke—learn to live their lives again. TIRR was ranked by U.S. News & World Report as the best in Texas and third best across the United States for 2020-21. It was the 30th consecutive year that TIRR Memorial Hermann has been ranked in the top 10 nationally.

At Children's Memorial Hermann, medics treat the smallest of premature babies as well as children who have neurological disorders and brain tumors, congenital heart problems, and cerebral palsy, among others.

Memorial Hermann has recently opened Community Resource Centers at two of its acute-care hospitals. These centers, open to the entire community, are designed to remove some of the obstacles that keep people unhealthy in American society. When people come for help, they have access to fresh and healthy food and can get assistance finding insurance coverage, safe housing, or transportation if that is what they lack. These efforts go beyond the scope of traditional health care, but they fall in line with Memorial Hermann's goal to create a healthier community.

Memorial Hermann prides itself on being a good place for its employees to work. The city's daily newspaper, the *Houston Chronicle*, has named Memorial Hermann one of its Top 100 Workplaces for 10 years in a row. Ultimately, though, the greatest honor for Memorial Hermann is the tributes and thanks from patients who have received life-saving treatment and interventions at its care facilities.

In January 2011, U.S. Representative Gabrielle Giffords was transferred to Memorial Hermann-Texas Medical Center's Neuroscience Intensive Care Unit after she was shot in the head at point-blank range in Arizona. After a portion of her skull was removed to relieve brain swelling, she was brought to Houston and TIRR Memorial Hermann to begin the long journey of recovery. "Everyone really went out of their way to do everything they possibly could to make our experience at TIRR Memorial Hermann as positive and productive as possible," said Giffords' husband, U.S. Senator Mark Kelly.

Liz Guice, mother of three-year-old accident victim Grayson Guice, has called Memorial Hermann-Texas Medical Center the "best hospital on planet Earth" after Grayson was airlifted by a Life Flight helicopter to the hospital, where a trauma surgeon and two pediatric surgeons performed an operation to remove a potentially fatal ceramic shard that had penetrated his inner organs. "The emergency medical services, Life Flight, the doctors, nurses, and Child Life specialists—they all showed tremendous compassion," said Liz Guice. "They are all geniuses."
www.memorialhermann.org

Above: A rally in New York City, 2013, in support of
amendments to the Violence Against Women Act of 1994.

THE BATTLE AGAINST DOMESTIC VIOLENCE

The Office on Violence Against Women is a crucial component of the Department of Justice that helps administer justice and strengthen services for the victims of domestic and sexual abuse

An office in the United States Department of Justice, the Office on Violence Against Women (OVW) provides federal leadership in developing the national capacity to reduce violence against women and administer justice for and strengthen services to victims of domestic violence, dating violence, sexual assault, and stalking.

In 1994, Congress passed the Violence Against Women Act (VAWA) in recognition of the severity of crimes associated with domestic violence, sexual assault, and stalking. Established in 1995, OVW administers financial and technical assistance to communities across the country that are developing programs, policies, and practices aimed at ending violence against women.

"From the time it was first enacted in 1994, the Violence Against Women Act has represented a multifaceted approach to strengthening responses at the local, state, tribal, and federal levels to domestic violence, dating violence, sexual assault, and stalking," says Laura L. Rogers, the OVW's former Acting Director. "In addition to providing federal grant funding to support communities across the country, VAWA and its subsequent reauthorizations have made many improvements to federal law, from stronger criminal laws to housing protections for victims to greater accountability for domestic violence committed on tribal lands, to name just a few."

OVW administers both formula-based and discretionary grant programs, established under VAWA and subsequent legislation. The four formula programs are STOP (Services, Training, Officers, Prosecutors), SASP (Sexual Assault Services Program), State Coalitions, and Tribal Coalitions. The discretionary programs work to support victims and hold perpetrators accountable through promoting a coordinated community response.

Funding is awarded to local, state, and tribal governments, courts, non-profit organizations, community-based organizations, secondary schools, institutions of higher education, and state and tribal coalitions. Grants are used to develop effective responses to violence against women through activities that include direct services, crisis intervention, transitional housing, legal assistance to victims, court improvement, and training for law enforcement and courts.

Since its inception, OVW has awarded more than $8.1 billion in grants and cooperative agreements and has launched a multifaceted approach to implementing VAWA. By forging state, local, and tribal partnerships among police, prosecutors, judges, victim advocates, health care providers, faith leaders, and others, OVW grant programs help provide victims with the protection and services they need to pursue safe and healthy lives, while simultaneously enabling communities to hold offenders accountable for their violence.

"OVW works tirelessly to support those who have been affected by domestic violence," says Rogers. "Last year alone, it awarded over $488 million to support coordinated community responses to domestic and sexual violence. These funds also help provide education and prevention resources critical to ending domestic violence. Domestic violence is more than just physical violence. It can include sexual, psychological, and emotional abuse. Domestic violence intimidates, assaults, and often is an attempt at controlling a partner. In their lifetimes, one in five women will experience physical violence by an intimate partner. One in seven men will share the same experience."

On any typical day, numerous calls are made to domestic violence hotlines nationwide. The past year has been particularly difficult for many people. Countless challenges, including a global pandemic, have made it extremely difficult for victims to physically escape their abusers or even call for help. Social-distancing precautions have made for fewer vacancies at shelters and limited the availability of resources and services to victims. However, advocates for domestic violence victims have striven to continue providing the help that these survivors desperately need.

"OVW continues to work tirelessly with its partners to end domestic violence," says Rogers. "The challenges it faces are constantly evolving, and it will continue to have conversations to find solutions to combat them. It will discuss new approaches for law enforcement, more sweeping victim service approaches, and how to increasingly engage men as part of the solution."

EPILOGUE

The 19th Amendment's 2020 centennial has been characterized by incredible breadth and creative activity. Yet it arrived differently than anyone expected, reimagined by increasingly urgent calls for racial justice and the shock of a global pandemic. These forces remodeled programs and events to be effective online and stretched the observance into 2021. Issues of health and equity heightened ongoing concerns about racism and voter suppression. Some feared that the American voting system was itself in peril. In many eyes, the right to vote looked newly precious. We gained a fresh admiration for the century of struggle waged by American suffragists.

The articles and images in *A Vote for Women* remind us that the story of woman suffrage was both protracted and complex. The movement evolved, reshaping American society and politics as women demanded equality. Suffragists ran campaigns (often multiples) in every state and U.S. territory. Their desire to vote grew from and intersected with a wide range of reform movements, from abolition to temperance to workers' rights and immigration issues. Women of every age, class, race, ethnicity, sexual preference, and marital status engaged with the crusade, though not necessarily on the same terms. The people and the organizations were imperfect, as is every human endeavor. We today decry the sexist notions some suffragists clung to, the racism some stooped to, the strains of xenophobia commonly visible. The centennial pushed us to re-examine our own efforts, trying not to make the same mistakes.

We also marvel at the unflagging persistence and the courage of so many women, some of whom devoted their lives to win the vote for women. Suffragists remade themselves as they remade America, pushing toward the equality of the founders' dreams. Many did not give up activism in 1920 but applied the ideas and skills they had learned to newfound goals. Carrie Chapman Catt founded the League of Women Voters to engage and educate new voters and continue to advocate for reforms. Mary Church Terrell and other women of color persevered to be able to exercise their rights, fueling the nascent civil rights movement. Alice Paul authored the Equal Rights Amendment and took up a cause that 21st century feminists continue to pursue.

As we read the stories in this volume and contemplate the images, hope builds for our present-day striving toward equality, whether it be with the voting rights movement, Equal Rights Amendment, MeToo, Black Lives Matter, or the myriad other missions in our sights today. We look with fresh eyes at our own times, even at ourselves, and reconsider how to build the future we want.

The long battle for the ballot looked different at the 25th anniversary in 1945, the 50th anniversary in 1970, the 75th in 1995, and now at the centennial of the 19th Amendment in 2020. Every generation has utilized the suffrage saga for its own purposes. Whether we are calling for women's rights in a new United Nations, forging a women's liberation movement, hammering out a worldwide platform for equity, or celebrating the first female U.S. vice-president, the drive toward a more perfect union connects us with the suffrage story, indeed, with the story of America.

"As we read the stories in this volume and contemplate the images, hope builds for our present-day striving toward equality, whether it be with the voting rights movement, Equal Rights Amendment, MeToo, Black Lives Matter, or the myriad other missions in our sights today"

APPENDICES

WOMEN'S SUFFRAGE TIMELINE

1776

New Jersey adopts a constitution that allows all residents who own a specific amount of property to vote, without reference to gender or race. Thus, unmarried or widowed women (Black and white) and Black men could vote if they met the other requirements. Married women could not vote because legally they could not own property.

1787

The United States Constitutional Convention is held at what is now Independence Hall in Philadelphia from May to September. At the convention, it is decided that states have the right to determine qualifications required to vote.

1790

The Acts of the 15th General Assembly of New Jersey refer to voters as both "he" and "she."

1807

The New Jersey Legislature limits the vote to "free, white, male citizens."

1838

Kentucky passes a statewide woman suffrage law allowing female heads of household to vote in elections deciding on taxes and schools.

1840

Elizabeth Cady Stanton, Lucretia Mott and other American women are permitted to attend the 1840 World Anti-Slavery Convention in London as spectators, but are not allowed to take part.

1846

A New York State Constitutional Convention is held between June and October. Six property-owning women from the state petition the convention, demanding "equal, and civil and political rights" enjoyed by white men in the state. Their demands are denied.

1848

A Woman's Rights Convention is held in Seneca Falls, New York, in July, organized by Elizabeth Cady Stanton and attended by more than 300 people. One hundred of the attendees sign the "Declaration of Sentiments," which includes a call for women's access to the vote.

1849

A Michigan Senate committee proposes that the state adopt universal suffrage. The proposal dies in committee because woman suffrage is viewed as "unusual" and "needless."

The first state constitution in California extends property rights to women.

1850

The first National Woman's Rights Convention is held in Worcester, Massachusetts. Almost 1,000 men and women from 11 states attend. A strong alliance is formed with the abolitionist movement.

1851

Sojourner Truth gives her "Ain't I A Woman" speech at the Woman's Rights Convention in Akron, Ohio, on May 29.

1854

The Territorial Legislature of Washington considers a law granting women the right to vote. It is defeated by a single vote. Shortly after, the legislature passes a law stating that "no female shall have the right of ballot or vote."

1857

The U.S. Supreme Court rules in Dred Scott v. Sandford that the U.S. Constitution is not meant to include Black people as citizens. The Dred Scott decision is later overturned by the 13th and 14th Amendments to the U.S. Constitution.

Iowa's new state constitution includes "white" in the description of who can vote.

1861

The U.S. Civil War starts in April. Suffrage activity across the country is minimal, as people focus on the war effort until the war ends in 1865.

1862

Women in Oregon who are widows and have children and taxable property win the vote in school elections. Women of color are excluded because the Oregon constitution restricts voting to whites.

1866

The 11th National Woman's Rights Convention is held in New York City. Black and white attendees form the American Equal Rights Association to argue for universal suffrage: access to the ballot "irrespective of race, color, or sex."

The election laws in Washington Territory allow "all white citizens" to vote, opening the ballot again to women.

1868

The 14th Amendment is adopted and states: "All persons born or naturalized in the United States, and subject to the jurisdiction thereof, are citizens of the United States and of the State wherein they reside." Women, therefore, are citizens (unless part of a group excluded from this amendment). After this, questions of what rights and responsibilities come with citizenship are debated. In subsequent court actions, "citizens" and "voters" are defined exclusively as male.

1869

At its annual meeting in May, the American Equal Rights Association undergoes a painful split due to disagreements over the proposed 15th Amendment, which would enfranchise Black American males. Some suffragists argue in vain for a suffrage amendment that includes women.

Ultimately, the National Woman Suffrage Association (NWSA) is established by Elizabeth Cady Stanton, Susan B. Anthony and others to achieve the vote through a constitutional amendment.

The American Woman Suffrage Association (AWSA) is founded and led by Lucy Stone. The group works for woman suffrage through amending individual state constitutions.

In a historic first, women in Wyoming Territory win unrestricted suffrage in December.

At a state women's suffrage convention in St. Louis, Missouri, Virginia Minor argues that the 14th Amendment grants women the vote by right of citizenship.

1870

In February, women over 21 in the Utah Territory win full suffrage rights.

The 15th Amendment becomes law, giving Black men the right to vote. It prohibits exclusion from voting "on account of race, color, or previous condition of servitude." In response, many former Confederate states begin to pass Jim Crow laws that disenfranchise Black and poor white men from voting through poll taxes, literacy tests, and other restrictions.

1871

Victoria Woodhull becomes the first woman to address a U.S. House committee; she speaks to the House Judiciary Committee, arguing women's right to vote under the 14th Amendment. The committee disagrees.

The Anti-Suffrage Party is founded.

1872

The Equal Rights Party nominates Victoria Woodhull for president of the U.S. Her platform supports woman suffrage and equal rights. Frederick Douglass is nominated as her running mate but never acknowledges the nomination. They receive a very small percentage of the vote.

In St. Louis, Missouri, attorney Francis Minor suggests that the 14th Amendment can be read as including woman suffrage. Suffragists decide on a "New Departure" to test this theory by attempting to vote. Virginia Minor is not allowed to register to vote. She and her husband sue.

Susan B. Anthony is one of 16 women in Rochester, New York to vote in the presidential election. Afterwards, Anthony is arrested and charged with voting illegally. Her case is heard by a federal judge who fines her $100, which she does not pay.

Sojourner Truth appears at a polling place in Battle Creek, Michigan, demanding a ballot to vote; she is turned away like many other women.

An African American woman and three white women in Portland, Oregon turn out to vote in the presidential election. The election judge accepts their ballots but does not put them into the ballot box. Their votes are not counted.

1874

In Minor v. Happersett, the Supreme Court rules that the 14th Amendment does not give suffrage to any citizen. The defeat turns the suffrage movement's focus on the states.

The Woman's Christian Temperance Union (WCTU) is founded. Under Frances Willard, it becomes an important proponent in the fight for woman suffrage but makes the liquor lobby a strong opponent of women's rights.

1876

Susan B. Anthony and Matilda Joslyn Gage disrupt the official Centennial program at Independence Hall in Philadelphia, presenting a "Declaration of Rights for Women" to the Vice President.

1878

Senator Aaron Sargent of California introduces an amendment recognizing women's right to vote. When the 19th Amendment passes in 1920, it has the exact same wording: "The right of citizens of the United States to vote shall not be denied or abridged by the United States or by any State on account of sex. Congress shall have power to enforce this article by appropriate legislation."

1880

Thirteen women in Syracuse, New York register and vote in a local election, the first to do so after the state's women won local voting rights.

Mary Ann Shadd Cary establishes the Colored Women's Franchise Association in Washington, D.C. The organization links suffrage to political rights as well as education and labor issues.

1881

At its National Convention in Washington, D.C., the WCTU formally endorses woman suffrage in the belief that women will vote to protect their homes from evils like alcohol. They support limiting access to the vote to those who can pass an educational test.

The first volume of *The History of Woman Suffrage* is published by Elizabeth Cady Stanton, Susan B. Anthony, and Matilda Joslyn Gage as an attempt to record the movement's origins. Five more volumes follow.

1882

The U.S. Senate forms a Select Committee on Woman Suffrage to consider "all petitions, bills, and resolves asking for the extension of suffrage to women or the removal of their legal disabilities."

1883

The Washington Territorial Legislature passes a law granting the vote to: "All American citizens, above the age of 21 years, and all American half-breeds, over that age, who have adopted the habits of the whites, and all inhabitants of this territory above that age... Whenever the word 'his' occurs [in this law], it shall be construed to mean 'his or her,' as the case may be." White women and Metis (indigenous people who have assimilated into white society) are able to vote in the territory until 1887, when the Washington Territorial Supreme Court invalidates the law.

1884

The U.S. Supreme Court's logic is that Native Americans are citizens of Indian nations, not of the United States even if they have given up their tribal affiliation and culture.

1887

Kansas women become able to vote in municipal elections state-wide.

The U.S. Senate defeats the women's vote amendment.

The Dawes Act grants U.S. citizenship to Native Americans, but only those willing to give up their tribal membership, lands, and culture. Despite being citizens, Native Americans are still considered "wards" of the federal government, and therefore generally forbidden to vote in U.S. local, state, or federal elections.

1888

Elizabeth Cady Stanton, Susan B. Anthony and others establish the International Council of Women at a meeting in Washington, D.C. The organization advocates internationally for women's rights, including suffrage.

1889

Voters in Washington state consider adding woman suffrage to the new state constitution. The suffrage measure fails to pass.

1890

NWSA and AWSA merge to form the National American Woman Suffrage Association (NAWSA). The Association focuses on securing suffrage at the state level.

Wyoming is admitted to the Union, the first state with a constitution including woman suffrage. The action coincides with the start of what is known as "the Progressive Era," in which the issue of woman suffrage becomes part of mainstream politics.

The American Federation of Labor declares support for woman suffrage.

1892

Olympia Brown founds the Federal Suffrage Association to campaign for woman's suffrage.

1893

For the first time, male voters in Colorado pass woman suffrage after a successful state-wide voter referendum on the issue.

1894

A petition with 600,000 signatures is presented to the New York State Constitutional Convention to approve woman suffrage but the convention votes 97 to 58 against.

1895

The first National Conference of the Colored Women of America convenes. From this meeting comes the National Federation of African-American Women. These groups focus on woman suffrage as well as other issues affecting Black women.

1896

Utah becomes a state in January with woman suffrage included in its new constitution.

The National Association of Colored Women's Clubs (NACWC) is founded by Mary Church Terrell, Ida B. Wells-Barnett, Frances E. W. Harper, and others. Members advocate for woman suffrage and women's rights.

In November, Idaho voters approve of adding woman suffrage to the state constitution, making it the fourth equal suffrage state.

1898

The Territory of Hawaii is established. Woman suffrage is explicitly left out of the territorial constitution.

1902

The First Conference of the International Woman Suffrage Alliance is held. Women from 10 nations meet in Washington, D.C. to discuss organizing around international woman suffrage.

1903

Emmeline Pankhurst and her daughter Christabel establish the Women's Social and Political Union in Great Britain. Their militant tactics inspire U.S. suffragists including Harriot Stanton Blatch and Alice Paul.

The Women's Trade Union League (WTUL) is established at the annual convention of the American Federation of Labor. The WTUL argues for woman suffrage as a means of improving working conditions and is instrumental in fostering the support of working men for woman suffrage.

1906

Harriot Stanton Blatch establishes the Equality League of Self-Supporting Women (later the Women's Political Union). Members are professional and industrial working women, emphasizing the connection between woman suffrage and labor.

1908

Members of New York City's Women's Progressive Suffrage Union march from Union Square to the Manhattan Trade School. Denied a permit and despite police attempts to break it up, the Union finishes its march. This is the first suffrage parade in New York City.

1909

The National Association for the Advancement of Colored People (NAACP) is established. The NAACP becomes an important organization in the fight for suffrage and civil rights, both for women and for Black men in the South.

Women workers in New York City observe National Women's Day on February 28, in part demanding women's right to vote. Now held on March 8, it is celebrated around the world as International Women's Day.

In England for graduate study, Alice Paul joins Pankhurst-led protests, is arrested seven times, and imprisoned three times; she endures forcible feeding 55 times in her final jail term.

1910

The Women's Political Union organizes its first suffrage parade in New York City.

Around 10,000 people gather in New York City's Union Square at what was then the largest woman suffrage demonstration held in the United States.

Washington voters support a woman suffrage amendment to the state constitution. The measure passes with nearly 64 percent support.

1911

The Triangle Shirtwaist Factory Fire in New York City results in the deaths of 146 workers, most of them young immigrant women. The tragedy spurs increased collaboration between working women and middle-class reformers, who advocate for woman suffrage as a way to change working conditions.

At least 3,000 people take part in the second New York City suffrage parade. It concludes with a rally in Union Square, which is attended by around 10,000 people.

California voters approve a woman suffrage measure on the state ballot. Women narrowly win the vote across the state with 50.7 percent of the vote. California becomes the sixth equal suffrage state.

The National Association Opposed to Woman Suffrage (NAOWS) is organized. Its members included wealthy, influential women, some Catholic clergymen, distillers and brewers, urban political machines, Southern congressmen, and corporate capitalists.

1912

The third New York City suffrage parade attracts 20,000 marchers and half a million spectators. Mabel Ping-Hua Lee rides in the brigade of horsewomen that leads the parade.

Oregon and Arizona adopt woman suffrage after referenda, while Kansas women win full suffrage as part of a state constitutional amendment.

In Michigan, after suffrage passes on the first count, alcohol lobbyists, angered by WCTU support for woman suffrage, demand a recount. The recount, which many believe was tampered with, shows a defeat of woman suffrage by 700 votes.

1913

Ida B. Wells-Barnett establishes the Alpha Suffrage Club, the first Black women's suffrage organization in Illinois.

The Alaska Territorial Legislature passes woman suffrage as its first order of business following the establishment of the Alaska Territory. The vote becomes available "to such women as have the qualifications of citizenship required of male electors." It excludes Alaska Natives.

The first national Woman Suffrage Procession fills the streets of Washington, D.C. on the eve of Woodrow Wilson's presidential inauguration. The beautiful spectacle draws as many as half a million spectators. Paraders are attacked by mobs but no arrests are made.

Parade organizers Alice Paul and Lucy Burns found the Congressional Union to fund their work leading NAWSA's Congressional Committee.

On June 26, Illinois women win the right to vote in presidential elections (presidential suffrage).

1914

After NAWSA removes committee leaders Alice Paul and Lucy Burns, the two reshape the Congressional Union into a rival national suffrage organization.

Suffrage Day on May 2 is marked by parades and demonstrations throughout the country.

Male voters in Nevada and Montana approve woman suffrage, making 11 equal suffrage states, all in the West.

The U.S. Senate votes on the "Susan B. Anthony Amendment" that would allow women to vote. It is defeated.

1915

The U.S. House of Representatives defeats the woman's suffrage amendment by a vote of 174 to 204.

The Alaska Territorial Legislature recognizes the right of Indigenous people to vote on the condition they give up their tribal customs and traditions.

Forty thousand women and men march in New York City's pre-election suffrage parade. Many women are dressed in white and carry placards calling for Votes for Women.

Referenda fail in four large Eastern states: New York, New Jersey, Pennsylvania and Massachusetts.

1916

Alice Paul launches the National Woman's Party (NWP) as a suffrage lobbying group made up of women voters in western states. The NWP merges with the Congressional Union in 1917.

NAWSA launches demonstrations at both the Republican and Democratic Party Conventions.

Suffragist Jeannette Rankin is elected to represent Montana in the U.S. House of Representatives. She is the first woman elected to Congress.

1917

"Silent Sentinel" pickets organized by the National Woman's Party appear at the gates of the White House in January. The women's protest becomes controversial once war is declared; some are arrested beginning in June. More than 150 women eventually serve time in jail, where all endure wretched conditions, many engage in hunger strikes, and some are force-fed. All are eventually released after a public outcry about their treatment.

In April, the U.S. enters World War I. NAWSA declares that it will support the war effort; the NWP remains neutral.

Women in Michigan and Rhode Island gain access to the vote for U.S. president.

Arkansas women win the right to vote in primary elections.

Voters in the state of New York approve full woman suffrage with 59 percent voting in favor.

1918

In January, President Woodrow Wilson signals his support for the suffrage amendment.

Representative Jeannette Rankin opens debate on the suffrage amendment in the House of Representatives. The 19th Amendment narrowly passes and it moves to the U.S. Senate.

In September, President Wilson addresses the Senate about passing the 19th Amendment at the end of World War I. The Senate bill falls two votes short of the two-thirds majority required.

A majority of male voters in Michigan, South Dakota, and Oklahoma approve woman suffrage for a total of 15 equal suffrage states.

1919

The NWP initiates a new series of demonstrations, including lighting "Watchfires for Freedom" in January to maintain political pressure on the Senate.

Both Houses of Congress pass the 19th Amendment and it moves to the states for ratification. By the end of the year, 24 of the required 36 states have ratified it.

1920

Carrie Chapman Catt, president of NAWSA, founds the League of Women Voters. Most state suffrage associations become LWV chapters.

After three quarters of the state legislatures ratify, the 19th Amendment is certified into law on August 26 by the U.S. Secretary of State. American women win full voting rights.

1923

The NWP begins to campaign for what becomes known as the Equal Rights Amendment. "Equality of rights under the law shall not be denied or abridged by the United States or by any State on account of sex." It is introduced in Congress every year from 1923 to 1972, when it is finally passed and sent to the states with a ten year deadline for ratification.

1924

The U.S. Congress passes the Indian Citizenship Act defining Native Americans as U.S. citizens, but citizenship does not necessarily include the right to vote. Many states continue to disenfranchise Indigenous people; some states responded to the act by passing laws designed to keep Native Americans from voting.

1926

Zitkala-Ša establishes the National Council of American Indians to lobby for education and civil rights for Native people—including access to the ballot.

1928

Oscar De Priest, the first African American elected to the U.S. House of Representatives since Reconstruction, credits Black women's votes for his success. He takes office in March 1929.

1929

Literate women in Puerto Rico, a U.S. Territory, are able to vote. This is extended to all women in Puerto Rico in 1935.

1935

Suffragist Mary McLeod Bethune organizes the National Council of Negro Women, a coalition of Black women's groups that lobbies against job discrimination, racism, and sexism.

1941

The United States enters World War II. WAC and WAVE are established as the first women's military corps.

1943

The Magnuson Act repeals the 1882 Chinese Exclusion Act and Chinese immigrants, including women, are able to become U.S. citizens (though rights of property ownership remain restricted). Some already in the U.S. are able to naturalize. The quota for entry visas to the U.S. issued to Chinese citizens is set at 105 per year.

1952

The Immigration and Nationality Act becomes federal law, abolishing direct racial barriers to U.S. immigration and allowing Japanese and Korean people, as well as those from other Asian nations, to naturalize as U.S. citizens for the first time.

1952

Democratic and Republican Parties eliminate women's divisions.

1955

Rosa Park's arrest leads to the Montgomery Bus Boycott and a renewed movement for Black civil rights, including the right to vote.

1960

The Civil Rights Movement builds in the South; young voting rights activists lead sit-ins and demonstrations.

1962

Native Americans gain voting rights in all states.

1964

The 24th Amendment to the U.S. Constitution is ratified. It formally abolishes poll taxes and literacy tests as barriers to voting.

1965

President Johnson signs the Voting Rights Act into law, prohibiting racial discrimination in voting. Later amendments to the Act expand its protections.

1966

The National Organization for Women is founded by Betty Friedan and others to support the Equal Rights Amendment and "full participation in the mainstream of American society now."

1968

The Civil Rights Act of 1968 prescribes penalties for certain acts of violence or intimidation in certain circumstances. This includes interfering with a person's access to the vote.

1970

Demonstrations on the 50th anniversary of women's suffrage fill the streets across the country with a Women's Strike for Equality marking the emergence of the women's liberation movement.

1971

The 26th Amendment prohibits states and the federal government from preventing U.S. citizens who are at least 18 years old from voting based on their age.

1972

The Equal Rights Amendment (ERA) is adopted by both Houses of Congress and goes to the states for ratification. Thirty-eight states are required to ratify the Amendment for it to become law. It has, so far, failed. As of 2020, 38 states have ratified, but since the original deadline has passed, it is currently in legal limbo. Legislation to correct this problem is introduced in 2021.

Title IX of the Education Amendments of 1972 prohibits sex discrimination in schools or any education agency receiving federal funds.

1981

Sandra Day O'Connor is appointed the first woman justice of the U.S. Supreme Court justice.

1990

The Americans with Disabilities Act forbids discrimination against the differently-abled in all areas of public life, including voting.

2020

Throughout the year, the nation honors and celebrates the 100th anniversary of the 19th Amendment and women's right to vote. Commemorations continue into 2021.

2021

Kamala Harris becomes the first female vice-president of the United States.

CREDITS

Contributors

Kerri Lee Alexander

Cathleen D. Cahill

Sheri J. Caplan

Sarah H. Case

Elyssa Ford

Susan Goodier

Ann D. Gordon

Kristina Graves

Sharon Harley

Nancy Hayward

Jennifer Helton

Allison Lange

Katherine M. Marino

Debra Michals

Robyn Muncy

Johanna Neuman

Arlisha R. Norwood

Jeanette Patrick

Heather Munro Prescott

Christine L. Ridarsky

Emma Rothberg

Sally Roesch Wagner

Images

Archive Photos/Getty Images

Bain News Service/Buyenlarge/Getty Images

Bettmann Archive/Getty Images

Bob Nye/NASA/Donaldson Collection/Getty Images

Buyenlarge/Getty Images

Chicago History Museum/Getty Images

Chip Somodevilla/Getty Images

Cincinnati Museum Center/Getty Images

Corbis/Getty Images

Fine Art Images/Heritage Images/Getty Images

FPG/Getty Images

Gado Images/Alamy Stock Photo

Granger Historical Picture Archive/Alamy Stock Photo

Hulton Archive/Getty Images

Interim Archives/Getty Images

John Olson/The LIFE Picture Collection via Getty Images

Kean Collection/Getty Images

Ken Florey Suffrage Collection/Gado/Getty Images

Keystone/Getty Images

Library of Congress/Corbis/VCG via Getty Images

Library of Congress/Interim Archives/Getty Images

Mayer/Buyenlarge/Getty Images

Minnesota Historical Society/CORBIS/Corbis via Getty Images

Nawrocki/ClassicStock/Getty Images

Paul Thompson/Topical Press Agency/Getty Images

PhotoQuest/Getty Images

Pictorial Press Ltd/Alamy Stock Photo

Science History Images/Alamy Stock Photo

Universal History Archive/Universal Images Group via Getty Images

UPI/The LIFE Images Collection via Getty Images/Getty Images

Other images are the copyright of Alamy, Getty Images, or individual organizations.

Articles

The following articles were originally published by the United States Women's Suffrage Centennial Commission (WSCC) as a part of the WSCC blog, The Suff Buffs, in the series, "On Their Shoulders: The Radical Stories of Women's Fight for the Vote." The United States National Park Service now hosts the series:

Women's Suffrage Before 1848

How Chinese American Women Helped Shape the Suffrage Movement

The following articles were originally commissioned by the National Conference of State Historic Preservation Officers in partnership with the United States National Park Service as part of the 19th Amendment Centennial Commemoration and are part of the series, "The 19th Amendment and Women's Access to the Vote Across America," edited by Tamara Gaskell:

The Fight for a Right to Vote

The Influence of Other Social Movements

Flexing Feminine Muscles

African American Women and the 19th Amendment

Woman Suffrage in the West

Woman Suffrage in the Midwest

Woman Suffrage in New England

Woman Suffrage in the Mid-Atlantic

Woman Suffrage in the Southern States

The International History of the U.S. Suffrage Movement

Footnotes and Bibliographies

For article notes, references, and bibliographies, go to the following online sources:

Women's Suffrage Before 1848
www.nps.gov/articles/000/the-prequel-women-s-suffrage-before-1848.htm

The Fight for a Right to Vote
www.nps.gov/articles/introducing-the-19th-amendment.htm

The Influence of Other Social Movements
www.nps.gov/articles/the-necessity-of-other-social-movements-to-the-struggle-for-woman-suffrage.htm

Flexing Feminine Muscles
www.nps.gov/articles/flexing-feminine-muscles-strategies-and-conflicts.htm

African American Women and the 19th Amendment
www.nps.gov/articles/african-american-women-and-the-nineteenth-amendment.htm

How Chinese American Women Helped Shape the Suffrage Movement
www.nps.gov/articles/000/mabel-ping-hua-lee-how-chinese-american-women-helped-shape-the-suffrage-movement.htm

Woman Suffrage in the West
www.nps.gov/articles/woman-suffrage-in-the-west.htm

Woman Suffrage in the Midwest
www.nps.gov/articles/woman-suffrage-in-the-midwest.htm

Woman Suffrage in New England
www.nps.gov/articles/woman-suffrage-in-new-england.htm

Woman Suffrage in the Mid-Atlantic
www.nps.gov/articles/woman-suffrage-in-the-mid-atlantic.htm

Woman Suffrage in the Southern States
www.nps.gov/articles/woman-suffrage-in-the-southern-states.htm

The International History of the U.S. Suffrage Movement
www.nps.gov/articles/the-internationalist-history-of-the-us-suffrage-movement.htm

Women's Political Participation After 1920: Myth and Reality
www.womenshistory.org/articles/womens-political-participation-after-1920-myth-and-reality

Legislating History
www.womenshistory.org/exhibits/legislating-history

Tracing the Roots of Women on Wall Street
www.womenshistory.org/articles/tracing-roots-women-wall-street

The Women of NASA
www.womenshistory.org/resources/general/women-nasa

ABOUT THE WVCI

The 2020 Women's Vote Centennial Initiative (WVCI) was created to promote the 100th anniversary of the 19th Amendment and American women winning the constitutional right to vote. Founded in 2015, WVCI brings together individuals from national institutions, leaders of non-profit groups, scholars, and grassroots organizers to raise the visibility and increase the impact of this historic anniversary.

Our mission is to encourage efforts to commemorate the centennial of the 19th Amendment across the country, educate the public on the legal and social advances resulting from the amendment, acknowledge the inadequacies of the movement and the amendment's implementation, and stimulate dialogue concerning the ongoing fight for equal rights.

WVCI operates through a volunteer Steering Committee, with the nonprofit National Women's History Alliance as the fiscal agent. We have been joined in our work by our Task Force Partners, a wide range of organizations and individuals who collectively represent the various segments of the historic woman suffrage movement, contemporary women's organizations, centennial groups and committed individuals.

WVCI's 2020centennial.org website serves as a central organizing and information-sharing clearinghouse on the broad range of programs, exhibits, artistic works, and governmental and grassroots activities in states and localities around the country. In addition, we have hosted a series of "Women and the Vote" panel discussions and webinars in Washington, D.C., many in partnership with the National Archives. We promote all of these events on social media and post them online. WVCI designed and sells centennial pins, magnets, and bookmarks, provided monetary awards to state History Day essay winners, and partnered with St James's House on this centennial tribute, *A Vote for Women*.

The 2020 Women's Vote Centennial Initiative honors the brave and committed suffragists in American history as we commemorate their legacy and continue the unfinished business of creating a more equal and just society.
www.2020centennial.org

WVCI Steering Committee

The Steering Committee is made up of scholars, historians, educators, and leaders of women's organizations.

Nancy E. Tate, Co-chair
Krysta Nicole Jones, Co-chair
Lucienne Beard
Robert P. J. Cooney, Jr.*
Lisa Kathleen Graddy
Page Harrington
Ann Lewis
Molly Murphy MacGregor
J.D. Zahniser

Alyssa Norwillo, web and social media manager

A Vote for Women book liaison

WVCI Task Force Partners

Alice Paul Institute
American Bar Association
Arkansas Women's History Initiative
Better Days 2020
Civically Re-Engaged Women
ConSource (The Constitutional Sources Project)
Elizabeth Cady Stanton Hometown Association
Elizabeth Cady Stanton Trust
Girl Scouts of the USA
Glen Park Neighborhoods History Project
Inez Milholland Centennial
Jane Addams Hull-House Museum
Jewish Women's Archive
League of Women Voters
Lower Eastside Tenement Museum
Matilda Joslyn Gage Foundation
Morgan State University
National Archives
National Collaborative for Women's
  History Sites
National Council of Women's Organizations

National Museum of American History
  Smithsonian Institution
National Museum of American Illustration
National Museum of American Jewish History
National Susan B. Anthony Museum & House
National Trust for Historic Preservation
National Woman's Party
National Women's History Alliance
National Women's History Museum
Olympia Historical Society and Bigelow House Museum
One Woman, One Vote Film Festival
Page Harrington & Company
President's Commission on the Celebration of Women
  in American History (March 1, 1999)
St James House Group
St James's House
Staten Island Museum
Turning Point Suffragist Memorial
UCLA Department of History
University of Maryland Baltimore County
University of Wisconsin, Office of the Librarian
Virginia Museum of History and Culture
Wentworth Institute of Technology
WETA-TV
Woman Suffrage Media Project
Women's Activism NYC
Women's Rights National Historical Park
Women's Suffrage Celebration Coalition of Massachusetts
Workhouse Arts Center
Zeta Phi Beta Sorority

Acknowledgements

We want to acknowledge the following organizations and individuals who have assisted WVCI: National Women's History Alliance, National Woman's Party, Fallon Worldwide (Minneapolis), Helen Bing, Ellen DuBois, Edward R. Hearn, Esq., Allison Kodroff, Jennifer Krafchik, Anna Laymon, Anna Marcus, Julie Silverstone, and the Arthur & Elizabeth Schlesinger Library.

ST JAMES'S HOUSE

ABOUT THE PUBLISHER

St James's House is part of the SJH Group, a world-leading creative media organization that delivers bespoke solutions to a global client base. Comprising five unique publishing companies—St James's House, Artifice Press, Black Dog Press, SJH Publishing and Cargo Media—the group's diverse range of industry-leading imprints encompasses a vast breadth of expertise, from history and government to global business, art and architecture to luxury lifestyle.
www.stjamess.org

Acknowledgements

The publisher would like to thank the WVCI Steering Committee for its considerable support in the production of this book. We are also grateful to the National Park Service, the National Women's History Museum, the Women's Suffrage Centennial Commission, and the National Women's History Alliance, as well as the government departments and offices, sponsor organizations, and writers that feature herein, for their support and contributions, without which this book would not have been possible.

St James's House
St James's House
298 Regents Park Road
London
N3 2SZ
United Kingdom

Telephone: +44 (0)20 8371 4000
Email: publishing@stjamess.org

Richard Freed, Chief Executive
richard.freed@stjamess.org

Stephen van der Merwe, Managing Director
stephen.vdm@stjamess.org

Garry Blackman, Group Commercial Director
garry.blackman@sjhgroup.com

Richard Golbourne, Sales Director
r.golbourne@stjamess.org

Stephen Mitchell, Head of Editorial
stephen.mitchell@stjamess.org

Aniela Gil, Head of Design
aniela.gil@stjamess.org

John Lewis, Deputy Editor

Jochen Viegener, Senior Designer

INDEX